STRENGTHS-BASED CHILD PROTECTION

Firm, Fair, and Friendly

Strengths-based, solution-focused practice is rapidly becoming a preferred approach to the difficult work of child protection. However, despite the demand for this type of protection practice, there has been a distinct shortage of training resources to help students and practitioners working in this area.

In *Strengths-Based Child Protection* Carolyn Oliver provides an original, accessible, and practical research-based model that focuses on the key to success in this field: the worker-client relationship. Oliver's long and varied front-line experience in child welfare, along with research based on surveys and interviews with 225 child protection workers, provides the grounding for the firm, fair, and friendly model. Presenting a rich synthesis of case studies, reflective questions, and exercises, this volume provides a much-needed guide that enables students and practitioners to conceptualize and implement strengths-based practices in a positive and meaningful way.

CAROLYN OLIVER is an adjunct professor in the School of Social Work at the University of British Columbia as well as the Strategic Policy Advisor for Canada's largest urban Aboriginal child protection agency.

CAROLYN OLIVER

Strengths-Based Child Protection

Firm, Fair, and Friendly

UNIVERSITY OF TORONTO PRESS
Toronto Buffalo London

ISBN 978-1-4875-0114-3 (cloth)   ISBN 978-1-4875-2123-3 (paper)

∞ Printed on acid-free, 100% post-consumer recycled paper with vegetable-based inks.

Library and Archives Canada Cataloguing in Publication

Oliver, Carolyn, 1970–, author
Strengths-based child protection : firm, fair, and friendly / Carolyn Oliver.

Includes bibliographical references and index.
ISBN 978-1-4875-0114-3 (cloth).   ISBN 978-1-4875-2123-3 (paper)

1. Social work with children – Canada. 2. Child welfare – Canada. I. Title.

HV745.A6O45 2017   362.70971   C2016-907754-3

This book has been published with the help of a grant from the Federation for the Humanities and Social Sciences, through the Awards to Scholarly Publications Program, using funds provided by the Social Sciences and Humanities Research Council of Canada.

University of Toronto Press acknowledges the financial assistance to its publishing program of the Canada Council for the Arts and the Ontario Arts Council, an agency of the government of Ontario.

Canada Council **Conseil des Arts**
for the Arts **du Canada**

ONTARIO ARTS COUNCIL
CONSEIL DES ARTS DE L'ONTARIO
an Ontario government agency
un organisme du gouvernement de l'Ontario

Funded by the   Financé par le
Government   gouvernement
of Canada   du Canada   Canada

Contents

Foreword

Towards a Strengths-Based Practice That Actually Works in Child Protection

Child protection is the most challenging work in the human services because it is the most scrutinized, most publicly contested work a social worker can do. Child protection work is also precious, and helping professionals often make a lifetime commitment to the work precisely because it is all about helping the most vulnerable children in our societies. Being so scrutinized, child protection systems around the world have become more risk averse and proceduralized, which in turn has led to services becoming more expensive, more families being taken to court, and more children being placed in care for lengthier periods. Perhaps most worryingly, practitioners who love the work report increasing rates of burnout, and staff retention rates have diminished. Experienced practitioners who have resigned will usually say they left not because of the challenges they faced with families but because of their frustration at working in a system that had become more focused on procedures than people.

Being so scrutinized, there is a constant impulse, even longing, among child protection organizations to find some sort of magic-bullet solution to child protection problems. This desire leads us on a constant quest for the next model, method, assessment tool, or policy that will solve the problem. In reality, child protection problems always involve complex human and social interactions; the work is uncertain, and our best work is always done knowing that this is an inexact science and we constantly have to be reflective and self-critical. As Eileen Munro has observed, "the single most important factor in minimising error in child protection practice is to admit that you may be wrong" (Munro, 2008, p. 125).

Munro's maxim applies equally to practitioners who think they know the truth about what is wrong and what must be done in a particular family and to agency leaders who want to assert the value of a particularly policy, framework, theory, or model. I say this to underline to advocates (and opponents) of strengths-based child protection approaches that exploration of strengths-based work must always be nuanced and must always be grounded in the everyday systemic, organizational, and practice realities of what it's like to actually do this work.

At worst, proponents of strengths-based child protection ideas and practice have come off as being on some sort of holy crusade, who frame strengths as "good and right" and harm, danger, and risk as "bad." I resist such naive advocacy of strengths-based approaches in child protection because the development of effective strengths-based child protection organizations and practice is enormously complex and requires courage, compassion, and rigour, not evangelic colonization of high moral ground.

The title of this book, *Strengths-Based Child Protection: Firm, Fair, and Friendly,* is so important in this regard. In child protection we seem to constantly struggle with a supposed disjunction between being forensic and professionally rigorous on the one hand and building relationships, drawing on strengths, and involving parents and children in the work on the other. This can lead to a false demarcation between the "tough" forensic professionals who gather evidence of harm and danger and substantiate maltreatment and the "caring" strengths-based professionals who work together with families. Quite simply, both polarities are dangerous because there is no such thing as a risk-free child protection intervention. In this work we will always take court orders and make removals, and we also know how often our alternative care systems fail the children we remove. Equally, we always have and always will build relationships and look for strengths in parents and families who face huge problems, but to do this without a rigorous focus on child safety leads quickly to naive practice.

The reality is that to do child protection work well we need a mind like a steel trap infused with the compassion of Buddha. This is also what makes child protection work exciting: Just when you think you know what you're doing, the work takes you to your next level of incompetence and asks you to think deeper and do better.

The Signs of Safety approach, of which I am a co-developer, depends, as any strengths-based child protection method must, on analytic acuity. Western social workers often get very sloppy when they think about strengths. When listing strengths, child protection practitioners typically focus on professional priorities such as parents attending appointments, completing services, or undertaking urine analyses. Children are *not* made safe by these things, and we tend to value them as strengths not because we can see they make a difference for children but because they are things we can easily count. Meaningful strengths and safety for children are *always* actions of everyday practical and emotional care for the child in the places and relationships in which they live.

Focusing on the detail of everyday care provided to children and distinguishing between strengths and safety in relation to danger is the heart of forensic strengths-based child protection practice. This is the intellectual rigour and emotional intelligence we need to focus on. I have recently had the privilege of becoming involved with several Cambodian child protection agencies that support social workers working with families in absolute poverty. These professionals get it. When I ask them what they like about the parents they are working with, they say things like "Dad wants the children to go to school" and "no matter what happens, this mum and dad always make sure their kids get good food at least once a day." When asking these Cambodian social workers about times when the parents have made the child safe when danger was present, they say things like "when Dad is drunk at night, Mum will walk the six children two miles to the village leader's home to sleep there, and even though he's angry Dad will let them go."

My close colleague and mentor Susie Essex – who taught me how to work collaboratively with the most complicated disputed child abuse cases (Turnell and Essex, 2006) and to explore harm, danger, strengths, and safety forensically and compassionately – sums it up simply when she says, "in this work we need to be both firm yet hugely kind." It has always been thus and always will be, and this book is exploring this exact territory.

Whatever theory or model of child protection one favours, the critical question that always needs be asked is how do these ideas and practices actually land in the real world of child protection organization and practice? The people who have the best insight into whether any particular approach makes a difference are the practitioners delivering the services as well as the parents and children on the receiving end. Ideas and methods that look fantastic on the top floor of a head office or in a university often tend to come unstuck in everyday practice.

I want to congratulate Carolyn Oliver for preparing a book that elegantly distils a complex body of research and work. Most importantly to me, Carolyn has undertaken this work alongside front-line practitioners, who are the most taken-for-granted group and most under-researched population in children's services. This book explores strengths-based child protection practice from the direct experience of practitioners and builds its theory from their lived experience about what works and what doesn't. This is courageous and demanding academic work, and throughout the book Carolyn's integrity and intelligence shines through, as does her acuity and commitment to the challenges of what it's like to actually do child protection work.

To make any sense of strengths-based thinking and practice in child protection you have to address the fundamental questions:

- How can the practitioner use their authority skilfully and still work collaboratively with parents?
- How can the practitioner bring rigorous professional knowledge about harm and danger and at the same time approach parents and extended family as people who bring strengths, resources, and solutions?

This book tackles these issues head on and frames answers based in practice and in language that will resonate with child protection professionals everywhere. This book significantly extends our professional thinking about how to do child protection and how to research and build theory together with practitioners. Anyone who wants to do child protection practice more rigorously and more compassionately should read this book. It won't provide answers to all your struggles and questions, but it will undoubtedly help you envision and think more deeply about doing this work skilfully and well.

Dr. Andrew Turnell
Perth, Western Australia

Acknowledgments

My thanks to all those at the British Columbia Ministry of Children and Family Development who shared your precious time and experience to make this book possible, in particular to Doug Hughes and Jayn Tyson. Thank you to Dr. Grant Charles for your constant support and astute advice, and to Dr. Sheila Marshall, Dr. Richard Sullivan, and Dr. Shafik Dharamsi for your guidance. Thank you to John, Sue, Stephen, and Alison for setting me on a path, and to Kim Dooling and Susan Kroft for helping me walk it. Finally, thank you to Matthew and Georgia – for pretty much everything.

STRENGTHS-BASED CHILD PROTECTION

Firm, Fair, and Friendly

Introduction

As the sun sets on a cold November afternoon, a young child protection worker finally spots the house she has been looking for in this run-down neighbourhood. For more than an hour, she has been trying to hide both that she is lost and that she is too scared to ask for directions. She is acutely aware that she looks like a social worker, with her briefcase and sensible shoes. Above all, she is tired and anxious about what lies behind the front door. This is an unannounced visit, and she can remember little about the family who live here beyond the report made to her office this morning. A daycare worker had called to say that a young boy had arrived with unusual facial bruising and a fear of his father. Nobody knows what is going on, and it is the worker's job to find out. She takes a deep breath, looks around to make sure no one is watching, and does not knock on the door. She taps it, inaudibly. Without pausing for a response, she slips her calling card under the door and tiptoes away.

Why This Book Matters

The young worker in this story was me. Since starting on the child protection front lines over twenty years ago, I have consistently been seen as a good worker. I moved quickly into positions in which I was given both the most complex cases and responsibility for training and supporting others. I was known to be responsible, caring, and capable. I generally did a good job, and yet there were many times when I did not act like the child protection worker I wanted to be. I avoided client contact, hid my true intentions, back-pedalled on my position, and used parents' words against them.

I was not alone. Over two decades practising and teaching within the child welfare systems in the United Kingdom and Canada, I have heard many workers confess to less than ideal relationships with the parents with whom they work. We have known for a long time that the quality of the helping relationship is one of the most important factors in bringing about change and that maintaining this relationship while also exercising statutory authority can be extremely hard. Balancing responsibilities to care for and control clients has always been one of the central challenges of the child protection role.

Then, at the end of the 1990s, the stakes were raised with the introduction of strengths-based child protection approaches. These focus attention on the worker-client relationship as the "principal vehicle for change" (Turnell & Edwards, 1999, p. 47). They have only increased the need for authentic collaborative worker-client relationships in which the worker shows up both physically and emotionally. They have made it more important than ever to avoid that fake knock on the door and to stay present, trustworthy, compassionate, and hopeful for those with whom we work.

This book was prompted by the realization that, as child protection agencies across the United States, Canada, the United Kingdom, Australia, and New Zealand embrace strengths-based practice, many workers struggle to establish the relationships on which the approach relies. It can be hard to practise strengths-based child protection in the way in which it is typically described in textbooks. It is tough enough to stay positive and emotionally available for the people we love – think of the times you have unfairly focused on a loved one's mistakes or stormed away from someone whose company you cherish. It is even tougher when you feel overwhelmed, undervalued, and at odds with the other party. This is the way child protection workers often feel as they negotiate too many cases, too little support, and ambivalence or anger towards parents who may have hurt or neglected their children. Their statutory authority to remove children from their families means that they are often viewed with fear and suspicion. In these conditions, even workers who have subscribed to the values and mastered the techniques of strengths-based practice might need a little help with the worker-client relationship required to consistently enact those values and techniques.

What This Book Does

This book tells the story of my research with 225 front-line workers in a large Canadian child protection agency (Oliver, 2014). I asked what we might learn from the workers who appeared to have success-ful strengths-based child protection relationships. What did they do? What attributes, experiences, beliefs, practices, situations, and supports enabled them to do it? I also asked what we might learn from those who struggled with or rejected the approach, so we might continue to adapt strengths-based practice to the unique context of child protec-tion practice and to better support front-line workers. The outcome is a model for the strengths-based worker-client relationship that is con-gruent with the statutory child protection role and supports a range of strengths-based child protection approaches. Applicable to all clients and all situations, it can help workers approach relationships with cli-ents in a way that fosters strengths-based values and a professional identity as a strengths-based child protection practitioner.

The study was unique for providing both a quantitative analysis of attitudes towards strengths-based practice and an in-depth qualitative exploration of the ways in which child protection workers interpreted the ideas of strength-based practice in relationships with their clients. Other studies have sought to answer whether workers implement the approach (some do, some think they do but don't, some don't) and whether it has good outcomes (probably yes). Some have described workers' responses to the approach (generally positive) and clients' per-ceptions of it (also generally positive). There are many examples in the literature of workers taking a strengths-based approach, but there is lit-tle understanding of how typical these workers are within their agencies and what makes it possible for them to work in a strengths-based way.

This book, however, is not simply a story about a study and its out-comes. It is intended to help current and future statutory child pro-tection practitioners reflect on their understanding of strengths-based child protection practice, to rehearse the core components of a success-ful strengths-based child protection relationship, and to analyse what they need to implement it. The goal of this book is to support work-ers so they can move beyond *understanding* strengths-based practice to *doing* it. The goal of the model described in this book is to help them move one step further, from *doing* strengths-based practice to *being* strengths-based child protection practitioners.

The structure of this book supports this process. The first section sup-ports the choice to identify as a strengths-based child protection practi-tioner by discussing early evidence of the approach's potential and the reasons it is needed. The second section helps readers recognize com-mon interpretations of strengths-based practice that are incompatible with the child protection role. It illustrates why these are poor choices on which to base an identity as a strengths-based child protection practitioner. This should help readers loosen their grip on these interpretations and prime them for a more appropriate model of the strengths-based worker-client relationship. The third section presents this model: "firm, fair, and friendly practice." This section relates each component of the model to what is known about effective practice with users of child protection and other mandated services, and it explains how strengths-based practice can be enacted with all clients and in all child protection situations. The final section helps readers consider the educational and organizational supports needed to do "firm, fair, and friendly practice" and to sustain a professional identity as a strengths-based child protection practitioner.

Learning exercises at the end of every chapter are designed to help readers reflect on the way they work, develop their understanding of how to relate to child protection clients in a strengths-based way, and embed the approach into their professional identity and daily practice. The reflective questions can be used as the basis for individual reflection or for group reflection and discussion in the workplace or classroom. These questions draw on educational research suggesting that effective reflection helps learners access their emotional responses as well as their cognitive beliefs and attitudes (Korthagen & Vasalos, 2005). What workers feel is as important to professional decision-making as what they think (Gambrill, 2006; Munro, 1999). This means that effective learning supports help learners access, assess, and prepare for their emotional responses to difficult situations as well as to rationally analyse their way to solutions.

The learning exercises are informed by the 5 R model of reflection (Bain, Ballantyne, Mills, & Lester, 2002). This model suggests that transformative reflection needs to engage learners at the levels of 1) reporting specific experiences, 2) responding to those experiences, 3) relating those experiences to other experiences and knowledge, 4) reasoning through the issues involved, and 5) reconstructing the knowledge to inform future practice. Each level provides the cognitive "scaffolding" to help learners move to the next (Ryan, 2013). It can be hard for teachers, facilitators, and supervisors to move beyond talking about what strengths-based practice is to help learners wrestle with how to enact it in challenging working environments. The goal of the reflective questions in this book is to support learners to reflect deeply about what they have read and for it to inform their future practice.

Case studies throughout the book are designed to help readers link what they are reading to their current and future clients. The case studies were written without a great deal of biographical detail in the hope that readers will add the information that makes them most relevant to their local community, culture, and context. These case studies are developed in role-play exercises that support readers to build their skills piece by piece. The exercises offer readers the opportunity to practise and rework their relationships with clients, each time adding more components of the "firm, fair, and friendly practice" approach.

Who This Book Is For

This book is for child protection practitioners and students who hope to become child protection practitioners. It is also for practitioners in other health and social care disciplines who want to better understand their child protection colleagues or to apply strengths-based practice with their clients. The learning exercises are intended to be useful to people with all levels of experience in the child protection field, to help novices think about and rehearse how they might apply strengths-based practice when they enter the child protection workforce, and to help experts reflect – in team-based discussions, advanced education, or private study – on ways to reinforce strengths-based skills and values in their daily practice.

The book is aimed primarily at readers from Canada, the United States, the United Kingdom, Australia, and New Zealand as well as readers who are interested in child protection practice in those countries. These are the countries in which strengths-based child protection practice has been most widely implemented. The child protection systems in these nations also have much in common. They emerged in response to the same broad social, economic, and political trends and have been shaped by the same liberal and neo-liberal political values that promote the privacy of family life and the efficiency of the market (Dingwall, Eekelaar, & Murray, 1995; R. Hetherington, 2002; Myers, 2004). In each of these countries, strengths-based solution-focused practice has been hailed as a corrective to a deficit-based investigative approach and a solution to the ineffectiveness of agencies managing a growing number of child protection reports amid shrinking resources. Service delivery models and cultures certainly differ across and within these nations, as do the methods workers employ and the resources they are offered. The ways in which "child," "abuse," and "neglect" are defined in legislation varies, and there are important differences in the demographic characteristics of the clients served. However, in each of these countries you will find child protection workers performing roughly the same role and facing the same challenges (Featherstone, White, & Morris 2014; Lonne, Parton, Thomson, & Harries, 2008). This is why this book draws on research from, and has something to say about, the child protection practice across this broad geographical area.

What This Book Does Not Do

It is important to acknowledge the limitations of this book. In the countries it covers, practice within statutory child protection agencies has tended to systematically exclude or pathologize the voices of non-dominant cultural communities (Armitage, 1995; Chand, 2000; Jimenez, 2006; Trocmé, Knoke, & Blackstock, 2004). Many of those communities have deeply established traditional practices and social networks that support the safety and well-being of their children, and these are not well reflected in the research on which this book is based. Some have now assumed the legal authority to operate statutory child protection services for their children, and many have embraced strengths-based practice. In Canada, for instance, culturally specific statutory agencies serving Indigenous communities appear to be furthest ahead in implementing strengths-based practice. Practitioners and Elders in these agencies have much to teach us about how to make strengths-based child protection practice work. This is an area about which we need to ask more questions and listen carefully to those who answer.

This touches on the question of the relevance of the information in this book. The study on which this book is based was conducted in one statutory child protection agency in one part of Canada: 225 front-line workers took part, but the model of strengths-based child protection practice that came from the study was described by only four. Why should somebody in New Zealand or Australia or America or the United Kingdom or even the province next door listen to what four workers in a particular part of Canada had to say?

The answer lies in how these workers were similar to each other and different from everyone else. They were the only four people in the study who described being able to establish strengths-based child protection relationships with all their clients at all times. In contrast to their peers, they fully identified as strengths-based child protection practitioners, and their deep commitment to enacting strengths-based values appeared to carry through into every aspect of their daily work. Others struggled to make strengths-based practice fit with the clients and situations they encountered in child protection work. These four workers did not. All four described creating strengths-based relationships with their clients in the same way, and this way was markedly different from the ways in which their colleagues approached these relationships. It appeared to make strengths-based child protection practice work. This deserves attention.

I make no claims that the findings described in this book are generalizable to other agencies. It would require a great deal of research to establish that, and my view is that those with whom we work do not have the luxury of waiting for these studies. We are faced with a real problem: Strengths-based child protection practice appears both to hold a great deal of promise and to be difficult to implement consistently. Applied researcher Sally Thorne comments that in research designed to address such knotty practice problems, we need knowledge that is timely, even if this means that the evidence supporting it is not yet as strong as we would like. This knowledge is initially best classified as sitting "somewhere between fact and conjecture" (Thorne, 2008, p. 15). It might be compared to "the clinical wisdom of a passionate and thoughtful expert practitioner for whom a similar understanding had been acquired through extensive pattern recognition and reflective practice observations"(Thorne, 2008, p. 169). That is the kind of knowledge this book puts forward.

The book presents a model that springs directly from front-line practice experiences. It is well supported by a range of empirical and theoretical evidence for how to make good relationships in child protection and similar professions. It is a model with which front-line workers can experiment. I invite the reader to evaluate the ideas on which it is based for the ways in which they fit with what we know of good child protection practice, the ways they resonate with personal experiences, and the ways they support the development of the kind of effective, meaningful worker-client relationships of which we can be proud.

A Note about Language

In this book, the term "child protection practice" is used to describe the work, governed by statute, involved in assessing and responding to reports that a child may have been, or is likely to be, abused or neglected. This work is also commonly called "child welfare" and "child safeguarding" practice. The term "client" is used to describe the children, parents, and family members who are the users of child protection services.

SECTION ONE

Setting the Scene

"I know what those outside the profession could not know: that this is one of the most challenging and exciting jobs one could wish for, with a potential to actually change the lives of some of the most vulnerable children in society."

(Hope, 2011, p. xi)

Chapter One

Child Protection Practice

The role of statutory child protection workers in Canada, the United States, the United Kingdom, Australia, and New Zealand is to respond to concerns that a child has been or may be abused or neglected within their family. These concerns may come from the child or family members, but more typically they come from members of the broader community, like neighbours, teachers, health-care workers, or the police. The child protection worker's job is to assess the reported concerns and work with the child's caregivers, family, and community to ensure the child receives at least a minimally acceptable standard of care and safety.

Statutory child protection practice developed in social work agencies staffed and led by social workers. While workers now enter the profession from a broader range of academic disciplines, a great deal of the job still involves what might be seen as the standard social work tasks of providing information, offering emotional and practical supports, educating, advocating, and linking clients to professional services and community resources. The primary statutory duty is to the child, whose safety and well-being must be assessed, supported, and monitored. The focus of the worker's attention, however, is often on the adults surrounding the child (Ferguson, 2016; Jobe & Gorin, 2013). Workers carry a legislated responsibility to make all reasonable efforts to support the child to be cared for within the family. Securing the child's safety and well-being is widely seen as a matter of making, supporting, and monitoring plans with the child's parents, the allies of these parents, and the other professionals involved in the family's life.

Child protection workers may well be perceived by their clients as helpful (Ghaffar, Manby, & Race, 2012; Schreiber, Fuller, & Paceley, 2013), but they do not depend on that perception. Workers also carry considerable statutory authority to intervene in their clients' lives without their consent. If necessary to mitigate the risk of significant harm to a child, workers can turn to the courts for legal orders to monitor a child's welfare, to limit contact between an adult and child, to determine where the child lives, or to mandate parental compliance with services. Workers will present the arguments for infringing parental rights to the court, with detailed evidence of the failure of less intrusive measures to provide the child with a safe environment. Court orders typically last a matter of months. Workers return to court at intervals to report progress towards addressing the child safety concerns and, if needed, to request a new order. If family members are assessed as being unable to meet the somewhat nebulous standard of "good enough parenting" (Choate & Engstrom, 2014) within a reasonable time frame and negotiations for alternative arrangements fail, it is the child protection worker's role to initiate a legal process to transfer parental rights and responsibilities from the child's parents to the state or other caregivers.

This ability to draw both on mechanisms of support and mechanisms of control leaves child protection workers operating in a grey area of "semi-compulsion" (R. Hetherington, 1998). The threat of court intervention is ever present, although it does not dominate contacts with most clients. There is some evidence that clients can forget that workers have loyalties to the courts (Regehr & Antle, 1997), as the discomfort many workers feel about the extent of their authority leads them to emphasize their "helping" role (Bar-On, 2002; Bundy-Fazioli, Quijano, & Bubar, 2013; R. Hetherington, 1998; van Nijnatten, Hoogsteder, & Suurmond, 2001). However, this authority is always in the background; the offer of support comes with the often unspoken caveat that if it is rejected, the client might be compelled to accept services anyway. Few clients of child protection systems can be deemed to be truly voluntary (Calder, 2008b). They are typically referred by others, find themselves required to meet expectations laid down by others, and feel disadvantaged in the face of the considerable power wielded by the worker on whom they are supposed to rely (Bundy-Fazioli, Briar-Lawson, & Hardiman, 2009; Dumbrill, 2006).

Tipping Towards Control

During the 1980s, each of the nations covered in this book experienced a growing recognition that the delicate balance between care and control inherent to the child protection worker's role had tipped too far in favour of control. This was partly due to the demand for child protection services outstripping the supply. On the demand side, there was a rapid rise in referrals throughout the 1970s and 1980s. Reporting of abuse and neglect had become mandatory across the United States and in some Canadian and Australian jurisdictions. Public awareness of child abuse and neglect increased dramatically over this period, with lurid media coverage of problems with child protection systems and the first official enquiries into the deaths of children they served (Ayre, 2001; Parton, 1979). Until the middle of the century, child protection work was primarily concerned with child neglect, "delinquency," and only the most egregious cases of physical abuse. Then, the articulation in 1962 of "Battered Child Syndrome" (Kempe, Silverman, Steele, Droegemueller, & Silver, 1962) led to a surge of reports from medical professionals about injured infants and young children. Within a few decades, the child protection worker's domain had expanded further to include "nonorganic failure to thrive, Munchausen by proxy syndrome, and sexual abuse including child prostitution and pornography" (Doek, 1991). As concerned commentators put it at the time, child protection workers were expected to intervene with "practically every physical and emotional risk to children" (Newberger & Bourne, 1978).

The supply of child protection workers and resources fell far short of what was needed to meet this soaring demand. Fuelled by concerns from the political Right about government inefficiency and lack of accountability, child protection agencies reorganized in the 1980s to reflect the neo-liberal idea that public services were best run according to market principles (Croft & Beresford, 1994). The result was financial cuts, the contracting out of support services, and the introduction of a "residualist" approach in which only the most in need of service were seen as worthy of intervention (Parton, 1994, 1998; Scarth & Sullivan, 2007). This left front-line workers with little in the way of practical support to offer families. One American study found that even when concerns were sufficient to warrant a court order supervising the child, families received on average only five visits, "after which the case is closed or forgotten in the press of other business" (Besharov, 1985). Most cases were closed without services being provided (Parton, 1997).

The drive to ration scarce resources increasingly meant that only families who had been "investigated" and found to have a child "at risk" could access services (Waldfogel, 1998). This shifted the focus of the worker-client interaction. Rather than existing to identify and provide appropriate supports to meet the needs of children and their families, its purpose became to facilitate an investigative process that could feel very much like police work and, indeed, was often done in close collaboration with the police (Howe, 1992; Parton, 1997). The worker-client relationship increasingly began not with "how can I help?" but "what did you do?"

The increasing use of the adversarial legal system in child protection cases meant that the rights of parents and their children were often framed as being in conflict. The goal of child protection services came to be seen as the protection of children from their parents rather the promotion of healthy functioning within the family unit (Howe, 1992). In child welfare literature of the period, parents were frequently described as untrustworthy, dangerous, and unable to engage in a helping relationship. Abuse and neglect was reframed as the deliberate acts of deviant parents who required the coercive use of mandated authority. One paper advised that "the lack of normal conscience and behavioural control, the dangerous and repetitive acting out of these adults, the unreliability of their promises all make authoritative intervention imperative for the protection of children" (L. M. Anderson & Shafer, 1979); another commentator opined that for these parents, coercion "may actually be therapeutic; that is, they need the pressure of protective services or the court to enable them to focus on the problems" (Faller, 1985). By the mid-1990s, the increasing emphasis on the "control" function of child protection work meant that, typically, "clients are expected to comply and conform; they are not diagnosed, treated or cured. If they know the rules, it's up to them to decide whether or not to abide by them" (Howe, 1996, p. 88).

Throughout this period there were, of course, individual workers who exercised their authority with compassion, who believed wholeheartedly in the capacity and dignity of clients, and who provided them with a great deal of support and care. I know this because I have met these workers and heard their stories in every office in which I have worked. Researchers have brought us the voices of child protection clients who said they felt valued and cared for by their workers (Winefield & Barlow, 1995) and of child protection workers who saw nurturing as important to their role (Davis, 1995). It was not until the 1990s, however, that systematic attempts to correct the tilt towards worker authority became evident in front-line practice.

Tipping Back Towards Partnership

During the 1990s, what has been called a "partnership" approach to child protection was introduced (Christenson, Curran, DeCook,

Maloney, & Merkel-Holguin, 2008; Comer & Vassar, 2008). This saw the implementation of a raft of policies promoting greater attention to parents' rights to actively participate in decisions about their children. Since the 1989 Children Act led the way in the United Kingdom, such rights have been enshrined in legislation across Canada, the United States, Australia, and New Zealand. The introduction of strengths-based child protection practice can be seen as an important component in this refocusing on a more collaborative approach.

The push to shift the focus of child protection from policing to parental partnership and participation has resulted in the implementation of new family involvement strategies, like the family group decision-making conference (Crampton, 2007). This strategy brings together members of the child's family and community in a facilitated process to determine how best to support the child's safety and well-being. An element of great symbolic as well as practical value is the requirement that professionals leave the meeting after the child protection concerns have been described. Family members and their non-professional supporters then develop their own solutions to child protection concerns. While workers are still responsible for determining whether these solutions are adequate, their role becomes less about dictating their terms and more about supporting families to turn these solutions into reality.

Another pillar of the partnership approach has been the widespread introduction of a "differential response" to child protection reports (T. Hetherington, 1999; Kyte, Trocme, & Chamberland, 2013; Marshall, Charles, Kendrick, & Pakalniskiene, 2010; Merkel-Holguín, Kaplan, & Kwak, 2006; Trocmé, Knott, & Knoke, 2003). How the approach is delivered differs across jurisdictions (Conley, 2007), but common to all is the idea that investigation is no longer the default response to all child protection reports or the threshold for families to receive services (Waldfogel, 1998). At its simplest, differential response means that different types of reports are met with different responses. While, for instance, reports regarding serious physical injury or sexual abuse might still be investigated, neglect reports might be met with a more collaborative approach. This typically involves an assessment and a plan focused on meeting family-identified needs without any need to formally substantiate that child abuse or neglect has occurred (Kaplan & Merkel-Holguín, 2008; Merkel-Holguín et al., 2006).

These processes have helped rebalance the child protection role somewhat, although child protection work can still be extremely intrusive. One recent UK-based study found workers routinely inspecting the bedrooms of children and their parents, checking the pedigree of household dogs, and exercising "an authoritative element that goes into the depths of families' most private spaces and intimate lives" (Ferguson, 2016, p. 4). While some rebalancing is still required there is little argument that child protection workers need to access a range of supportive and directive strategies if they are to be ethical and effective. Good child protection work involves both care and control. But what does this mean in practice?

Case Examples

Consider the following four phone calls to child protection services:

1 A neighbour calls to say that there is fighting again next door. Through the thin walls he can tell that Joe is drunk again. He can also hear the sound of breaking furniture, insults being thrown, and a young child's voice crying for it to stop.
2 A teenager calls in tears. His name is Craig. He wants to kill himself.
3 A mother, Shauna, wants counselling for her post-partum depression. She says she is at her breaking point and is worried that she will hurt her baby if he does not shut up.
4 A school counsellor seeks guidance after nine-year-old Katy accidentally let slip that her father has been pressuring her for several months to have "proper sex" with him.

While names and details have been changed, these reflect real situations to which I responded as a child protection worker. In exercises throughout this book, readers will have the chance to create their own strengths-based ways of managing each situation. I offer my responses here not as a demonstration of exemplary strengths-based practice, but as an illustration of the range of actions front-line practitioners typically perform as they exercise their dual care and control role.

In response to any child protection report, one of the first tasks is to assess and deal with any immediate risk to the child. In the cases above this meant:

1 Calling the police and asking them to urgently attend Joe's home to intervene in the fighting and assess the safety of the child.
2 Keeping Craig talking on the phone until he began to question whether he did indeed want to die and had agreed to tell me his

whereabouts. I also slipped a note to a colleague, asking her to contact emergency mental health workers, and helped the teenager prepare himself for their imminent arrival.

3 Helping Shauna to calm down and brainstorm whom she trusted to help her in her current crisis. I also called the friend she suggested and asked her to go to the home and stay there until the next day, when a social worker might be able to better assess the situation and a support worker might relieve the immediate burden of childcare.

4 Discussing the report about Katy with the police sexual offences unit before interviewing the nine-year-old at school. I also talked to the school counsellor about the disclosure and how she might support Katy for the rest of the day. I then drove to Katy's mother's place of work, to break the news of the report and assess her ability to keep Katy safe, supported, and apart from her husband while we investigated the concerns.

After addressing any immediate safety issues, the next step is to conduct a fuller assessment of the child's safety and well-being. This will support the worker to make an informed decision about the child's need for services or protection. This assessment usually starts with talking to the parents and interviewing or observing the child. Sometimes it is conducted jointly with the police and, in the event of physical or sexual injury, may involve arranging for the child to be medically examined. The worker will often talk to those who know the child's situation best; this might include members of the child's immediate family, cultural or religious community, teachers, daycare staff, or the family doctor.

What happens next? The range of possible options is illustrated by these four cases:

Joe's situation was complicated. When the police arrived at the home that day, they found him very intoxicated and in the midst of a fist fight with a male friend. Joe's three-year-old grandson, Sam, was curled up on his bed. Assessing that there was no sober adult available to care for Sam, and unable to elicit the names of any alternative caregivers from Joe or his friend, the police brought the child to the office. From there, I took him to an emergency foster home.

I returned Sam to the care of a sober and apologetic Joe the next day, with an agreement in place that Joe would continue to work with child protection services to get supports in place for himself and his grandson. During the subsequent child protection assessment, it emerged that Joe had cared for his grandson since Sam's mom had dropped him off and disappeared two years previously. Joe was struggling to manage parenting, a lifelong addiction to alcohol, and a great deal of grief and anger at losing his daughter and also his wife some years before. Joe's own daughter had grown up in government care and had had plenty of involvement with child protection services since Sam's birth. In all this, several things were clear: Joe was wholeheartedly committed to his grandson, and the boy was healthy and well loved.

I attempted to meet with Joe to figure out a workable plan, but he became increasingly elusive. I tried to explore ways to develop a family-led solution, but Joe appeared to be totally isolated from his family and broader community network and to have no interest in re-establishing good relations. At Joe's request I arranged for Sam to be transported to and from daycare and advocated for a change of housing so he could move away from the people he blamed for many of his problems. Joe refused to work with any other services and appeared little interested in any kind of support.

Throughout this work I made regular visits to Sam's daycare and worked with health and early childhood education services to have him assessed and accessing extra supports. He was significantly developmentally delayed. I remember fielding numerous concerned phone calls about him and having many professional meetings. I remember talking to Joe through his closed front door and trying to assess whether he would be sufficiently sober to care for Sam at the end of the daycare day. And I clearly remember the conversation when I finally told Joe, after another incidence of violence, that Sam was coming into care.

The immediate focus of my work was then on helping identify an appropriate foster home by drawing on the relationship I had made with Sam to advocate for his unique needs. I moved him into the foster home and tried to visit as often as possible. I spent a great deal of time trying to engage Joe in working towards his grandson coming home and in arranging for visits between Joe and Sam that more often than not Joe did not attend. Like the social workers before me, I struggled to find the key to obtaining his collaboration. Eventually, we agreed on a compromise: Joe put me in touch with his estranged sister, who ended up gaining custody of Sam. Through her, Sam gained a stable and loving caregiver who could reconnect him to his community and to the grandfather he adored.

What of the other cases? Craig was assessed by the emergency mental health team as being in no immediate danger of suicide and was taken home to the care of his parents. I talked to this team, Craig, and his parents, and I determined both that he had no intention of killing himself and that his parents were doing everything that a reasonable parent could do to meet his needs. I held one session in which he and I talked with his parents about the issues that were bothering him. Leaving them with a suicide safety plan and the numbers of parent-teen mediation resources, I closed the case.

I worked with Shauna for the next year, visiting with her at home to provide emotional support through her ups and downs and to assess her care of the baby. We had meetings with her psychiatrist, her best friend, and the public health nurse. We negotiated an agreement that if ever she felt unable to care for her baby, the protection agency would support her friend to become the temporary caregiver. Once it was clear that her mental health had stabilized and her baby was flourishing, I closed the case.

Finally, nine-year-old Katy. Her mother, Ada, did not believe that Katy had been sexually abused but suggested that the girl stay with a trusted aunt until things had blown over. I participated in a comprehensive joint police and social work investigation and applied for a court order to ensure there was no contact between father and child. With the police proceeding with criminal charges, I had many conversations with Ada, initially alone and then with her daughter, to help them process what had happened and talk about the future. I connected both mother and daughter to a counselling organization, who helped Ada support her daughter so the girl could move back home, as she very much wanted to do. Things did not always go smoothly; at one point Katy came into care when her father briefly moved back into the home, against legal orders, the safety plan, and everything I thought we had been working towards. He moved out again, however, and by the time he pled guilty to the criminal charges, I felt confident in the assessment that Ada was able to protect her daughter. I then closed the case.

These stories are intended to show the diversity of the child protection role. In the course of a typical week, child protection workers may conduct home, daycare, and school visits to observe and interview children deemed to be at risk or in need of support. They may take a child in foster care out for lunch or visit them at home to help them make sense of a difficult piece of their life story. They will typically spend more time with the child's parents and other adults in the child's circle, exploring with them the concerns, eliciting their views, assessing parenting, developing plans, monitoring progress, and providing emotional support, education, and links to other agencies. They might supervise a parent's interactions with a child in care, write letters to advocate for resources, assess the capacity of another family member to support the parents, or convene a family meeting.

Child protection workers also spend a great deal of time managing their relationships and communication with other professionals (Parton, 2008; Reder & Duncan, 2003). Whether in face-to-face meetings, by phone, or by email, they share information with the police, teachers, educational support workers, mental health professionals, family doctors, public health nurses, and other professionals involved in the family's life. They may attend court, presenting the evidence for plans to monitor children, restrict a parent's access to their child, or remove or return a child to a parent's care. If an order is made for the child to come into care on a permanent basis, their focus will shift to collecting the information and doing the planning work necessary to find the child a new living situation that is as permanent and appropriate as possible. This might involve extensive work with the child's family or community network or with foster or adoptive families and the professionals who work with them.

Finally, child protection workers do a lot of paperwork, completing referral forms, compiling reports, and keeping records of their work and the families' situations. The tendency for people to turn to the written record whenever service quality is questioned has promoted the position, increasingly taken in enquiries and accountability processes, that "if it is not written down it did not happen" (O'Rourke, 2010). Child protection workers are expected to document every case-related move. A recent study found child protection workers in the United States spending four to six hours of each working day interacting with different information and communication technologies (Wilson, 2013). For many, it is an uphill battle to step away from their desks and do the relational work with clients that brought them into the profession in the first place.

Reflective Questions

1 What surprises you most about the description of the child protection role in this chapter?
2 How does this description fit with your personal experience or theoretical understanding of child protection work?

3 As you think about the case examples and your own values, skills, and aspirations, what parts of the child protection role appeal to you? Why?

4 As you think about the case examples and your own values, skills, and aspirations, what parts of the child protection role seem most challenging? Why?

5 A feature of child protection work is the combination of caring and controlling roles.

   a) In which other relationships in your life do you combine care and control?

   b) What helps you navigate these dual relationships?

   c) Describe in as much detail as possible the kind of relationship you might seek to develop with the parents of a child on your caseload.

6 Imagine you are recruiting for your local child protection agency.

   a) Write the job description for a child protection worker. What does the role entail? What responsibilities and tasks would you include?

   b) Now imagine that the child protection role could be exactly as you *wish* it to be, without any constraints. What tasks and responsibilities would you add or remove?

   c) How and why do the real and ideal job descriptions differ?

   d) What qualities and experience would you seek in candidates for each position?

Chapter Two

Strengths-Based Practice

"Though the recipe is uncomplicated, as you will see, the work is hard."
(Saleebey, 2006, p. 1)

The many advocates for strengths-based practice paint it as a transformative new approach that has the potential to empower service
users and practitioners alike. Its critics see it as an excuse to ignore
structural problems and offload public responsibilities onto service-
users' shoulders (Gibbons & Gray, 2002; Gray, 2010, 2011; Roose,
Roets, & Schiettecat, 2014). Its originators complain that many things
done in the name of strengths-based practice are not strengths-based
at all (C. Rapp, Saleebey, & Sullivan, 2005). Yet, within the relatively
short period of a decade, social work textbooks have been rewritten
to include strengths-based practice as a core approach that has been
implemented in child protection agencies across Canada, the United
States, United Kingdom, Australia, and New Zealand. Several well-
articulated strengths-based models have been developed specifically
for use with mandated clients in statutory child welfare agencies. To
understand these models, it is important to step back and consider
their roots. Where does strengths-based child protection practice come
from? What was strengths-based practice before it came to child protection work?

The Kansas Approach

Strengths-based practice originated in the United States as a social work
approach for working with people with serious and chronic mental

illness (Kisthardt, 1997; Macias, William Farley, Jackson, & Kinney, 1997; C. Rapp & Chamberlain, 1985). It was the result of a major refocusing of mental health services from the 1950s onward. During this period, many large psychiatric institutions closed, and the perception that residential treatment was to be used only in the event of crisis emerged. Former residents of psychiatric institutions were resettled in the community and relied on community-based day treatment programs and individual therapy for their mental health support (Kisthardt, 1997; Macias et al., 1997; C. Rapp & Chamberlain, 1985). Missing from the new service model, however, was the help these people often needed to secure and maintain their community-based housing, income, education, and relationships.

Support for these challenges of daily living was sometimes offered on an ad hoc basis by day treatment or residential treatment staff (Macias et al., 1997). It sometimes fell under the remit of highly paid therapists who typically had little interest in such work (C. Rapp & Chamberlain, 1985). Sometimes it was provided by mental health case managers, whose role was to link clients to scarce community resources. Their work was primarily problem focused and telephone based. They rarely knew their clients well, as developing meaningful relationships tended to be seen as the special preserve of therapists. Not surprisingly, many clients fell through the cracks (Kisthardt, 1997; C. Rapp & Chamberlain, 1985).

In response to these systemic problems, Rapp and his social work colleagues at the University of Kansas School of Social Welfare developed the strengths case-management approach (Kisthardt, 1997; Modrcin, Rapp, & Poertner, 1988; C. Rapp, 1993; C. Rapp & Chamberlain, 1985; Weick, Rapp, Sullivan, & Kisthardt, 1989). The approach had the following key elements:

1 It reframed the case manager–client relationship as a therapeutic intervention. In the "service-broker" case-management model, case managers only had to know clients sufficiently well to get referrals made and the work done. In the strengths case-management approach, the working relationship became central and was promoted as a key factor in the reduction of hospital admissions and psychiatric symptomology.
2 It got case managers out of the office and off the phone to meet regularly with clients in their homes and other community settings. In this model of "aggressive outreach" (Modrcin, Rapp, & Poertner, 1988), case managers accompanied clients, both psychologically and

physically, into the community to forge the links they needed for successful community living.

3 It focused on clients' strengths and goals rather than pathology. The approach was shaped by the twin beliefs that social work's emphasis on problems aggravated these problems, and that clients could direct their own case planning (Weick et al., 1989). Case managers and clients worked together to systematically assess the client's strengths and goals using personal planning tools. The work was oriented to these client-identified goals.

4 It framed all clients as having the capacity for continual growth and human behaviour as being highly responsive to changes in the environment (C. Rapp & Chamberlain, 1985). This challenged the prevailing belief that people proceed along a fixed developmental path set by their personality, pathology, or past experiences. Later, key theorists drew on research in the areas of health and wellness, resilience, and human development to counter ideas of an inevitable route from adversity to pathology (Saleebey, 1996, 2012).

5 It framed the environment as rich in health-promoting resources (Modrcin et al., 1988). As was later written, "in every environment, there are individuals, associations, groups and institutions who have something to give, something that others may desperately need: knowledge, succor, an actual resource or talent, or simply time and place" (Saleebey, 2012, p. 20). A primary task of the strengths case manager was to help clients connect to these resources, most of which were found outside the official network of professional "helping" services.

Strengths case management was created as an approach for people in a particular role (case managers) to use with a particular group of people (adults with mental illness). By the early 1990s, however, it had developed into a general social work perspective that was applicable to all social work clients (Saleebey, 1992, 2006). Dennis Saleebey, a colleague of Rapp's at the University of Kansas, took the principles underlying strengths case management and articulated them as a general attitude, standpoint, or orientation to identify and pursue clients' strengths and goals rather than to focus on their deficits and problems (Saleebey, 1997; Staudt, Howard, & Drake, 2001). While this standpoint was quickly applied in work with "elderly people, youths in trouble, people with addictions, even communities and schools" (Saleebey, 1996, p. 296), it was slow to be translated directly to work with families

(Early & GlenMaye, 2000). It was only with the addition of solution-focused ideas that the potential for strengths-based child protection work was realized.

The Solution-Focused Approach

In 2006, Rapp and his colleagues at the University of Kansas identified four approaches that met their criteria to be called a strengths-based approach and had some empirical support (C. Rapp et al., 2005). The first, strengths case management, has been discussed. The second and third approaches they identified were the "individual placement and support model of supported employment" (Becker & Drake, 2003; R. E. Drake, Bond, & Becker, 2012) and the "asset-building model of community development" (Green & Haines, 2012; Kretzman & McKnight, 1993), neither of which has had a widespread impact on statutory child welfare work. The fourth was "solution-focused therapy" (Franklin, Trepper, McCollum, & Gingerich, 2012; Miller, Hubble, & Duncan, 1996), which profoundly influenced the development of strengths-based child protection practice.

Like strengths case management, solution-focused therapy emerged in the United States in the 1980s as a response to pressures for more cost-effective mental health services (de Shazer, 1982; de Shazer et al., 1986). It developed, however, very separately from the Kansas strengths approach. There are no references to strengths case management or the strengths perspective in the early solution-focused literature. Solution-focused theorists did not cite the same theoretical influences as those who wrote about the strengths perspective and strengths case management. Solution-focused therapy was intended to be used in clinic-based therapeutic work with adults and families, and it proposed a worker-client relationship that was quite different from that envisaged by the Kansas school.

Solution-focused therapy was the product of two decades of work to develop a brief therapy model that was more effective than simply offering shortened versions of conventional therapeutic treatment. The work was started by therapists at the Mental Research Institute in Palo Alto, California. They developed the Focused Problem Resolution model (Weakland, Fisch, Watzlawick, & Bodin, 1974). This model was radical for offering clients no more than ten sessions of therapy and for focusing on changing present, observable behavioural interactions rather than mining the past for the causes of a client's difficulties. It framed problems as interactional and situational rather than the product of individual psychopathology. This meant that the therapist's role was to interrupt the habitual thinking and behaviour patterns that maintain the problem. A small change in either – a new behaviour or even just the relabelling of a behaviour – had the power to trigger significant change.

These ideas were the starting point for the development of solution-focused therapy by Steve de Shazer and his colleagues at the Brief Family Therapy Centre in Wisconsin (de Shazer, 1982). Their greatest innovation was to reject brief therapy's focus on problematic behaviours to focus instead on solutions. Their position was that clients are always inherently motivated to solve their problems. When they arrive in the therapist's office, and even before, clients are already taking action that manages, mitigates, or resolves these problems. The therapist's job is to identify and amplify these client-generated solutions.

The belief that clients are best motivated to achieve solutions grounded in their habitual ways of thinking and behaving means that solution-focused therapists need to accept and work with the client's view of reality. However, they also need to introduce sufficient "news of a difference" (de Shazer, 1982, p. 8) to expand the client's behavioural or cognitive responses to the problem. Solution-focused therapists borrow from Milton Erickson the art of using implicit, indirect, and para-doxical interventions to induce small cognitive or behavioural changes without directly challenging the client's frame of reference (Haley, 1993). Solution-focused therapists typically first compliment the client's current behaviour or perspective before offering new information or strategic suggestions that will worry at but not threaten that perspective and invite a new way of thinking or behaving about the issue:

> We do not attempt to transform potentially resistant clients into cooperative ones by influencing techniques ... As they reflect, puzzle, and struggle to answer solution-focused questions, new possibilities for doing something different often emerge and cooperation naturally happens. (De Jong & Berg, 2001, p. 372)

Solution-focused therapists challenge the client's construction of problems as continuous and reinterpret taken-for-granted behaviour and assumptions as a matter of client choice. Their focus is not on revisiting the problem situation but on exploring what the client does from session to session that is different. Focusing on narratives of strengths and success reinforce the client's motivation to choose what works, and these new interpretations open up new possibilities for action. As Miller and de Shazer wrote,

> The solution-focused language game is designed to persuade clients that change is not only possible, but that it is already happening. It is, in other words, a rhetorical process designed to talk clients into solutions to their problems. (Miller & de Shazer, 1998, p. 7)

Solution-focused therapists use particular questioning techniques to elicit detailed descriptions of the client's goals and successes (De Jong & Miller, 1995). These include:

- **Miracle questions:** Clients are asked to imagine what life would look like if the problem situation was resolved. For instance, a miracle question to a client who is refusing to engage with their worker might be "Imagine you wake up tomorrow and a miracle has happened and our relationship is exactly as you would like it to be. What would you notice? What would tell you things are different between us?" The detailed description of the imagined ideal situation offers both therapist and client a picture of what to aim for.
- **Exceptions questions:** These elicit detailed descriptions of what is happening when the problem is less severe. A father might be asked about the times when his relationship with his teenage son is not full of the conflict that brought social workers to his door. For example, "It's clear that you don't fight 24/7. When do you not fight? When was the last time you got along better? What was happening then? Who was there? What did you do?" His answers will give clues to how to build on what he and his son are already doing right and about the conditions that support greater harmony.
- **Coping questions:** Clients are asked to describe what is going on when they cope well with their challenges. Like exceptions questions, they elicit descriptions of the strengths and strategies clients already use and can build on. A mother describing a long history of depression might be asked, "How have you coped with all this over the years? What has kept you going?" Her answers might help her get in touch with the strengths and resources that often get lost when we tell our stories.
- **Scaling questions:** Clients are asked to rate a dimension of the problem situation along a scale of one to ten and then to imagine

what they need to achieve a rating that is one point better. A child might be asked to rate on a scale of one to ten how prepared she feels to go home and then to identify what it would take to move her one point higher on the scale. In the details of her answer lie the key strategies and resources needed for a safe return.

- **Relationship questions:** Clients are asked to put themselves in the shoes of another person and to describe the situation from that person's perspective. Clients who feel they are failing at life might be asked, "How would your best friend describe you?" or "What would your partner say are your best qualities?" Such questions encourage clients to reconsider their own story, expanding it to include the things in the stories of others about which they might feel some pride.

Embedded in the details of the answers to all of these questions are the strategies that clients believe in, the strengths they draw on, and the resources they employ. By articulating these strategies, strengths, and resources, clients lay claim to them, generating both a clear plan of how to resolve their issues and the motivation to achieve that plan.

Dealing with Authority

Whether they know it or not, strengths-based child protection workers often draw on both the Kansas and solution-focused traditions. This is because the strengths-based child protection approaches that have been developed specifically for statutory settings are primarily informed by solution-focused therapy, borrowing its focus on goals and many of its questioning techniques. Yet many child protection workers also bring to their workplace an understanding of the Kansas strengths approach, which they will have learned during their social work education or from reading they have done and training they have received in generic strengths-based approaches.

If solution-focused therapy were a perfect expression of the Kansas strengths approach, child protection workers would have little difficulty combining what they know about strengths-based practice with what they know about solution-focused work and applying the whole package to the task of keeping children safe. If the Kansas approach and child protection solution-focused models were entirely congruent, the only point in quibbling about theoretical distinctions between the two traditions would be to preserve the accuracy of the historical record. The fact that the two traditions developed almost entirely without reference to each other would be unimportant, and it would make sense to conflate them, as some academics now are, by talking about a strengths *and* solution-focused approach and drawing on references from both the Kansas and solution-focused therapy literature (Jack, 2005; Lietz, 2011; Skrypek, Idzelis, & Pecora, 2012; Skrypek, Otteson, & Owen, 2010). The difficulty with this, however, is that the Kansas and solution-focused traditions differ on a point of central importance in child protection work – the use of authority – and propose different worker-client relationships as a result.

The Kansas tradition arguably has a less complicated relationship with worker authority, framing it as the opposite of the client self-determination that lies at the heart of the strengths approach. As the original Kansas team wrote,

> It is impossible for even the best trained professional to judge how another person should best live his or her life. The nonjudgmental attitude in social work dictates that not only should social workers not judge but that social workers cannot judge. (Weick et al., 1989, p. 353)

Client self-determination was so central in the development of the strengths approach that in the early days, case managers were required to be "preprofessional personnel" (C. Rapp & Chamberlain, 1985, p. 419). In the first studies they were social work students (Kisthardt, 1997; C. Rapp & Chamberlain, 1985) or workers with no human services experience or advanced degrees (Modrcin et al., 1988). This was part of a deliberate attempt to ensure that case managers truly felt that they had something to learn from their clients (Kisthardt, 1997). Professional authority simply got in the way of perceiving clients as the experts and directors of their own plans. While strengths-based practice was never intended to avoid the uncomfortable reality that many of those with whom it was used were involuntary participants (Graybeal, 2001), its architects paid relatively little attention to the question of how to assert authority within this approach.

In solution-focused therapy, the therapist's authority is framed very differently. The approach sprang from the brief therapy tradition in which the therapist is an expert who delivers directives, tasks, and reinforcing messages for strategic ends:

> Since we as therapists are by definition experts, giving authoritative instructions on both thinking and acting, another pervasive element of

paradox is created by the fact that ordinarily we do so only tentatively, by suggestions or questions rather than direct orders, and often adopt a "one-down" position of apparent ignorance or confusion. We find that patients, like other people, accept and follow advice more readily when we avoid "coming on strong." (Weakland et al., 1974, p. 9)

This idea has remained influential in solution-focused therapy. Delivering "compliments" before making suggestions, for instance, is a strategy to help clients feel sufficiently understood so they might accept the therapist's authority. Put another way,

simply, the start of the therapeutic message is designed to let clients know that the therapist sees things their way and agrees with them. This, of course, allows the clients to agree easily with the therapist. Once this agreement is established, then the clients are in a proper frame of mind to accept clues about solutions, namely, something new and different. (de Shazer et al., 1986, p. 8)

Taking a "one-down" position in which clients are promoted as the expert on their own situation circumvents client "resistance." When reluctant clients are mandated to attend therapy, it is not uncommon for the solution-focused therapist to play a double game in relation to power. By allying with the client on the question of "how can I help you convince them you are doing well?" (De Jong & Berg, 2001), therapists both claim the authority to report on the client's progress – a very powerful position – and position themselves alongside the client as subordinate to other powerful decision-makers.

It is not surprising that practitioner authority plays a greater role in solution-focused therapy. In contrast to strengths-based case management and the strengths perspective, the approach developed largely through work with involuntary clients (De Jong & Hopwood, 1996). Many of the clients of the Brief Family Therapy Center were referred or mandated to attend by public agencies like courts and child welfare agencies (Berg & Miller, 1992). None of this negates the fact that solution-focused therapy is underpinned by an authentic belief in the capacities of all clients. It simply means that the discourse of partnership is more complicated than with the Kansas strengths approach. In solution-focused therapy it is both a core value and a strategic manoeuvre.

This matters because the relationship between practitioners and their own authority is of central importance in child protection work.

As will be seen in the following sections, the different stances on worker authority expressed in strengths-based and solution-focused traditions play out dramatically in front-line practice.

Reflective Questions

1 What are the main differences between the Kansas strengths approach and the solution-focused approach?
2 Think of your own understanding of strengths-based practice. What readings, teachings, or personal experiences led to this understanding? Does it fit best with the Kansas strengths approach or a solution-focused approach?
3 What are the advantages and disadvantages of each approach for child protection work?
4 With which approach do you feel most comfortable? Why?
5 Think of Craig, the teen who called in a suicidal crisis in the previous chapter. He has been assessed by the emergency mental health team as no longer a danger to himself and has been sent home to the care of his parents.
    a) If you were working through a Kansas strengths approach, what actions might you take with the family?
    b) If you were working through a solution-focused approach, what might you do?

Chapter Three

Strengths-Based Child Protection Practice

"[It] does not set problems in opposition to a strengths and solution-focus, nor does it frame forensic, rigorous professional inquiry as something that diminishes or erases the possibility of collaborative practice. Quite simply, the best child protection practice is always both forensic and collaborative and demands that professionals are sensitised to and draw upon every scintilla of strength, hope and human capacity they can find within the ugly circumstances where children are abused." (Turnell, 2010, p. 21)

Many child protection workers seek to practice in a strengths-based way simply by taking the principles and techniques of strengths-based or solution-focused practice discussed in Chapter 2 and applying them in their daily work. Others will follow one of several clearly articulated models of strengths-based practice that have been developed specifically for child protection settings. No matter which route they choose, their challenge is to focus on strengths, support client self-determination, and build collaboration at the same time as they assess risk to the child, make judgments as to parental capacity, and exercise their statutory authority.

When doing any form of strengths-based child protection practice:

- Child protection workers hold child safety and well-being as an explicit goal. In the spirit of the strengths-based approaches discussed in Chapter 2, workers support parents' right and capacity to make decisions, to identify their own solutions, and to set their own goals. However, they only do so when these actions align with the goal of child safety and well-being.

- Child protection workers systematically assess and reinforce clients' strengths, thereby building client motivation and helping clients expand their perception of and access to available options. However, they also assess threats to the child's safety and well-being in order to evaluate and manage the likelihood that a child will be abused or neglected.
- Child protection workers help clients identify and connect with personal, family, and community resources. However, they also use both their access to formal professional services and their statutory power when these become a necessary resource to support child safety.

Insoo Kim Berg and Susan Kelly's work with statutory child welfare agencies in Michigan laid the foundations for strengths-based child protection practice (Berg, 1994; Berg & Kelly, 2000). Their approach clearly drew on solution-focused therapy rather than the work of the Kansas school, and this should come as no surprise in light of Insoo Kim Berg's background. She was a therapist at the Brief Family Therapy Center, where solution-focused therapy began; her partner, Steve de Shazer, is commonly seen as the godfather of solution-focused work; and her mentor, John Weakland, developed the brief therapy model from which solution-focused therapy evolved. The work in Michigan demonstrated how solution-focused principles and techniques could be applied at each stage of the child protection process, from the first phone call to placing a child out of the home or closing a case.

In 1991, Berg and de Shazer travelled to Perth, Australia, where they worked with Andrew Turnell, a brief family therapist and social worker, and Stephen Edwards, a child protection worker (Turnell & Edwards, 1999). Turnell and Edwards went on to develop the Signs of Safety® approach in collaboration with statutory child protection workers in Western Australia (Turnell, 2012; Turnell & Edwards, 1999; Turnell, Lohrbach, & Curran, 2008). The Signs of Safety approach articulated the principles of strengths-based child protection practice and provided child protection practitioners with a process to follow as they applied six practice elements and an assessment and planning tool at different points in the life of a child protection case.

Signs of Safety is now the most commonly used model of strengths-based solution-focused child protection practice. It is supported by an extensive network of licensed trainers and consultants, and in 2012 it had been implemented in 50 to 100 jurisdictions across Australia, New Zealand, Canada, the United States, and Europe (Bunn, 2013; Turnell, 2012). In 2014, the approach was being used in statutory agencies in the Canadian provinces of British Columbia, Ontario, and Manitoba and across the state of Western Australia. Three years earlier, a survey of risk-assessment tools in the United States had found eleven states using the Signs of Safety approach, three as their sole model for practice and eight in conjunction with the Structured Decision Making risk-assessment model (Harbert & Tucker-Tatlow, 2012). Some jurisdictions had developed hybrid practice models that drew on the ideas of Signs of Safety but no longer went primarily by the Signs of Safety name (Harbert & Tucker-Tatlow, 2012). A survey the same year found thirty-nine English local authorities using Signs of Safety, interested in using it, or with staff trained to use it (Bunn, 2013). With a survey response rate of only forty-four per cent, it is likely that the approach was being implemented more widely.

While Signs of Safety has garnered the most attention, it is not the only strengths-based approach developed specifically for statutory child protection settings. The best-researched alternative is Solution-Based Casework (Antle, Barbee, Christensen, & Martin, 2008; Antle, Christensen, van Zyl, & Barbee, 2012; Barbee, Christensen, Antle, Wandersman, & Cahn, 2011; Pipkin, Sterrett, Antle, & Christensen, 2013; van Zyl et al., 2014). Also known as Family Solutions, it was developed with front-line child protection workers in Kentucky and implemented in that state, Washington state, and some parts of Florida, New Hampshire, and Tennessee (Barbee et al., 2011). It integrates solution-focused therapy, family life cycle theory, and relapse prevention theory. It encourages workers to normalize child welfare problems as a response to challenges faced by all families at different stages in the parenting life cycle. It helps them identify the patterns of behaviour, thinking, or feeling that sustain child welfare problems, in addition to searching for the exceptions to those problems, and for the family's solutions, strengths, and goals.

The contrast between Signs of Safety and Solution-Based Casework illustrates the ways in which the various strengths-based child protection approaches tend to differ. Some approaches, like Solution-Based Casework, incorporate other theories and perspectives. The inclusion of relapse prevention theory, for instance, means a Solution-Based Casework assessment includes a detailed accounting of the behavioural patterns leading to unwanted outcomes for the child.

Shear (2015) describes how workers using this approach might track the details of events culminating in the moment a stepfather punches his three-year-old. They would explore the stepfather's frustrations of the previous day, his attempts later that evening to cope with those frustrations by smoking drugs, his angry mood on waking, and how his anger turned to violent rage when the boy spilled his juice. By taking the time to track sequences like this, the worker can help unpack the causes and triggers for problematic behaviour in order to identify how behaviour might change. Signs of Safety adheres to a more "purist" solution-based approach. The assessment process covers three questions – What are we worried about? What's working well? What needs to happen next? – but a general statement of the problem is sufficient answer to the first. Digging for details is limited to the latter two questions. The minutiae of the problem sequence is not required.

The second difference between strengths-based child protection approaches lies in the extent to which they have been operationalized through the development or integration of unique practice tools. The Signs of Safety approach, for instance, has evolved to incorporate visual mapping tools like the Three Houses (Weld, 2008) and Words and Pictures (Turnell & Essex, 2006). These were designed specifically to engage children and family members in strengths-based safety-focused discussions. Solution-Based Casework has developed tools to support workers to make plans that include behaviourally specific goals both for individual family members and for the family as a whole (van Zyl et al., 2014). Strengths-based child protection approaches differ in the intensity of their focus on strengths, in their tools, and often in the language they employ. They are remarkably similar, however, in the principles and working relationship on which they rely.

Principles

Strengths-based child protection approaches are grounded in the following principles:

1) The client is a respected partner in creating safety for the child.
Clients are respected as fully participating partners at all stages of the case. They are seen as an expert on their life who, if given the opportunity,

will lead the worker towards solutions. The worker's job is to establish a collaborative partnership in which the client's perspective can be understood and validated. Workers need to accept that this perspective likely differs from their own. True strengths-based collaboration requires workers to be open to the ideas of others. This means suspending assumptions and adopting a "not-knowing" stance of curiosity.

2) Every family has strengths on which the solutions to child protection problems can be built.
It is assumed not only that parents wish to parent well, but that there are already many times when they do parent well. Within each family lie strengths and solutions that help them do this. This means one focus of the work is identifying and developing the strengths and solutions that families use or want to use. Another focus is exploring the conditions in place when parents do a good job, in order to pinpoint the resources and supports that will help families to make the best use of their strengths and solutions.

3) The goal of the work is the future safety of the child.
The work is oriented not to the past (what happened?) but to the present (what can be done now?) and to the future (what will increase child safety moving forward?). Answering these latter questions involves assessing risks to the child, but this does not rely on a complete understanding of past problems or a parental admission of wrongdoing. The details of past abuse and neglect are important only in so far as they link to an assessment of the child's future safety.

4) The work is driven by clients' motivation to achieve their own goals.
It is assumed that clients are motivated to work towards their own goals and that more often than not these goals, identified in the context of a child protection intervention, will support the overarching goal of increasing child safety. It is always possible to find common goals on which a working partnership can be built; with the least collaborative client something as simple as wanting to see the end of the worker's involvement can be a powerful motivator to address risks. Goals are kept small, achievable, and related to specific new behaviours described in detail. This is because goal achievement is inherently motivating and small changes can trigger significant personal and systemic change.

5) Solutions, and the motivation to achieve them, are the product of the worker-client interaction.

The way a problem is discussed opens or closes the door to different solutions and builds or impedes client motivation to achieve those solutions. Workers can create an expectation of change by framing problems as temporary, solutions as accessible, and clients as having capacity. Because both motivation and goals are co-constructed through the worker-client interaction, every interaction is a potentially powerful intervention, and the worker-client relationship is central to the work.

6) Coercion and partnership are not mutually exclusive.

The worker possesses a great deal of power and needs to exercise statutory authority if the child's safety cannot be secured without it. However, the use of coercive force can coexist with ongoing efforts to construct a genuine partnership informed by both the client's and worker's perspectives.

7) The worker strategically uses the tools of solution-focused therapy in the interaction with the client.

The approach is more than simply a perspective. It requires the use of a toolset of solution-focused questions (exceptions, scaling, coping, and miracle questions) throughout the casework process (Oliver, 2014; Oliver & Charles, 2016).

Worker-Client Relationships

In strengths-based child protection practice, the worker-client relationship is critically important. The approach moves away from the idea that protection work is first and foremost a technical endeavour in which good practice can be achieved by completing the assigned tasks, following the procedures, and mastering the correct techniques. The key to effective work is the quality of the connection between worker and client in a relationship that is "the principle vehicle for change" (Turnell & Edwards, 1999, p. 47). It is through this relationship that the client develops a sense of validation, personal competence, and trust in the helping process and that the worker elicits the best information. It is through this relationship that the client and worker co-construct solutions and the motivation and means to achieve them.

The worker-client relationship is so central to strengths-based child protection work that it is worth taking time to unpack how this relationship is supposed to look. What kind of worker-client relationship can support the collaboration with families and the dual focus on client strengths and child safety required from strengths-based protection workers who are operating from a position of authority? The study described in this book offers new answers to this question. Prior to the study, the most detailed answers could be found in the case descriptions and advice offered by the approach's key theorists – Turnell and Edwards and Berg and Kelly. They painted a picture of the kind of worker-client relationships to which strengths-based child protection practitioners might aspire.

This picture is of a purposeful, goal-centred relationship for which the worker is primarily responsible. It is a relationship in which the worker moves continually between expressing empathy for the client and establishing expectations, between being led and leading (Turnell et al., 2008). It is one in which the worker wields considerable power, hypothesizing future goals before even meeting with the client and using the client's goals as "leverage" for cooperation (Turnell & Edwards, 1999). The worker guides interviews with structured communication, therapeutic questioning techniques, and cognitive-behavioural strategies of rehearsal and reinforcement (Turnell & Edwards, 1999). As Berg and Kelly (2000) explain, "What we can do is to influence clients in such a way that they believe it is in their desire and in their best interest to change. This is all done with talking" (p. 80).

The same authors go on to say,

> Ask the client to explain the events as she sees them, without correcting her or arguing with her, however outrageous her story seems. Then – much later – you follow her logic and push it to an extreme, it will come to sound pretty incredible to her also. (Berg & Kelly, 2000, p. 88)

Acceptance of clients' perspectives is grounded in a genuine respect for their point of view, but it is also a clinical strategy to promote behavioural or cognitive change. It is worth noting that while workers are transparent in the discussion of goals, there is no requirement that they be open about their theoretical positioning and use of these clinical techniques. There is nothing wrong with front-line social workers taking this kind of strategic leadership-from-behind role or expertly using therapeutic techniques. Research into the effectiveness of solution-focused therapy suggests that this approach is a helpful way to support people to resolve their problems (Bond, Woods, Humphrey, Symes, & Green, 2013; Corcoran & Pillai, 2009; W. J. Gingerich & Eisengart, 2000; W. J. Gingerich & Peterson, 2013). The difficulty is that it makes for a complex relationship when workers are also required to genuinely support client self-determination, step out of the expert role, and present their authentic self.

Descriptions of strengths-based child protection practice suggest that the worker-client relationship relies as much on workers' genuine curiosity, openness, and warmth as on their clinical skills in eliciting and working with the client's position. Workers are advised to "maintain humour, hope and gratitude. Do not take yourself too seriously" (Berg & Kelly, 2000, p. 73). Strengths-based child protection practice seems to require a willingness to engage in a reciprocal and spontaneous relationship in which there is nothing contrived about the worker's caring and curiosity. This is illustrated by Turnell et al.'s (2008) story of a social worker confronted with a screaming and swearing one-eared father during an investigation who, after answering his demand that she "f*** off" with the request to know when she can "f*** back," then proceeded to say, "I couldn't help notice the fact that you hardly have a left ear, and if you don't tell me how that happened I don't think I'll be able to concentrate on what we have to talk about" (p. 105). The worker-client relationship that is central to strengths-based practice engages the whole worker, not just the professional persona.

To add to the complexity, this is a relationship in which workers may need to assert their authority in a very explicit way (Turnell & Edwards, 1999). The classic textbooks on strengths-based child protection practice describe its use with families in which the risk to children is high, collaboration is low, relationships do not always proceed smoothly, and children are brought into care. They illustrate the times when workers must act against their client's wishes in order to fulfil their statutory responsibilities to gather information, assess risk, and make decisions to support child safety. Strengths-based workers must be straightforward about the child protection concerns, their role, expectations, and the possible consequences of the client's choices. Workers' use of this authority is judicious and gentle; practitioners are advised that "making your requests in a calm, quiet firm voice makes them difficult for clients to resist" (Berg & Kelly, 2000). Nevertheless, it is very real.

In strengths-based child protection practice, this explicit use of mandated authority is balanced by the worker's willingness to be wrong and to respect clients' capacity to make their own decisions. Workers must always see their perspective as incomplete and open to revision while being sufficiently sure that they can take decisive action when required. Workers have to "hold at least five different stories in their head at one time" (Turnell & Essex, 2006, p. 38) and carry judgments lightly in order to work with clients' interpretations of their difficulties. Workers must hold their own interpretation in abeyance for as long as possible but be prepared to act on that interpretation against the client if they decide there is no other way to secure the child's safety.

Even on paper, the strengths-based worker-client relationships looks complex. How then do workers navigate it in practice?

Implementing Strengths-Based Child Protection Practice

The early evidence suggests that strengths-based approaches work well in child protection settings. There is probably no better place to assess their effectiveness than in Western Australia, the birthplace of the Signs of Safety approach. In a 2010 survey (Department for Child Protection, 2010) eighty-eight per cent of participating child protection workers said they found the approach useful or very useful, and eighty per cent reported that it had made a positive difference in their practice. An online survey two years later found eighty per cent of respondents rating the approach as useful or very useful (Department for Child Protection, 2012). The two surveys found workers reporting that the approach had had a range of positive effects, including supporting greater client participation, voice, and collaboration; enabling clearer goals to be set; supporting clearer articulation of information and more transparent decision-making; and helping clients come to a better understanding of the impact of harm. In both 2010 and 2012, nearly two-thirds of respondents reported that using Signs of Safety had increased their job satisfaction.

Similar findings were reported from an independent evaluation of the implementation of the Signs of Safety approach in the Borough of Copenhagen Child and Family Services led by Holmgård Sørensen in 2009 (as cited in Turnell, 2012). Between 2005 and 2008, 380 workers were trained in the approach, and the study found over seventy per cent of the 171 workers interviewed saying Signs of Safety had changed the way they worked with families and increased their focus on family resources. Sixty-nine per cent reported that they used the approach with families. Just over half said it had increased their inclusion of family strategies and solutions, and just under half said they now gave families more responsibility.

The positive response to strengths-based child protection practice is not just from workers. Clients also appear to appreciate the approach. Researchers in Minnesota interviewed twenty-four parents of children whose child protection cases had recently been closed and whose workers had utilized a Signs of Safety approach (Skrypek et al., 2012). Two-thirds reported that their worker had taken the time to get to know them and had clearly described child protection concerns. All described their worker engaging in key strengths-based processes like helping them identify a "safety network," identifying their strengths, and collaborating with them in safety planning. Half of these parents described their participation in particular Signs of Safety strategies like scaling and using the Three Houses tool (Weld, 2008). Two-thirds of interviewees reported their relationship with their worker had been consistently positive or had improved over time. Many "used terms such as 'friendly,' 'professional,' 'respectful,' 'good listener,' 'fair,' and 'non-judgmental' to describe their worker" (Skrypek et al., 2012, p. 2), and a few even equated the working relationship to a kind of friendship. When the same research team interviewed external stakeholders in the child protection system like lawyers, doctors, and police, these professionals appeared to confirm the impression that the approach increased collaboration with parents as

> in essence, under Signs of Safety, the responsibility shifts to the parent to identify the solution. According to stakeholders, rather than working behind the scenes to find a solution for the family, Child Protection is working with families to help them find their own strengths and create their own safety nets. (Idzelis Rothe, Nelson-Dusek, & Skrypek, 2013, p. 28)

There is early evidence to suggest that this increased partnership between families and workers may translate into better outcomes for children. An independent report into Signs of Safety in two Minnesota counties that have used the approach since 1999 and 2000 described improvements in such outcomes as the rate of entry into care and the recidivism rate (Idzelis Rothe et al., 2013). In Kentucky, a series of studies suggested that workers who were more highly trained in Solution-Based Casework and used it more had better case outcomes. When compared to a team in which the supervisor received only one day of training in the model, a team in which all members received five days of training and twenty-four monthly consultations secured greater cooperation from families, achieved more goals, and saw fewer child removals and referrals to court (Antle et al., 2008). When 4,559 child protection cases were categorized into the two groups of high adherence and low adherence to Solution-Based Casework, researchers found the high-adherence cases to have better outcomes in child safety, permanency, and well-being (Antle et al., 2012). A study in Copenhagen claimed that in a sample of sixty-six child protection cases, strengths-based safety planning reduced the placement of children by almost fifty per cent in comparison to a control group (Holmgård Sørensen, 2013).

The difficulty with these studies is that they give only one piece of a complex implementation story. The research may point to improved outcomes, but it is very hard to isolate their cause. The Signs of Safety approach was implemented in Minnesota shortly after other radical changes in service delivery, like the introduction of a differential response policy and Structured Decision Making tools. This makes it impossible to conclude that it was specifically the use of a strengths-based approach that prompted the improved outcomes for children. The Kentucky research team have identified a link between Solution-Based Casework and better outcomes, and they have interrogated this link to identify sixteen specific components of the approach that predict better outcomes (van Zyl et al., 2014). However, they stop short of claiming that such links are causal. It is possible that an unidentified third factor was at work – maybe the teams trained in Solution-Based Casework did better simply because they felt better supported than others, or maybe workers used Solution-Based Casework most faithfully with clients who were easier to engage and more amenable to change no matter what approach was used. Maybe it was a factor other than the application of Solution-Based Casework that made the difference. It is hard to know. Certainly there is reason to believe that strengths-based child protection practice may be good for workers, clients, and the children they care about. However, a great deal more research is needed to establish an ironclad basis for this claim.

The same is true of studies suggesting that strengths-based practice has been positively received by professionals and clients. They tend to give little insight into how representative these happy professionals and clients are. Only forty-two of the one hundred parents initially approached to participate in the study into client perceptions of Solution-Based Casework consented to be contacted by researchers (Skrypek et al., 2012). This first approach was often made by the parent's worker, making it is possible that only those most positive about their experience participated in the study. There is a similar problem with the Western Australia and Copenhagen studies with front-line workers, and indeed with the study on which this book is based. The results of the first study were based on a seventeen per cent response rate, with only 251 responses to invitations sent to 1,460 staff. The results of the second were based on data from forty-five per cent of the workers trained. While some workers appeared to be using the Signs of Safety approach to good effect, it is not clear how typical they were and impossible to gauge the views of non-participants.

The positive picture of implementation is based to a significant extent on small-scale and descriptive studies (Bunn, 2013), which have tended to focus on what works and stories of success (Keddell, 2012; Shennan, 2006). Much of what has been written has been produced by workplace leaders charged with implementing Signs of Safety (Hogg & Wheeler, 2004; Lohrbach et al., 2005; Shennan, 2006; Turnell et al., 2008; Wheeler & Hogg, 2012). This means we have accounts that are rich in real-world knowledge and a deep understanding of, and commitment to, strengths-based child protection practice. It also means that we need to work to create space for dissenting voices and to hear the perspectives of those who have been less successful with the approach.

There are clearly implementation challenges. In Minnesota, Signs of Safety was first introduced in Olmsted County in 1999 and became part of statewide training in 2009 (Idzelis Rothe et al., 2013; Skrypek et al., 2010). An independent study found inconsistent implementation, with workers deterred from using the approach by a lack of trust in its efficacy, in the capacity of the families, and in their agency's commitment to implementation efforts (Skrypek et al., 2010). Inconsistent implementation of Solution-Based Casework was a consistent finding in Kentucky (Antle et al., 2008; Antle et al., 2012), partly due to "challenges of the shift from a pathology-orientation to a solution-focused and strengths-based perspective ... and the struggle to understand complex elements of the model" (Antle et al., 2012, p. 344). In Arizona, nearly half the families participating in a study of strengths-based in-home child welfare services described their worker as having demonstrated very little in the way of strengths-based practice (Lietz, 2011), while in Belgium, child protection workers individualized problems and pathologized clients in a way that was highly inconsistent with their claims to be taking a strengths-based approach (Roose et al., 2014).

A key problem in implementation seems to be difficulty enacting strengths-based values. A commitment to real partnership and a belief in the capacity of all is hard to detect when workers say of their clients, "Probably, you have been hurt so much in the past that it is impossible to reach a state of emotional well-being in your own life" (Roose et al., 2014, p. 8) or "I would like to see residents have more of a sense of accountability and less of a sense of entitlement ... because you see selfishness, and I remind them of how lucky they are" (Grant & Cadell, 2009, p. 428). Both comments were made by workers who were, in theory, implementing strengths-based practice. They fuel broad concerns that much social work done in the name of strengths-based practice is not strengths-based at all (Blundo, 2001, 2012; Grant & Cadell, 2009; C. Rapp et al., 2005. As Rapp, Saleebey, and Sullivan lament,

> Since the strengths model has gained currency, many people are claiming they are "doing strengths." Sometimes that seems to mean "being nice to people" or having a small section at the bottom of an assessment form calling for a listing of strengths. (2005, p. 81)

Since we have the early evidence that strengths-based practice can work well on the child protection front lines, these implementation difficulties constitute a real problem. It is a problem that the study described in Chapter 4 was designed to explore.

Reflective Questions

1 What are the seven principles of strengths-based child protection practice?
2 To what extent do these principles fit with what you know, from personal experience and/or your theoretical knowledge, to be
   a) good generalist strengths-based practice?
   b) good child protection practice?
3 Think back to Shauna's case. You are doing a 9 a.m. home visit the day after Shauna called the emergency line to say that she was at her breaking point and worried she would hurt her baby if he did not shut up. Her friend stayed with her overnight and needs to leave in a couple of hours to get to her lunchtime shift at the local coffee shop. What might you do or say during the home visit to put into practice each of the principles of strengths-based child protection practice?

4 On a scale of one to ten, where one is not confident at all and ten is extremely confident, rate each of the seven principles of strengths-based child protection practice to indicate how confident you are that you can apply it with *all* child protection clients. Explain your ratings.
5 What do you think you would need to increase your confidence to enact each principle by one point?

Chapter Four

Hearing from the Front Lines

This chapter describes the study that led to the ideas on which the book is based. The study asked front-line child protection workers in a large statutory Canadian agency whether and how they use strengths-based practice and what helps and hinders them in their approach. The goal of this chapter is to give enough information so readers can put those ideas in context and understand the basis for the claims made, leaving the more academic details of the study to be read elsewhere (Oliver, 2012, 2014; Oliver & Charles, 2015, 2016).

The study was grounded in the firm belief that one of the best ways to understand whether and how an approach works is to ask those responsible for putting it into practice. This does not mean that their view is the only "truth"; they can only report their perceptions of what they do. Clients, judges, supervisors, or anyone else looking at the work from another perspective may well see things differently, but workers' perceptions are important. If those charged with enacting an approach do not perceive it as useful, it is not likely to get very far.

The evolution of strengths-based approaches has been driven from the beginning by this kind of practice knowledge. The strengths perspective developed through direct work with mental health clients, and solution-focused therapy was the brainchild of practising therapists. The foundational strengths-based child protection approaches were co-developed by front-line child protection workers within statutory agencies. Strengths-based practice assumes that clients are experts on their own lives and know what they need to succeed. My study assumed that front-line practitioners are experts in their own practice and that they, too, know what they need to succeed.

The Context

The study took place in British Columbia, a western Canadian province that spreads over 922,509km^2 of land. To give some sense of how large that is, California, Arizona, and Nevada could nearly fit within its borders. The United Kingdom and Ireland together are about a third of its size, and it equates to about one seventh the size of Australia. It has a population of 4.4 million people, 4.8% of whom identified as Aboriginal in the 2011 Census (Statistics Canada, 2012).

The study was conducted with the branch of the provincial government responsible for statutory child welfare services, the Ministry of Children and Family Development. Its staff assess concerns about child abuse and neglect, support families to mitigate those concerns, monitor their progress, and provide guardianship and adoption services to children in its legal care. These services are provided to all children in the province, with the exception of some Indigenous children who are served by agencies delegated to deliver services to a specific Indigenous community. At the time of the study, ministry staff worked out of approximately 429 offices located across British Columbia.

The Ministry of Children and Family Development introduced strengths-based practice in 2003. This was two years earlier than the Minnesota jurisdictions of Carver County and Olmsted County, which are "often identified as two of the longest-term implementers of the Signs of Safety framework anywhere in the world" (Idzelis Rothe et al., 2013, p. 6). The approach was intended to underpin the introduction of differential response and the work of the newly created Family Development Response (FDR) teams. Workers on these teams were trained in solution-focused questioning and in the Signs of Safety model. They were to offer family-centred strengths-based interventions informed by assessments of child protection concerns that were more collaborative than the typical investigation response could provide (Marshall et al., 2010).

The following decade saw strengths-based practice promoted as the preferred response to child protection concerns. By 2008 it was embedded in agency policy and basic training, and all child protection workers were expected to implement the approach (J. Wale, personal communication, July 31, 2013). It is important to note that the ministry did not subscribe with great fidelity to Signs of Safety or any other practice model. Written material supporting the policy referenced Saleebey's strengths-based ideas as well as Turnell and Edwards' work.

Training promoted the general principles, working relationship, and solution-focused questioning techniques of the approach rather than strict adherence to one particular interpretation.

Agency policy required that workers "use strengths-based, solution-focused communication techniques when discussing the family's situation and exploring possible solutions ... take an approach to planning that recognizes that families are experts regarding what interventions or services will be most supportive to them ... [and] recognize that family members have strengths upon which they can draw as they work towards the kind of positive change that will improve the safety of the child/youth and the family's overall well-being" (Ministry for Children and Family Development, 2012, p. 53).

In addition to giving every new worker at least two days of training in strengths-based child protection practice, the ministry launched major training initiatives across the province in 2006, 2008, and 2011. By the time the study was conducted in 2012, the agency had had nearly a decade to embed the approach into its policies and expose workers to strengths-based roles. The chances were good that a study in this agency would throw light on the ways in which strengths-based practice was used on the child protection front lines.

The Study

The purpose of the study was to answer two questions:

1 Do child protection workers apply the ideas of strengths-based solution-focused practice and, if so, how?
2 What do child protection workers perceive as helping and hindering them in this process?

The answers to these questions were sought using a mixed methods approach. The data were collected from front-line child protection workers via an online survey and in-depth interviews. The quantitative data provide a picture of the broad trends of strengths-based child protection implementation at the time. They illuminate patterns in workers' attitudes and opinions and the extent to which workers knew about and used strengths-based practice. The qualitative data flesh out this picture with detailed descriptions of the ways in which workers experienced and understood the approach. Their thoughtful interpretations and analysis of strengths-based practice enabled the study to go beyond simply describing *what* was going on, to offer insights into *why* things were as they were.

Survey

All child protection workers in the agency had their own computer, which they used on a daily basis for tasks like recording client data and accessing resources. This made an online survey one of the most efficient ways to contact such a large and geographically scattered workforce (Dillman, 2007). An original fifteen-question survey was developed from the strengths-based child protection practice literature. With an eye to increasing participation and respecting the workload carried by front-line practitioners, it was designed to take no more than ten minutes to complete.

A link to the survey was emailed to all 824 front-line employees who carried the legal authority to undertake the full range of child protection duties. The link was live for one month. In order to protect the confidentiality of their responses, the survey was hosted in an encrypted and password-protected format by an independent survey company. An important message conveyed in the promotional material for the study was that nobody from the agency would have access to the raw data or to any information that might disclose the identity of those who took part. This kind of study only works if participants feel able to be honest and to talk about practice as it is rather than how their employer or the textbooks tell them it should be.

Interviews

Seventy front-line child protection workers volunteered to be interviewed. Forty-two went on to give their formal consent to interviews, and, of these, twenty-four workers participated in in-depth taped and transcribed discussions as to what strengths-based child protection practice meant to them. Interviewees were chosen to represent the broadest possible range of ages, experience levels in child protection and in strengths-based practice, team memberships, and beliefs about the relative difficulty and appropriateness of the approach. Other studies and early results from this study suggested these factors might be important.

In the early interviews, an interview schedule was used to ensure consistency in the questions asked. This kept in play all the avenues of enquiry that other studies, the survey responses, and practice experience had suggested might be important. As time went on, the interview questions evolved to explore recurring themes that called for more attention. Two workers were interviewed twice in order to capture their information across the full range of questions.

Analysis

Data analysis began from the time the first survey was returned. The number of different responses was counted and represented as percentages and average scores. More complex inferential operations examined whether different variables might be related. Was the rate at which workers said they used strengths-based practice related to their education, age, or type of team? Did knowledge of the approach predict how positively or negatively workers felt about its application? Correlations, ANOVAs, and chi square calculations helped explore these links.

The qualitative information from the survey and interviews was analysed using an Interpretive Description approach (Thorne, 2008; Thorne, Kirkham, & MacDonald Emes, 1997). The goal of Interpretive Description is to identify patterns in the data that help practitioners conceptualize practice problems in a new light, leading to more productive action. It enables researchers to draw on a variety of analytical approaches, so long as they do it logically. In this study, each distinct idea was coded inductively for its overt meaning and the actions, meanings, supports, and barriers connected to strengths-based practice. Information directly related to the research questions, like "supports for strengths-based practice," was grouped into larger categories, and some codes were summarized numerically (Sandelowski, Voils, & Knafl, 2009).

Much of the analysis happened through a back-and-forth process of comparing and contrasting coded data pieces to each other and to the entire data set to analyse for similarities and differences. This process is similar to the clinical reasoning used by front-line professionals (Thorne, 2008), as the researcher "alternates between asking 'what is going on?' and 'how does this relate to what else is known?'" (Oliver, 2012, p. 412). It results in similar codes being grouped into progressively larger, more conceptual categories and the initial broad categories being broken down as nuances within these categories become apparent. The emerging conceptual analysis was emailed to interviewees, and their comments were analysed to expand the analysis and assess the extent to which it was perceived as meaningful and relevant.

The end goal of this kind of analysis is a "research report that makes visible and accessible the clinical wisdom of a passionate and thoughtful expert practitioner for whom a similar understanding had been acquired through extensive pattern recognition and reflective practice observations" (Thorne, 2008, p. 169). This wisdom is presented in the form of a heuristic or mental shortcut that captures the main elements of the practice issue and is sufficiently memorable and relevant to practitioners to help them approach the issue more successfully. In other words, the hoped-for outcome of the study was a new way of looking at strengths-based practice that not only made sense to the participants because it was rooted in their experiences, but would help them and others in a similar position better implement the approach.

Participants

All 225 participants in this study were front-line child protection workers who carried the authority to investigate child protection reports and bring children into statutory care against the wishes of their parents. Their ages ranged from twenty-three to sixty-five years, with an average age of 41.9 years ($SD = 10.46$). Their years of experience as child protection workers ranged from zero to thirty-two, with an average of 8.41 years ($SD = 6.08$). They reported having between zero and forty years of experience doing strengths-based practice, with an average of 8.28 years ($SD = 6.81$). Sixty-eight per cent ($n = 153$) of survey participants held a bachelor of social work (BSW) qualification, eighteen per cent ($n = 41$) held a bachelor of child and youth care, and eight per cent ($n = 18$) held a master of social work (MSW). Five per cent ($n = 12$) held a different qualification, including degrees in the arts, psychology, education, and nursing.

The survey participants worked on different types of child protection teams. Twenty-one per cent ($n = 48$) were on an Intake team, working with families from the point at which the child protection report is received to the point at which it is determined that the child is at sufficient risk to need ongoing intervention. An additional five per cent ($n = 10$) worked on a Family Development Response team, doing the same kind of front-end work but only with families who do not present the more serious risks deemed to necessitate an investigation. Family Service teams undertake the more long-term work with a family; twenty-seven per cent ($n = 60$) of survey participants worked on one of these teams. Forty-five per cent ($n = 101$) of respondents worked on an

Integrated team. This was defined as a team that either works with families at all points in the life of a case or a team that includes colleagues from other fields, like addictions and mental health work. Finally, two per cent ($n = 5$) worked with a specific client group, like youth. There was no significant difference in the workers' ages, child protection experience, or strengths-based practice experience across these teams.

The profiles of the twenty-four interviewees are similar to that of the survey respondents. Their years of child protection experience range from zero to twenty-three, with an average of 7.17 years ($SD = 5.80$). They claimed between one and forty years of experience doing strengths-based practice, with an average of 9.79 years ($SD = 9.35$). One interviewee worked on an Intake team, two on a Family Development Response team, six on a Family Service team, fourteen on an Integrated team, and one on a Youth team. Seven were male and seventeen female. Sixteen workers had a bachelor's degree in social work, two had a master's degree in social work, and six had a qualification from another field, including psychology, counselling, medicine, and criminal justice. The final interviewee sample comprised eight people who agreed to the survey statement "strengths-based practice is hard to do in child protection," ten who disagreed, three who neither agreed nor disagreed, and one who did not complete the survey.

This picture of the study participants is far from complete. Important information about gender, location, cultural identity, and other common identifying characteristics was not collected. This is because participants in workplace research often worry about the consequences of expressing their honest views and will only speak up if they are sure they can do so anonymously (Scriven & Smith-Ferrier, 2003). To reassure participants in this study that their identity would be fully protected, some important questions about who they were had to go unasked.

Interpreting the Results

The survey was completed by twenty-seven per cent of the total 824 front-line workers carrying full child protection responsibilities for the agency. If this were a truly random sample, results could be said to represent the population of front-line child protection workers within the agency with a margin of error of 5.59%, 95% of the time. We do know that there was no significant difference between the average age of the participants and their non-participating colleagues. Beyond this, however, it is impossible to estimate the extent to which those who responded resembled or differed from those who did not. The study sample was not truly random, as it included only those workers who were willing and able to participate (Fricker, 2008). The views of non-participants remain unknown. The study also did not include independent observations of practice or corroboration from clients, supervisors, or case files. This meant there was no way to establish whether workers really acted in the ways they described.

These are normal problems in this kind of exploratory research and do not undermine the results (Palys & Atchison, 2003). They do, however, mean that caution is needed in interpreting them. The survey findings presented in this book are best seen as suggestive of possible patterns in the broader population of agency workers rather than firm evidence that these patterns existed beyond the sample. The interview findings are best viewed as expressing common experiences among the interviewees. It is left to the reader to reflect on the extent to which these resonate with, and offer a new way of looking at, their own experiences.

Reflective Questions

1 List possible sources of evidence for using one child protection approach over another.
2 What sources of evidence do you think are most persuasive? Why?
3 To what extent do you see the study described in this chapter as providing trustworthy evidence of strengths-based child protection practice? What are the study's strengths and limitations?
4 What other research or theories support taking a strengths-based approach to child protection?
5 Think about your personal experiences, values, and professional aspirations. What reasons do you have for attempting strengths-based child protection practice?

Section One Summary

Strengths-based and solution-focused ideas originated outside the field of child protection practice. While they have led to the development of several child protection–specific approaches, there is evidence that workers are having difficulty implementing these approaches consistently. This is a problem, in light of early research suggesting that both workers and their clients like strengths-based practice and that it may lead to improved outcomes for the children served.

One of the challenges of strengths-based child protection is that it requires workers to navigate complex relationships with their clients. The question of the worker's authority within that relationship is particularly problematic. The child protection role has always straddled responsibilities to care for and to control clients, and the ways in which workers have balanced those care and control functions have shifted over time and from place to place. The introduction of strengths-based practice is often interpreted as an attempt to recalibrate this balance, but different strengths-based traditions deal differently with the question of power, so the origin of the strengths-based ideas that workers are bringing to their work matters.

Do child protection workers apply the ideas of strengths-based practice? What supports them to do this and what gets in the way? What does strengths-based practice even mean when you have the power to remove someone's children? The study on which this book is based put these questions to front-line child protection workers. Their answers illustrate the importance of interpreting strengths-based practice in a way that is compatible not just with workers' supportive functions but also with their mandated authority. It led to a model for the worker-client relationship that supports workers to be strengths-based no

matter whether they are perceived to be helping or perceived to be med-
dling where they do not belong. Those anxious to explore this model
should jump ahead to Section 3. For others, we pause to consider interpretations of strengths-based practice that do not fit well with child
protection work. Recognizing which interpretations to avoid helps us
focus on which interpretation to apply.

SECTION TWO

Choosing Not to Use Strengths-Based Practice

"Practicing from a strengths orientation means this – *everything* you do as a social worker will be predicated, in some way, on helping to discover and embellish, explore and exploit clients' strengths and resources in the service of assisting them to achieve their goals, realize their dreams, and shed the irons of their own inhibitions and misgivings." (Saleebey, 2012, p. 3)

Chapter Five

The Question of Applicability

When the results from the online survey were analysed, a striking paradox became clear. While most survey respondents claimed to know about strengths-based practice, to like it, and to believe it to be a good approach for child protection, the vast majority said it could not be used with the clients and situations typically encountered in their day-to-day work.

Making sense of this contradiction requires us to look a little deeper. Every person who participated in the study reported knowing at least something about strengths-based practice, and just over three-quarters said they knew a good amount or a lot about the approach. Every person reported using it at least sometimes in their work, and eighty-three per cent said they used it most of the time or always. Knowledge and use of the approach did not vary with team type, age, or years of child protection experience. Remember that the agency did not subscribe to one specific strengths-based child protection model; their training and promotional material drew both from the Kansas and solution-focused traditions. Broadly defined as it was, strengths-based child protection practice had come to be viewed within this agency as a normal approach for child protection work. It was no longer seen as the preserve of a few specialists or of new trainees bringing innovative ideas into the workplace.

Workers did not only claim to apply strengths-based practice in a general or abstract sense. When asked to rate how often in the last ten conversations with adult clients they had used each technique, seventy-four per cent reported using the miracle question, seventy-seven per cent an exceptions question, eighty per cent a scaling question, and eighty-eight per cent a coping question. It is unlikely that these responses were entirely accurate – people tend to have difficulty recalling this kind of detailed information (Brace, 2008). The responses did, however, suggest that workers were familiar with these specific solution-focused techniques. The agency's attempts to embed the approach into practice through policy and training appeared to have had some success.

What of strengths-based practice's popularity? Eighty-nine per cent agreed with the statement that "strengths-based practice is a good approach for child protection work." Eighty-five per cent agreed that it increased the chances of success with clients. Only nine per cent felt that using strengths-based practice increased the risk to children. People felt more positive about the approach the more knowledge they had of it, the more frequently they used it, and the longer they used it. There appeared to be a great deal of buy-in.

These responses need to be interpreted cautiously, as it is possible that only those workers who felt most familiar with and positive about the approach chose to take part in the study. At no point in the study were participants provided with a definition of strengths-based practice, so what exactly it was that they said they knew about, did, and liked when they said they knew about, did and liked strengths-based practice is unclear. However, the responses do echo findings from other studies suggesting that strengths-based ideas are not only being used in child protection practice but are perceived by front-line workers as being valuable (Antle et al., 2012; Bunn, 2013; Department for Child Protection, 2010; Idzelis Rothe et al., 2013). That very few participants spoke out against using strengths-based practice suggests that it had come to be seen as relatively uncontroversial and that any work to support implementation did not need to focus on convincing child protection workers that strengths-based practice had merit. Participants seemed to have no trouble in seeing it that way.

The large majority of participating workers liked strengths-based practice, thought it was a good approach for child protection work, and said they knew about it and used it in their work. Yet only forty-four per cent thought the approach was right for all clients, and only forty-five per cent thought it was appropriate in every situation. Despite the general acceptance of, and support for, strengths-based ideas, seventy per cent of those who could be coded on the issue said there were child protection clients or situations for which the approach was simply not applicable.

These findings run contrary to the common claim that strengths-based practice can always be employed (Blundo, 2001, 2012; Corcoran,

2005; Graybeal, 2001). Those in the Kansas tradition describe it as a standpoint, a philosophical orientation to strengths or "an attitude and frame from which to engage those with whom we are working" (Blundo, 2001, p. 303). It is not an approach designed to be switched on and off as the situation requires. The same is true of the solution-focused approaches developed specifically for child protection settings. Forged from therapeutic work with mandated and "resistant" clients, these approaches were never intended to be used only with those who were particularly collaborative or possessed certain characteristics. They are promoted for use with all clients in all child protection situations. Why then, in this study, had so many workers decided that strengths-based practice was not a universal approach?

A Matter of Competence

It is likely that some workers in the study saw strengths-based practice as having limited use because they had not yet developed the competence and confidence to apply it in all situations. Those who saw it as being least applicable tended to be younger and to have the least knowledge of and experience with the approach. It is common when first using a new approach to apply it in very limited ways (Dreyfus & Dreyfus, 2005). As we develop confidence and see the new approach being useful, we begin to use it more often and more widely. Through experience, we develop what amounts to a mental database of examples of the approach being used in different situations (André & Fernand, 2008; Dreyfus & Dreyfus, 2005; Moulton, Regehr, Mylopoulos, & MacRae, 2007). As this database expands, so does our ability to adapt the knowledge it contains to a broader array of new situations.

It is perfectly normal to see strengths-based practice as having limited applicability in the early days of trying to use the approach. As we become more competent in connecting clients to their motivation, resources, and community, there should be fewer and fewer situations in which we feel using strengths-based practice does not work. This is one reason why the common recommendation for more strengths-based practice training (Antle et al., 2008; Idzelis Rothe et al., 2013; Lietz, 2011; Skrypek et al., 2010) is likely to be somewhat effective as an antidote to inconsistent implementation. In this study, however, practitioner age and strengths-based practice knowledge and experience had only a small effect on beliefs about the approach's applicability. The majority of practitioners did not see their competence as being a significant barrier, and approximately twice as many workers thought that strengths-based practice was easy as thought it was hard. Something apart from the normal learning process seemed to be at play.

A Matter of Choice

For many workers in the study, inconsistent implementation of strengths-based practice was a rational choice. It was not that they *could not* do it; they believed they *should not* do it. They had clear rules about the situations for which strengths-based practice did not apply.

Of the seventy per cent of survey respondents who said that strengths-based practice was not always applicable, 102 gave examples of the situations or clients for which it did not apply. It was deemed inappropriate for "child protection cases" (260[1]), "investigation cases" (198), with "mentally ill clients, clients where severe physical or sexual abuse has occurred, domestic violence. Severe substance using clients" (90), and "when there is court involvement" (319). Few respondents qualified their response with words like "some" or "sometimes" to suggest that strengths-based practice was inappropriate only for certain people within these client populations. Table 1 shows how participants deemed the approach inapplicable to entire categories of client with whom child protection practitioners tend to work.

At first glance these categories make little sense. Strengths-based child protection developed from solution-focused work with "resistant" clients. Its future-focus does not require worker and client to agree on what happened in the past, and its strength lies in its strategies to circumvent lack of collaboration. So why did nearly a third of respondents say it could not be done in the absence of collaboration and why did more say that client hostility or denial meant it no longer applied? Strengths-based child protection approaches are intended to focus on child safety, so why would it be problematic to use them when the child's immediate safety was a concern? The Kansas strengths-based approach originated with people with mental illness, and an important client group in the development of solution-focused therapy was people with addictions (Berg & Miller, 1992), so why would strengths-based practice be deemed inappropriate for people with these challenges? And

---

1 All study participants were allocated a code number. This number is used to attribute their quotations.

Table 1. When Strengths-Based Practice Is Not Appropriate ($n = 102$)

When Strengths-Based Practice Is Not Appropriate	Percentage of n
With clients who are not willing to work collaboratively	30
When the worker must act to secure the child's immediate safety	26
With clients with substance use issues	25
With clients with mental illness	21
With clients who are hostile or aggressive	18
With clients who deny concerns	14
With clients who sexually abuse	12
With clients who severely harm their child	10
With clients with a long history of child welfare involvement	7
With clients with limited cognitive capacity	5
In situations of family violence	4
With clients who are sociopathic or psychopathic	4
With clients who deliberately harm their child	2
With clients who are involved in criminal activity	2

finally, why would the type of abuse or the client's intentions, intellect, or criminal activity make the slightest difference?

The answers to these questions lie in the different ways in which workers defined strengths-based practice in child protection work. That they defined the approach differently is hardly surprising. Most had graduated from social work programs teaching the strengths-based perspective as a generic approach, some had received training in the Signs of Safety model, and others had received training that drew on both Signs of Safety and the Kansas approach. They worked in an agency that promoted the general principles and techniques of strengths-based practice but not one clear model to which they could all subscribe. They drew on their formal education as well as their personal reading, understandings of strengths-based practice held by colleagues and supervisors, and their experience of its enactment in this and other agencies. It makes sense that participants should bring a mixed bag of ideas about what being strengths-based means.

As the in-depth interviews with practitioners progressed, five distinct versions of strengths-based child protection practice became evident in practitioners' descriptions (Oliver, 2014; Oliver & Charles, 2015). Each interviewee's account of strengths-based child protection practice was consistent with one of these five versions. The versions are illustrated in Figure 1 and outlined in the following chapters as "relating therapeutically," "supporting client self-determination," "connecting to internal and external resources," "pursuing a balanced understanding," and

Figure 1. The five versions of strengths-based practice and the challenges they present

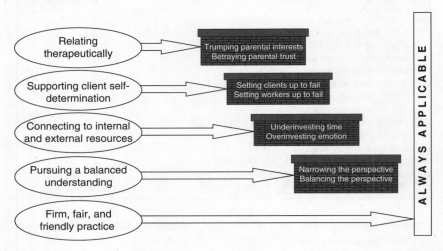

"firm, fair, and friendly practice." The labels reflect the core distinctive concern of each one.

Not one of these five versions can be dismissed as wrong. Each picks up on at least one significant strand of the diverse literature about the values and activities of strengths-based practice. There is every reason to believe that if interviewing had continued, more versions would have emerged. These five are instructive, however, because of the differences in their usefulness.

Only "firm, fair, and friendly practice" was entirely congruent with the child protection role (Oliver, 2014; Oliver & Charles, 2016). It was the only version that could be used with all clients in all situations and that could support workers to develop robust professional identities as strengths-based child protection practitioners. The other versions, grounded in the Kansas strengths tradition and relying on client self-determination, were simply not a good fit for statutory child protection work. These versions were unsuitable for many of the clients and situations encountered in a typical working day and had to be "switched off" at certain times or with certain people if practitioners were to keep children safe. Figure 1 illustrates some of the issues that got in their way. The overwhelming majority of child protection workers in the study were trying to use interpretations of strengths-based practice that could not survive the use of their statutory authority or the conditions in which they practised. In the remaining chapters in this section, we take a closer look at what they were doing and why it did not work out well.

Reflective Questions

1 When child protection workers say they like strengths-based practice but do not use it, what individual and structural issues might be to blame?
2 On a scale of one to ten, where one means you know nothing about it and ten means you know everything there is to know about it, rate your own knowledge of strengths-based child protection practice. Being as specific as you can, describe what you want to learn in order to rate yourself one point higher.
3 What connections do you make between your level of knowledge about the approach and your willingness to use it with all child protection clients?
4 To what extent do you think strength-based child protection is a universal approach? Identify your reasons with reference both to your personal experiences and your theoretical knowledge.
5 The study found workers using five different "versions" of strengths-based practice. Only one version of strengths-based practice could be used with all child protection clients. In what ways do you think that version is different from the others?
6 Take three minutes to create a mind-map that visually represents your current definition of strengths-based child protection practice.

Chapter Six

Relating Therapeutically

The "relating therapeutically" version of strengths-based practice was described by three interviewees. It was "all about the relationship" (266), but this was a very different worker-client relationship than that found in many child protection offices. It was a therapeutic alliance, whose primary function was to trigger changes in the client's ways of thinking and feeling.

The foundation of the therapeutic worker-client relationship was the workers' continual identification and acknowledgment of clients' strengths, resources, and capacities. Interviewees describing this approach really took to heart the solution-focused advice to start every session with "what is better?" (Berg & Kelly, 2000). By liberally complimenting client successes, they sought to provide encouragement and hope and to help clients reconnect to their innate resilience. Focusing on strengths brought them to the forefront of the client's awareness, making them more accessible. This was not simply a matter of being nice or supportive; it was a systematic attempt to increase the client's sense of agency, connection to their internal resources, and motivation to parent well.

In a "relating therapeutically" approach, the key to mitigating risks to the child was internal change on the part of the parent. Strengths-based interactions might, for instance, help clients feel empowered and more sure of their goal to parent well. This might increase their ability to take the necessary steps to address a long-standing problem or to access the help of those around them. The mechanism driving these secondary changes in the clients' behaviour and social systems was change in the clients' ways of experiencing themselves and the world around them. These emotional and psychological changes were the direct focus of the practitioner's attention within the kind of supportive working alliance more typical of one-on-one therapy than child protection practice.

This approach was rooted in the belief that clients entered the interaction with the worker feeling at least somewhat disempowered. This might be due to poverty, violence, or any other stigmatizing, traumatizing, or oppressive experience, including involvement with child protection services. As one worker said, building a strengths-based relationship "makes them feel like they're not totally sucking at everything in life" (266). The goal was empowerment, and the medium was the transformative worker-client interaction, leading to moments of catharsis and new understanding. Another worker explained the impact of identifying client strengths as

> I'm hearing things like "well no one's ever described it like that before," sometimes ... there's tears, and I don't base my practice on making people cry, but sometimes it's that light bulb moment where they're going "OK I am capable despite my dad, my mum, my great uncle, my whoever said that I was a loser," and they get and start to grasp that they can parent. (73)

The "relating therapeutically" worker-client relationship was characterized by empathy. Empathy helped the worker develop real insight into the client's challenges and potential solutions. When clients felt that their position was truly understood and acknowledged, they were more likely to be honest about their experiences. This gave the worker a deeper and more comprehensive perspective than was typical in child protection, allowing for assessments and plans that were more likely to be effective, since they were based in what was unique about the family's situation.

Empathy also helped "open up" the client to new perspectives, including recognizing concerns about their parenting. As one worker said, "I really think it's about the relationship. If they care about what their social worker thinks and they care about the relationship, then they're going to make that connection and that effort" (266). The thinking was that if clients did not have to fight for their strengths to be recognized, they would be more open to discussing their challenges. If they felt understood and accepted, they were more likely to try a new approach. This enabled the worker to provide information and an alternative perspective to help clients come to new realizations about their parenting. The worker could assume the role of guide, "showing them and explaining to them or talking to them about how it worked for them the first time around" (60) and "sharing wisdom ... showing them what a good parent is" (73).

"Relating therapeutically" drew heavily on the Kansas strengths-based tradition. It was the Kansas theorists who made the most of the ideas of resilience and empowerment and reframed the relationship between client and case manager as one of caring, collaboration, and great therapeutic potential. The difficulty is that "relating therapeutic-ally" workers were not always able to maintain their focus on the thera-peutic needs of the individual in front of them. They were rarely free to contract a therapeutic relationship on their own terms. The child, some-times the courts, and always the various levels of agency management were also involved. It was not unusual for the interests of one of these parties to trump the interests of the parent, and when this happened, the trust on which all therapeutic relationships rely was betrayed.

Trumping Parental Interests

Even in the best of conditions, with a skilled therapist and an engaged parent, the kind of therapeutic change envisaged in the "relating thera-peutically" approach can be a long time in coming. The clients of child protection agencies are typically extremely aware of the worker's power and cautious about disclosing vulnerability (Bundy-Fazioli et al., 2009; Dumbrill, 2006; Littlechild, 2008). Child protection workers rarely see themselves as therapists and lack training in therapeutic work (Yatchmenoff, 2005). They have been criticized for their competence in even basic counselling and communication skills; one UK study found child protection workers using closed questions twice as often as open questions, struggling to show empathy, and rarely using reflec-tive statements or identifying strengths (Forrester, Kershaw, Moss, & Hughes, 2008, p. 48). These are hardly conditions to foster rapid thera-peutic transformation.

A starving child cannot afford to wait too long for the parental insights necessary to put food on the table. A child who is being sexually abused in the home needs protective action far sooner than a therapeutic break-through is likely to take. Even when a child is not at immediate risk, court deadlines might not allow for an effective therapeutic relation-ship to run its course. In British Columbia, when children under the age of five are removed into care, their parents have only twelve months of court-ordered time to demonstrate the child can be returned home safely before the worker must initiate legal proceedings to permanently remove parental guardianship. This leaves little time for the therapeutic process to reap results. As one worker said,

> It's not like counselling or psychology or another job that doesn't have the same mandate, where you can spend as much time as you want with somebody, you can keep meeting up with them every week for years and you can make changes and movement, but we don't have that time, a lot of the time we don't have that kind of time. (266)

This version of strengths-based practice was frequently stalled by the reality that the worker needed to prioritize the safety of the child and the demands of the courts. When empathy, understanding, and the surfacing of strengths did not elicit in the child's parents the right kind of change in the right kind of time, it needed to be replaced with an approach that more directly addressed the child protection concerns. As one worker said,

> It may be that I can be strengths-based six months down the road, but through that initial period when the needs of the children are, and the safety of the child are, and the health of the child are, in jeopardy we kind of have to draw a hard and fast line as to what is acceptable and what is not. (73)

"Drawing a hard and fast line" signalled the end of "relating therapeutically" and the beginning of a more directive approach.

Respondents also blamed the interests of supervisors and managers for getting in the way of "relating therapeutically" worker-client relationships. Those above front-line workers in the organizational hierarchy were described as preoccupied with personal and organizational liability concerns. As one worker said,

> Supervisors are in a position to not use [strengths-based practice] as much because they are the ones that have to make the final call. They're the ones that are ultimately responsible if something happens to a kid and they're the ones that are most likely, in my experience, just to minimize what is going well and focus on what's not going [well]. And that's not a personality, it's just that's the job description that they're in. (266)

This was a problem when risk aversion from higher up the chain of command led to the rejection of plans that were crafted within the worker-client dyad but required management approval and resourcing.

Part of the difficulty was that supervisors and managers were too physically removed from families to experience them in the same way as the workers who were "relating therapeutically." They rarely did home visits, their client contact was largely limited to formal meetings, and they had little opportunity to develop the close, empathic worker-client relationships described by these interviewees. They appeared to have a hard time trusting the intuitive and nuanced understanding of families that resulted from these relationships but was tricky to capture in the written assessment tools on which management decision-making formally relied. Managers were described as

> all giving their own ideas and opinions as to how you should proceed and almost always it's far more intrusive than me at a front-line level who sees what's going on, who's right in the middle of the crisis ... who has a good understanding of the client, the client's strengths, the client's challenges, which are completely overlooked when they're sitting in an office, completely detached from the family dynamics ... [Managers do not understand] it's just rapport building, it's establishing a relationship, it's understanding their family dynamics which is very intrinsic, it's not just a cookie cutter thing. There are very many layers. (60)

The effect of the physical distance from families was exacerbated by an emotional distance from their lives. Managers are often seen as overly focused on the pursuit of efficiency, which has come to characterize contemporary child welfare systems (Gallagher et al., 2011; Harlow, 2003). The implementation of managerialism has increased demands on those in more senior child protection positions to ensure organizational performance through the implementation, monitoring, and audit of standardized procedures. It has seen the idea that good service delivery is founded on an intimate, relational knowledge of our families dismissed as an outdated indulgence. It promotes the view that

> the ideal new manager remains distant and controlled. He takes a critical stance towards the arguments presented and the established practices of others, drawing his own conclusions based on designated general decision rules [risk assessment, cost-benefit analysis and so on] rather than being swayed by sympathy to particular cases. (Meagher & Parton, 2004, p. 14)

Yet it is precisely this sympathy to particular cases and a deep attunement to the unique needs and strengths of individual families that underpins this version of strengths-based practice. When the worker-client relationship became the site of competing interests that had very little to do with parental insight, empowerment, or therapeutic change, plans were derailed, parental interests de-prioritized, and "relating therapeutically" ran aground.

Betraying Parental Trust

This version of strengths-based practice supported the creation of close worker-client relationships, but it almost inevitably led to their collapse if case planning changed and workers took action against parental wishes. One worker described these as "slap and tickle" (60) relationships that lurched unpredictably from a focus on therapeutic support to a focus on control. As she said,

> I see this with other workers around me that do ... kinda let that guard down, really develop a good strong relationship with those clients, only to have to turn around and take a very authoritative stance at some point. Completely sabotages that relationship then all you see is this hostility, defence, and it doesn't go away. So you could hold these files for ten years and because you developed a really strong relationship with them for the first three years and then all of a sudden had to remove their kids, they will never trust you again. And that trust is permanently severed ... I can have a wonderful, and I would say maybe a strengths-based perspective when I do work with one particular client one day, and then the next day I have to be the exact opposite. So it's really hard, and I feel like they even question like "Oh my God, is this gonna be a good day of hers or is this gonna be a bad day? Is she gonna come in and say something nice about me or is she gonna come and come in and say all these bad things? (60)

Workers' efforts to create a relationship in which clients felt whole-heartedly supported and deeply engaged in a therapeutic process meant that any use of their authority felt like a betrayal. Their focus on collaboration and the client's personal healing obscured the involuntary nature of the work. It was not that workers neglected to explain to their clients the basis of the relationship. All interviewees who described this version of strengths-based practice stressed the fact that in their very first contacts with clients they were very clear about their role, their authority, and the child protection concerns. Their subsequent struggles speak instead to how difficult it can be to forge worker-client relationships in the traditional therapeutic mould when key decisions are made by parties and in relation to parties outside of the therapeutic dyad. The emphasis on validating the client's perspective and building cooperation by amplifying client successes made it relatively easy to ignore the issue of mandated authority until they felt forced to attend to the competing interests of child, courts, supervisors, and managers. All too often workers' needs to take coercive action to safeguard a child's safety, to meet court deadlines, or to follow the instructions of superiors forced the issue of their power into a relationship that was not set up to withstand it.

These sudden shifts from a supportive to a coercive stance could have devastating consequences on worker and client alike. Interviewees described them leaving clients confused, betrayed, and struggling to reconcile the ideas that they were both replete with resources and unable to provide safety for their child. As one worker said,

> When I show up and I'm talking about their strengths, they're thinking ... "He's found three strengths but only one weakness so obviously three strengths is better than one weakness." And that's not the case ... I was giving a false impression with the family that "Oh, you're doing this so well, you're doing this so well, you're doing this so well; OK now I have to take your kids." That would make it hard for a family to deal with me when they're like "Why are you taking them? You just said I was doing this really well and this really well and this really well. How come now the end result is you're taking my kids?" So they're then left with confusion and anger at me and he's a dishonest social worker. (73)

All interviewees who interpreted strengths-based practice as "relating therapeutically" felt that it put them in the position of being dishonest. Their awareness that they might need to shift out of a strengths-based approach at any time left them feeling that they were offering clients "fake choices" (266) and "false encouragement" (73). Workers knew that if clients stopped collaborating, they held the power to mandate their involvement anyway. As one worker said of the focus on collaboration,

> The second they say "No," we're doing it anyway without your permission and now we're gonna be more intrusive and that's where I don't see why are we coming to them saying "It's with your permission and with your cooperation, we're gonna work together on this." When really it isn't,

we're gonna do that as long as you're willing to do that but the second you're not we're gonna do it anyway. And that I don't like, I find that kind of deceiving 'cos we're not really. It's surface and I think clients know that too. (266)

One way workers used deception to protect the therapeutic relationship was to pretend that the position being taken was always entirely their own. By failing to disclose that it had in fact been imposed by the courts, supervisors, or others with greater power, workers maintained the illusion that the relationship they had worked so hard to create with clients was a self-contained therapeutic space. As one worker explained,

Whatever information is being given to me from "higher-ups" is literally information that I'm regurgitating to the families. I don't agree with it, but I also feel that I don't have a choice ... I tell [it] to them as though this is something that I'm identifying for myself ... having to go in and pretend that what you're saying is really, truly how you feel about the family. (60)

Another common trick was to soften the concerns. Rather than risk the worker-client relationship feeling unsupportive and vulnerable to disconnection, workers chose to gloss over risks to the child. As one put it,

I feel like, OK I can't just come right out and say what we're worried about. Because I have to think of a way to frame it in a positive way. And I find that in my interactions I'm constantly thinking about how do I not use the word "not"? How do I use a different word for "hit" or something right? So I'm always just trying to think about how I can reframe it. And then by the end of the meeting I'll be like "Did I really say what I needed to say? Was I being too vague? Again was I trying to sugar-coat it too much?" To make it more palatable for the clients. And then does the seriousness of everything get lost in that? (203)

Another worker talked of having established such a supportive therapeutic alliance with one client that the man frequently called to discuss his ongoing problematic drug use. Together, worker and client put in place a support plan that saw the child being cared for by another family member during times of heavy use. Yet the worker felt her strengths-based approach encouraged the client to maintain a pattern of behaviour that would ultimately lead to an increase in risk for the child. She saw herself compromising her values, enabling bad parenting, glossing over the risks, depriving her client of important information as to the extent and seriousness of the concerns, and lowering the client's motivation to address the concerns. None of that felt good.

There is nothing new about this struggle to maintain honesty in helping relationships. As early as 1917, Mary Richmond, one of the founding figures of modern social work, talked of the "temptation to indirectness, subterfuge, concealment or ambiguity, in which you might drift in spite of yourself while striving to help" (Richmond, 1917, p. 109). Social workers are often uncomfortable with their power and frequently downplay or deny it (Bar-On, 2002; Bundy-Fazioli et al., 2013; R. Hetherington, 1998; van Nijnatten et al., 2001). Even before the introduction of strengths-based practice, concerns were expressed that clients of mandated social work services could translate their experience of a positive therapeutic alliance into the belief that their worker acted only for them (Regehr & Antle, 1997). Alternative loyalties to the child, the courts, and the employing agency are easily forgotten.

In all strengths-based child protection relationships there is a tension between therapeutic support for the client's narrative truth and the mandated requirement to piece together the historical truth for the legal and quasi-legal processes on which child protection depends. Strategies that work well in the context of a clearly defined therapeutic relationship can be difficult to translate to front-line relationships susceptible to being hijacked by the needs of others. These relationships can end in accusations of betrayal when therapeutic and forensic roles are not clearly differentiated (Greenberg & Shuman, 1997, 2007; Wright & Odiah, 2000) and clients feel tricked by empathy into disclosures that are later used against them (Strasburger, Gutheil, & Brodsky, 1997). In the "relating therapeutically" version of strengths-based practice, neither worker nor client was adequately prepared to manage this tension. The therapeutic character of the worker-client relationship tended to dominate until the need to attend to the interests of the child, the courts, and superiors forced the worker's statutory authority to the forefront. The worker-client relationship rarely survived this intrusion, and the need to be directive left the worker with no choice but to suspend the approach.

Relating Therapeutically

Founded on: acknowledgment of client strengths.
Characterized by: therapeutic nature of the relationship, empathy, the worker's gentle guidance.
Undermined by: competing interests, deception and loss of trust, the worker's use of authority.
Achieves child safety through: changes in parental insight, motivation, and capacity.

Reflective Questions

1 How is your definition of strengths-based child protection practice similar or different from "relating therapeutically"?
2 Child protection workers commonly attempt to build supportive, therapeutic relationships with clients. Why do you think this is so?
3 Think of a time when you felt "stuck" in a supportive position with someone.
    a) What made it difficult to shift out of this position?
    b) What did it teach you about how to avoid getting stuck in the future?
    c) If you have never had this experience, what do you think helps you avoid getting stuck in this way?
4 Think back to the case of Katy, the nine-year-old girl who disclosed sexual abuse from her father, Mike. Imagine that you have been working with her mother, Ada, for over a year now and Katy has returned to the home. You have come to feel very attached to Ada, and you know she feels the same way about you. Ada has told you that she feels you have a real friendship and that she values the way you support her and see her strengths. She has told you of a history of being betrayed by people and that it has been wonderful to be able to finally find someone who believes in her.

    After Mike was assessed as posing a high risk of physical and sexual violence to Katy, Ada reluctantly came around to seeing that he should have no contact with Katy and agreed to a legal order to that effect being put in place. Back in the early days of your work with her, you explained your role and authority but have not really needed to since. For a long time now the focus of your work has been on helping Ada feel confident in her role in protecting her daughter from this man. This has been most satisfying – you feel more like a counsellor to her than anything else and feel she is making great progress. You really do believe she can do this, and you have been struck by how much the two of you have in common. Today, however, you got clear evidence that Mike has been living in the home for the last two weeks.

    a) Describe how you might feel about the idea of confronting Ada with the information.

    b) What might make it difficult? What might make it easy?

    c) How would you go about this conversation with her?

5 With reference to your personal experiences and values and/or your theoretical knowledge, describe how you might establish relationships with clients that are supportive and therapeutic but avoid the pitfalls described in this chapter.

Chapter Seven

Supporting Client Self-Determination

The "supporting client self-determination" version of strengths-based practice was described by seven interviewees. It was all about facilitating clients to take as much control as possible of the plans to keep their children safe. Workers first identified the child protection concerns for the family, and they then used strengths-based practice to mitigate those concerns through strategies to engage clients' strengths and to foster self-determination. The key questions these strengths-based workers asked clients were "what do you need to resolve this problem?" and "how can I help you with that?"

This version of the strengths-based worker-client relationship was neither therapeutic nor transformational. It was instrumental – a means to the end of enabling clients to make effective safety plans. The worker facilitated clients to present their perspective, make choices about next steps, create plans, and connect to services. As much as possible, decision-making and resourcing for any action remained the responsibility of the family. As one worker said, "[I] try as often as we can to not drive the bus ... just kind of sit alongside the client, provide some direction, but the ideal situation is if they're the ones who are kind of in control" (72).

The focus of this approach was on keeping the intervention of the worker and their agency to a minimum. This meant using family and community resources in safety plans. It meant working to keep children out of care and using informal placements with relatives like aunts and grandparents instead of state-sponsored foster homes. It meant facilitating numerous meetings so the child's support network could craft their own solutions. Interviewees described family group decision-making meetings, in which the professionals left the room to enable the family to develop their own plan, as particularly strengths-based. So long as the child was safe, the less the worker became involved in the family's business the better.

Respect for the client's perspectives, plans, and strengths was the fundamental building block of this strengths-based worker-client relationship. Workers suspended their own judgment about the best way forward in order to support the family's right to resolve concerns in the way that worked for best for them. This required a great deal of listening to clients and those who knew them best. As one worker said,

> I think I give people the benefit of the doubt now. Y'know what I mean? I back off … I tell them it's really their responsibility, it's their children, they've got to get their act together, I can support them. They're going to go hundred per cent. I'll go to bat for them. That's what I do. And I spend time listening and I don't take sides. (89)

As much as possible, clients took the lead in setting goals and determining the strategies to meet them. Workers helped by eliciting the strengths and resources of the child, parents, extended family, and community. They might do this with solution-focused questioning techniques, like exceptions and scaling questions, or by completing formal strengths assessments. They might hold planning meetings and help the child's circle find ways to support the child's care. There was no question that identifying and acknowledging strengths in this way facilitated positive worker-client relationships, but its primary purpose was to enable clients to use the identified strengths and resources in plans to increase child safety.

This version of strengths-based practice drew primarily on the value, common to the Kansas and solution-focused traditions, of faith in a client's capacity. It retained their focus on the motivating power of goals developed by clients and embedded in their perspectives. It emphasised one of the central ideas of the Kansas school – the worker's role in connecting the client to a community rich in informal resources. The difficulty was that it was only effective with clients who were so high functioning, well-resourced, and motivated that they needed little help to address the child protection concerns. It set standards of family self-sufficiency that many clients were simply unable to reach. This set clients up for failure and exacted a high personal price from workers. It meant that the approach simply could not be used with many of those served in the course of a typical working day.

Setting Clients Up to Fail

A "supporting client self-determination" interpretation of strengths-based practice asked families to take primary responsibility not only for identifying a plan that addressed the child protection concerns but also for putting that plan into practice. All interviewees who saw it this way said the approach rarely worked for clients whose capacity was limited due to mental illness, addictions, developmental issues, or long-standing unresolved problems. These clients might not be able to come up with their own solutions and might find it hard to access the strengths and resources on which they could build an adequate safety plan. As one worker said,

> In child protection, I always struggle with ... when you're trying to give the parents that opportunity to come up with their own solutions, they can't or they don't. They don't know how to, they don't really know what resources are available or how, given their circumstances, they can achieve the goals that we're kind of expecting them to follow through on. So I find that hard. (203)

Clients of child protection services often feel overwhelmed by the challenges they face or traumatized by their experiences. It is not uncommon for them to struggle with multiple stressors, like "the 'toxic trio' of family violence, mental health problems and substance abuse problems" (Frederico, Jackson, & Dwyer, 2014, p. 106). One study of 405 children living with parental mental illness found forty-two per cent were also exposed to domestic violence and twenty-five per cent to parental drug or alcohol problems (Howe, Batchelor, & Bochynska, 2009). While many parents manage these challenges well, there is increasing evidence that children exposed to such issues are at risk of a range of negative outcomes that often see them referred to child protection services (Gorin, 2004; Hosman, van Doesum, & van Santvoort, 2009).

A parent involved in the child protection system and dealing with the combined effects of violence, addictions, and mental illness may well not feel that their difficulties are easily solved using their family's strengths and resources. These issues take a well-documented toll on cognitive capacity, coping skills, and the number of people available to offer support. This is not to say that these clients will not have strengths, resources, and very clear ideas about what they need. However, in order to access these, they may need a level of support from their social worker that goes considerably beyond respectful facilitation.

In this version of strengths-based practice, clients were left largely on their own to manage their difficulties. It was an interpretation that paid little heed to the deep structural roots of many child safety issues. Critics of strengths-based practice have identified the potential for it to be used in this way to individualize problems, to blame clients for broader societal ills, and to offload caring responsibilities onto families or, more accurately, the women in families (Gibbons & Gray, 2002; Gray, 2010, 2011). When the language of client capacity becomes linked to an organizational agenda of efficiency and retrenchment, even the most well-meaning strengths-based child protection practitioner can become punitive, as this worker explained,

> If families don't become self-supportive during our intervention process, our point of view is that they have to responsibilize themselves. When parents don't want to change, and get stuck in a repeated systemic pattern even when we have been reorienting their interactions, we conclude: "If you do not see what is under your nose, of course you're up a shit creek without a paddle." Our society can't take responsibility for that kind of problem. (Roose et al., 2014, p. 11)

It is hard to recognize this attitude as strengths-based, particularly when key strengths-based theorists have gone to some lengths to acknowledge that individual effort, insight, and resources cannot resolve all challenges. As Saleebey (1996) said, "Schizophrenia is real. Child sexual abuse is real. Pancreatic cancer is real. Violence is real" (p. 297). Often, the help needed to manage these problems is also very real.

"Supporting client self-determination" ignored the fact that many families need a great deal of support to parent safely and that this support may simply not be available through informal channels or other agencies. As Keddell (2012) states, in many cases "the idealized supportive extended family is a 'mythical family,' and social service agencies quite literally become this extended family in the absence of other supports" (p. 612). The misuse of the idea of client self-determination can lead workers to adopt an uncompromising stance about the need for children to be with their families, which results in them being returned to or left in unsafe homes (Turpel-Lafond, 2013). It does not take into account the fact that some children describe their time in care as necessary and welcome (Munro, 2011) and that some families value ongoing social work support (Ghaffar et al., 2012; Keddell, 2012).

Setting Workers Up to Fail

The gap between a family's needs and their ability to meet those needs with minimal social services help meant that with all but the most resourced clients, "supporting client self-determination" felt inherently risky. Workers were left with a great deal of anxiety about the children on their caseload. They worried that plans relied too heavily on family resources, were insufficiently robust, and left children in situations in which they could be harmed. The two supports that might have made this approach tolerable were absent. One was access to sufficient resources to support and monitor family-led plans. The other was a clear message from management that workers were not alone in carrying the burden of risk created by taking this approach in the absence of sufficient resources. Without these, workers described feeling set up to fail. As one recounted,

> By working with the family and keeping the kids in there often we have to tolerate an elevated risk level. And the challenge [is] to get management to support front line in developing balance, of balancing risk and behaviour and age of children, and trying to get to feel that you're not out on a limb and that you have the backing of your local team leader and local regional director and community service manager regarding some complex cases. (187)

Only one interviewee described a way to consistently implement this version of strengths-based practice in the context of inadequate resourcing and risk-averse management. Her strategy, however, dramatically increased her sense of being left out on a limb to manage risk alone. It was to take her casework underground, avoiding consultation with supervisors and oversight from managers. This strategy meant that her attempts to enact strengths-based practice were less likely to be sabotaged by others. She could facilitate families to develop and enact their own solutions with minimal interference. It may well have left the child in danger, however, and it certainly left her feeling unsupported and exposed:

> There's one particular case right now where I'm kind of freaking out a little bit about it, I think "Holy shit, I hope I did the right thing." I think I did

the right thing. I was told to do something different and I didn't ... and I'm kinda hoping the kid ... yeah there are, so rare, it's really like maybe once a year, once a year maybe in a file I go, "Ooh I hope that's OK." ... I've taken some big risks, and once in a while the risks are maybe a bit bigger than I would have bargained for. (72)

It is hardly surprising that workers were so aware of the level of risk implied by this version of strengths-based practice. The language of risk permeates contemporary child protection systems (Houston & Griffiths, 2000; Parton, 2011; Pollack, 2010; Scourfield & Welsh, 2003; Stanford, 2010). "Risk has become an institutionalized and reified concept which dominates the thinking of policy-makers, managers and practitioners" (Houston & Griffiths, 2000, p. 1). Parents are typically framed as risks to their vulnerable children, not as collaborators in the struggle to maintain healthy family functioning. How they enter and move through child welfare systems is determined largely by an assessment of the level of risk they pose to their child. Their very need for public services is painted by many on the right of the political spectrum as a risk to the neo-liberal ideal of the self-sufficient citizen, and this need is met with increased state surveillance and control. As part of this project, the remit of child protection workers has expanded from managing severe abuse and neglect to taking on a broad range of risks to children's emotional well-being and potential for economically productive adulthood.

Workers are well versed in this language of risk. They describe both their own and their clients' positions in terms of the risk they pose to others or are exposed to from others (Stanford, 2010). They themselves have often been framed as risks to efficient and effective public service delivery. As a result of child death enquiries, critical media attention, and the implementation of managerialism, they too have been subjected to increased surveillance, audit, and oversight. Whether in relation to a tragedy like the death of a child or a problem like not completing their paperwork, workers have frequently been blamed as individuals for issues that might be more usefully analyzed as failings of the whole system. The notions of blame and risk are woven into the fabric of modern child welfare. Against this background, it is hardly surprising that the tendency of the "supporting client-self-determination" approach to increase the worker's burden of individual risk exacted a high emotional toll.

This version of strengths-based practice left interviewees feeling exhausted and at times demoralized. It was hard to listen to all sides of a story and to play the role of peacemaker and facilitator in plans that might involve multiple family members. It was challenging to maintain a position of support for clients who did not take action to increase child safety or did not take action quick enough. As one worker admitted, "Quite honestly there are some where … there's no way I can be strengths-based anymore 'cos I feel like we've tried, and tried, and tried and I can't see a glimmer of hope" (203).

It was difficult to avoid stereotyping, cynicism, and directive practice when clients did not seem to be capable of exercising the self-determination on which this version of strengths-based practice relied:

> I've lost my patience with a family due to, you know, it's the tenth time and here we go again, and I've said, "No we're not having this discussion again, we're done, like, it's my way now, not talking about it." (407)

The point at which the worker needed to be directive was the point at which this version of strengths-based practice stopped. An approach founded on supporting client self-determination was simply impossible to reconcile with the restrictions put on client self-determination that are inherent to the coercive use of statutory authority. Interviewees talked of clients themselves not wanting to be "facilitated" or to hear about their strengths when the worker was taking action contrary to their wishes. They struggled with how to support parents to determine their own path when this conflicted with their assessment of the best interests of the child. As one worker said,

> While you're trying to have these [strengths-based] conversations with them … you find something happens and you have to step in and be, like, "Listen that plan's not working and I'm gonna have to bring them into care or they're gonna have to go somewhere else." It's a hard balance 'cos then they are, like, "The whole point of this was so that that wouldn't happen." (323)

Essentially a means of supporting a radical form of self-determination for clients, this version of strengths-based practice was deemed suspended at the point at which workers asserted their own control.

Supporting Client Self-Determination

Founded on: respect for client's perspectives, plans, and strengths.
Characterized by: family-led meetings and plans, minimal intervention,
the worker's facilitative role.
Undermined by: structural or deep-rooted problems, insufficient resources, worker concerns about managing too much risk, the worker's
use of authority.
Achieves child safety through: client-determined plans using strengths
and community resources.

Reflective Questions

1 How is your definition of strengths-based child protection practice
  similar or different from "supporting client self-determination"?
2 How comfortable are you with the idea of asking parents to develop
  and resource safety plans for their child? Describe the personal
  beliefs, fears, hopes, and experiences that inform your answer.
3 Think about how your answer to Question 2 might vary when
  clients experience different challenges or come from different social,
  economic, and cultural groups. What does this tell you about the
  assumptions you might make about client capacity?
4 How does this approach fit with the social work values that inform
  child protection work?
5 How does this approach fit with different ideas about the role social
  services should play in society?
6 You are at Shauna's house at 9 a.m. on the day after Shauna called
  the emergency line to say she might hurt her baby. She repeatedly
  says that everything is OK and that there is no longer any need to
  worry. Her affect is extremely flat, she looks very tired, and her
  hands shake throughout the one-sided conversation. She cannot
  explain what has changed since last night. She also can't describe
  any kind of plan or help that she might call on. However, she is
  resolute that she regrets calling you and does not need any help.
  The baby is sleeping soundly and looks well cared for. You are
  impressed by the number of cards from family and friends
  congratulating Shauna on the birth. The friend who was called out last

night to stay with Shauna is now anxious to get off to work. She tells you not to worry, and when you push her for more of a plan she breezily tells you she'll pop by later and that Shauna is not the type of person who needs social services – she comes from a nice middle-class family and can get by fine without government help.

   a) What factors might be stopping Shauna from developing an effective safety plan?
   b) How comfortable would you feel accepting Shauna's assurances that nothing more is needed?
   c) What do you need to say or do with Shauna to ensure both that the baby will be safe and that you are supporting Shauna's self-determination?
   d) How does your answer to (c) change the worker-client relationship described in a "supporting client self-determination" approach?

Chapter Eight

Connecting to Internal and External Resources

The third version of strengths-based practice combined ideas from the first two. Six front-line workers described it as a set of practices for connecting clients to their internal resources and a set of practices for connecting them to external resources in the family and community. It involved engaging clients in a trusting, empathetic, therapeutic relationship and also in a safety plan that mobilized the client's external network. Identifying, amplifying, and using clients' strengths was a key strategy to build both the relationship and the safety plan.

The foundation of this worker-client relationship was trust built through the worker's reliable and supportive presence. "Connecting to internal and external resources" required the investment of a great deal of "facetime" (999). Workers talked of being available to their clients on a daily basis, outside normal working hours, and whenever they were called upon. When asked to describe what strengths-based practice meant to her, one worker responded,

> I think being available 24-7 for [clients]. So coming in on a Saturday and calling them just to see how they're doing goes a long way. Staying, like, being there later at night and talking with them, attending activities in the community with them. Just spending more time with them, not just an hour and you do the intake, but actually spending more than a few hours a week with the family ... it's not just an 8:30 to 4:30 job. If you're doing strengths-based practice you're working at weekends, you're working at night, you're taking those calls. (156)

The amount of time dedicated to the approach was important because this version of strengths-based practice relied on the trust and intimacy born of being consistently present for clients, of getting to know them, of being there to listen and support. Workers described out-of-hours duties like staying late to supervise family visits and attending the school play of a child in care. In other approaches these tasks might be delegated to others. In this approach, they were important relationship-building activities and had to be done by the workers themselves.

An important role for the worker was simply to listen. As one worker said, strengths-based practice was "just a way to communicate with people where you sit down, you're open, you're not judgemental, you listen to their part, you support them on it, it's that active listening stuff" (999). This version of the approach included listening to clients' perceptions of challenges, to their suggested solutions, and to their views on planning and progress. To facilitate this process, workers asked solution-focused questions. As one worker said,

> When I think of strengths-based practice I think specifically of, you know, sort of like the strengths-based questions, like the scaling questions, the miracle question and, you know, like the coping questions, those kinds of things, but underneath that, underpinning that is sort of like the foundation of just, like, developing an empathetic rapport, you know, like through active listening and that kind of stuff. (189)

The ideal "connecting to internal and external resources" relationship was one of mutual trust in which clients felt able to turn to their workers for support and frank advice. This frankness was an important part of being a reliable presence; it meant clients could trust the information provided to them. In return, clients were expected to honestly disclose their challenges and feelings about possible solutions:

> Ultimately what I want to have ... is a client that, even though they think they might get in trouble, they're still going to call me. Like even though they might get in trouble for what they have to tell me, do you know what I mean? That they're still going to be calling me and saying, "Hey, you know, this is what happened" ... where if you need something you call me and we talk about it, and we get you what you need and then, you know, hopefully, eventually, in the end you won't need to call me anymore. (243)

There was a clear therapeutic purpose to the "connecting to internal and external resources" worker-client interaction. It helped clients open up to new perspectives, to access existing skills, to develop new skills, and to increase a sense of agency. The orientation to clients' strengths helped them feel validated, empowered, and hopeful about the results of their efforts to address risks to their child. Acknowledging the capacity of clients was a way of emotionally "pumping their tires" (216). This relational work was frequently described as having a transformative effect:

> I would talk about how she's doing a great job as a mum, and how she's doing the best that she can and that. And then she would get kind of weepy in the conversation and it was just, like, just validating who she is ... and it just seemed like she didn't really get that on her own, right? So for me to say that to her is like she kind of heard it for the first time. (189)

In this version of strengths-based practice, however, workers had a dual focus. While working therapeutically to strengthen clients' connection to internal resources like goals, abilities, and hope, they were also connecting clients to more tangible resources. They helped clients build networks of supportive people and places. This might mean accompanying them to community events, appointments, and resources. It might mean helping them access services by forging relationships with other professionals. It might mean holding family meetings. It did mean engaging with clients and their extended networks in a collaborative planning process in which plans were driven by what clients identified as helpful.

Once workers had been clear about their concerns, they saw themselves handing over power to the client and their community to meet the child's needs:

> I think also a lot of the stuff we're doing in strengths-based practice is we're trying to be really as least intrusive as we can with families, like involving families. Like extended family in planning, 'cos we do a lot of Family Group Conferencing now, and the Case Planning Conferences. Even just meeting with families, even trying to do things like having family members have custody of the children so they don't have to come into care. (268)

While workers had a significant role in forging relationships in which their clients felt safe, empowered, and able to engage in safety planning and connect to needed resources, the actual arrangements for a child were a matter for client self-determination. Clients and their communities were encouraged to control the direction of case planning, with the worker's role being to "follow their lead and brainstorm a little bit" (189).

This version of strengths-based practice came very close to the model of strengths-based case management developed by the Kansas school in the 1980s. It took up that model's central idea of social workers acting as "'travelling companions' to persons in need" (R. Rapp & Lane, 2012, p. 150). The approach involved walking beside clients, physically and emotionally, to connect them to the resources that might help them. The worker-client relationship was an important mechanism of change but was insufficient without assertive work to engage clients' communities to support their plans.

In combining the approaches described in the previous two chapters, "connecting to internal and external resources" presented workers with the worst of both of those worlds. On the one hand, case plans that were the product of the worker-client relationship were frequently derailed by decisions from above. They relied on an intimate understanding of the client's situation, to which managers and other parties had little access. When managers overruled these plans, they undermined the carefully nurtured relationship on which the approach depended. On the other hand, resource shortfalls left workers either unable to agree to client-generated and community-resourced plans or agreeing to them and being terrified about the level of unmanaged risk. Like the two before it, this version of strengths-based practice relied on a supportive and collaborative stance and could not work in all situations for reasons related to the context of child protection work rather than the willingness of the worker to use it. This willingness is also important, however, as a primary difficulty with this strengths-based approach was that it demanded a substantial and ongoing investment of time, energy, and emotional commitment. It frequently required more of the worker than the worker could give.

Underinvesting Time

Any approach requiring workers to develop intimate therapeutic relationships with their clients *and* productive relationships with multiple family and community members is going to take a great deal of time. This version of strengths-based practice could not be done quickly. It was often impossible to carry off when faced with constant pressure to just "get the job done" (216). As one worker said,

You have to give them the respect and the time to listen, and I think what makes strengths-based really hard is it takes so much time, right? So to have that time to build that relationship and work with families. And we don't have that time anymore to build those relationships. (999)

In this study, insufficient time was the most common barrier to strengths-based practice identified by survey respondents. Lipsky (2010) suggests that within public agencies, demand for service will always expand until capacity is reached. This makes lack of time an inherent feature of public service work.

The pressures on the time child protection workers have to spend with clients have arguably intensified over the last thirty years (Scarth & Sullivan, 2007; Smith & Donovan, 2003). Workers have been asked to spend more time performing administrative tasks, both to account for their own actions and to share information about children around professional networks (Parton, 2008). These information-management responsibilities have become a significant part of the job. One American study found front-line child protection workers spend four to six hours a day interacting with technology rather than with their clients (Wilson, 2013). Another found that time spent working directly with clients took up only thirty-two per cent of the working day (Weaver, Moses, Furman, & Lindsey, 2003). In Australia, child protection workers have talked of spending sixty to eighty per cent of their time attending to information-technology systems (Gillingham, 2014). This leaves little time to see and speak with clients, let alone to establish the intimate and trusting relationships envisaged by this strengths-based approach. As one interviewee said,

We just have so much paperwork, it's just mind boggling ... and sometimes I feel like you can't always do the best you want to 'cos you don't have the time. You don't have the time, so it's just managing fires, right, and piecemeal ... if I had just twelve files or something like that, twelve or fifteen, say, it would be great. (268)

That interviewee said she had twenty-seven "really active" files. Other study participants reported up to sixty. As one wrote, "With caseloads that high ALL they can do is respond to immediate risk and emergencies" (189). It is not clear whether these workers were talking about the number of children or the number of families; inconsistencies in the ways in which a "case" is defined have often hampered attempts to evaluate appropriate child protection workloads (Burns &

MacCarthy, 2012). It is clear, however, that the problem of insufficient time is due partly to the sheer number of families with which child protection practitioners are expected to work (British Columbia Government and Employee Services Union [BCGEU], 2014; Turpel-Lafond, 2014). A report into working conditions for child protection practitioners in British Columbia found

> less than one in five frontline child, youth, or family workers has a caseload consistent with best practices. Over 80% of surveyed ... workers have a caseload greater than 20 per month. Nearly half of all survey respondents (48%) reported working on over 30 cases. Ten percent of respondents reported caseloads that exceed 70. Nearly one-third of respondents (29%) were also carrying another worker's caseload at the time of the survey. (BCGEU, 2014)

These figures are worrying in light of recommendations that a reasonable maximum caseload is closer to sixteen to seventeen families (Yamatani, Engel, & Spjeldnes, 2009). They are worrying because high caseloads have frequently been blamed for workers' inability to adequately protect children, the inability of senior staff to provide adequate supervision, and workforce demoralization and burnout (BCGEU, 2014; Bennett et al., 2009; Bradley, Engelbrecht, & Höjer, 2010; Herbert, 2003; Laming, 2009). There is little doubt that high caseloads undermine practitioner capacity to engage in the intensive relational practice represented by "connecting to internal and external resources." When child protection workers face overwhelming demands they have been found to reinterpret strengths-based policies in ways that allow them to routinize their case management, de-prioritize anything not seen as a core function, and withdraw from client contact (Smith & Donovan, 2003). They deal superficially with some clients and neglect to attend to others (Burns & MacCarthy, 2012). It is hard to see how workers can establish the kind of relationships required for this version of strengths-based practice when they resort to survival strategies like these.

Overinvesting Emotion

Workers came to feel very close to their clients when they used a "connecting to internal and external resources" strengths-based approach. It was almost impossible to spend the many hours they did in the company of their clients without becoming deeply engaged. This made it hard to manage the emotional fallout when things did not go according to plan. As one worker said,

> I care about them as human beings, but sometimes you'll get, I think just because of the relationship or the helping relationship you have, like, sometimes there's a sort of a fondness that you have for a client, like, you know, like, you want to take care of them, like a mum almost, right? And sometimes it's not so good. Like I was just talking to our team leader about one of my files and I said: "… if we have to get more intrusive I want you to know I'm having a hard time with this. Because if we have to remove [the child] or something I don't feel good about it, because I care about this person, I don't want them to get hurt." (268)

All interviewees who subscribed to this version of strengths-based practice talked about their difficulties managing their emotional reactions to clients. One worker asked about paedophiles, "How do you find the positives of that person's nature when you just want to slit their throat?" (216). Another said, "How can I be strengths-based with somebody who, you know, who's beating up a woman … trying to be strengths-based, it's really tough, it's really, really tough" (268). "Connecting to internal and external resources" required them to keep cheering these clients on, to identify their strengths, and to maintain curiosity about their experience. They had not only to deeply empathize with their clients but also to spend considerable time listening to their experiences. As one worker said,

> I think 'cos you start getting emotionally attached and you start, I don't know, maybe getting angry or frustrated with the client, with the fam-ily … after you have someone for a while and they're constantly making complaints, they're constantly, like, you just never know what's going to happen when they come in. Are they going to be wanting to hug you or are they wanting to shoot you? Literally … it's exhausting. (156)

The emotional work of child protection can be hard to manage no matter what the approach, and anxiety is "like a vein which runs throughout the child protection process" (Morrison, 1997, p. 196). High caseloads, inadequate support, and daily contact with clients who have been traumatized or who are experienced as traumatizing take a heavy toll. Child protection workers experience high levels of burnout (D. G. Anderson, 2000; Boyas, Wind, & Kang, 2012; McFadden, Camp-bell, & Taylor, 2015; Travis, Lizano, & Mor Barak, 2016) and secondary traumatic stress (Conrad & Kellar-Guenther, 2006; Regehr, Hemsworth, Leslie, Howe, & Chau, 2004; Sprang, Craig, & Clark, 2011). A disproportionate number of front-line child protection workers are young and at the beginning of their professional careers (Healy, Meagher, & Cullin, 2009), which only increases the difficulties of coping with the emotional demands of the work (Boyas et al., 2012).

A "connecting to internal and external resources" approach seemed to leave workers particularly vulnerable to these challenges. Some have suggested that child welfare workers are at risk due to their high level of exposure to traumatizing material (Sprang et al., 2011). This version of strengths-based practice required an unusually high level of exposure, with very frequent client contact and an emphasis on listening to the client's experiences. The approach involved a close, empathetic worker-client relationship, and empathy has been described as a conduit for compassion fatigue (Figley, 1995, 2002). This explains why, once emotionally engaged, it was hard for these workers to step back and play a solely facilitative and supportive role with multiple family and community members. It explains why they so often talked of feeling exhausted and frustrated by their work, the system, and their lack of success:

> Empathy and sympathy turns to apathy when you've tried to assist parents in seeing the changes they need to make, and you have nice and tidy family plans and you've held [meeting] after [meeting] to encourage community members and family to step up to support the family and at the end of the day the parents aren't willing to do the work. It's hard to find the strength in that. (216)

Connecting to Internal and External Resources

Founded on: reliable, supportive presence.

Characterized by: dual focus on therapeutic relationship with the parent and facilitating community connections, the worker's listening role.

Undermined by: insufficient time, the worker's emotional reactions, the worker's use of authority.

Achieves child safety through: changes in parental insight, motivation, and capacity; client-determined plans using strengths and community resources.

Reflective Questions

1 How is your definition of strengths-based child protection practice similar or different from "connecting to internal and external resources?"
2 Think of Craig, the teenager who called in a suicidal crisis. You plan to work with him using a "connecting to internal and external resources" approach. You have met with him twice in the last week to try to develop enough trust so he will tell you how he feels and what he needs. The second time he showed you the local skateboard park and told you how good he felt when he was there. He doesn't have a skateboard, but there may be a way of getting one through a school program if you can put in a good word for him. You want to do this, as skateboarding seems to be an activity he is really excited about.

   You think you made a breakthrough with him during that last meeting – he really started talking about how he feels and what he wants. He has felt pretty sad for a long time and wants that to change. You told him about a group for youth with depression in the next town. He is willing to give it a go so long as someone can give him a ride. Neither of his parents can take the time off work so you are happy to take him there, at least for the first few sessions. He also wants some help with talking to his parents about their burdensome rules and with getting them to agree to a plan so he can go to his Aunt Helen's when he feels he can't cope. His parents don't like Aunt Helen, so that might be a tricky negotiation.

   Craig's parents have been very accommodating, although they are quite overwhelmed by their long working hours and now Craig's needs. You think it will take at least a couple of meetings with them and maybe Aunt Helen to develop a suicide safety plan that is sustainable for Craig. Craig's mom has said she feels quite depressed herself and in need of time away. Craig's dad is keen to get the whole family into counselling to "talk it all out." You want to support this and think they might qualify for service from the local Mental Health team, if you can make the referral and attend an intake meeting with them. You're not quite sure when any of this will happen; this is probably the lowest priority case of the thirty you are currently managing.
   a) What is your emotional response to this scenario?
   b) What problems do you foresee in working with the family in this way?

c) Imagine that while you are working with the family, Craig attempts suicide. How might you feel? What about your approach might help you or make it harder for you to cope with that?

3 Describe what you understand to be the working conditions within your local child protection agency.

a) To what extent do these support workers to implement a "connecting to internal and external resources" approach?

b) What organizational changes would you recommend to support this version of strengths-based practice?

4 What strategies, values, or attitudes might help you implement this version of strengths-based practice in the current working conditions in your local child protection agency. Evaluate the costs and benefits of employing these strategies, values, and attitudes.

5 What element of "connecting to internal and external resources" do you see as useful in your future practice? What elements would you discard?

Chapter Nine

Pursuing a Balanced Understanding

"Pursuing a balanced understanding" was the fourth version of strengths-based practice described in the study, and it was very different from the first three. It framed strengths-based practice as a set of beliefs about the work rather than a set of activities. When strengths-based practice is defined entirely in terms of what workers *do* with clients, the approach will never be universally applicable. In child protection work there are too many reasons for workers and clients to disagree on what is to be done, how it is to be done, and even on whether anything must be done at all. With "pursuing a balanced understanding," however, workers could be strengths-based far more of the time. All that was needed was to hold onto a certain way of thinking about clients, and this could largely be done irrespective of whether and how clients engaged in the work.

At the core of this approach was the attitude that all clients had both strengths and challenges and that worker action to increase child safety should be founded on the balanced exploration, deep understanding, and transparent expression of both. This search for strengths was not time limited and not a matter of simply completing an inventory of client resources and moving on. "Pursuing a balanced understanding" involved an ongoing process of believing in, finding, and focusing on client strengths to balance out the problem-focused narrative. This meant that even when parents refused to engage, workers still documented the positive family interactions observed by others, held onto the idea that these were people with capacity who desired the best for their children, and refused to "write them off" (236). They believed their continual focus on strengths increased client motivation, hope, and capacity and supported collaborative work to address the child protection concerns.

Workers went further than this, however, to actively question the validity of the problem-focused narrative. In the first three versions of strengths-based practice, the focus on strengths was a means to mitigate risks that went largely unquestioned. Workers laid out their understanding of the problems and then used strengths-based practice to attempt to address them in collaboration with the client. In "pursuing a balanced understanding," workers saw their whole perspective, including their belief that there may be risks to a child's safety, as needing interrogation.

Curiosity was the foundation of this worker-client relationship. It involved a more mindful and systematic commitment to "not taking anything for granted" (115) than that implied by the standard call for social workers to be open and non-judgmental. It was fuelled by a strong belief that there was always another way of seeing things and prompted continual questioning for the perspectives of the client and their network. A worker explained,

> I do try to take a look at the big picture and I often will ask a client: "Are there pieces that I'm missing?" ... it's really trying to get as thorough of a picture as possible of where the family is coming from. (116)

Part of seeing the big picture was understanding the contextualized meaning of client's behaviour. Angry clients were framed as people with rights who were simply expressing their needs. Parents' failure to attend meetings was described in terms of their broader challenges, like poverty and lack of transport. As one worker said,

> You have to be very mindful all the time ... You have to consider things like culture, poverty, mental health, structural barriers, these things that are so important. You can't just say, "Oh these are our expectations of you, we expect you to fulfil them." ... I think it's more about ... understanding [the family] within their environment and being very fair and balanced about how we see them in terms of all the possible barriers that they might be facing ... when parents are kind of experiencing anxiety or when, it could even be something as simple as they're very passionate about their children's education and they come off a certain way, strengths-based approach kind of helps the worker understand why the parent is behaving that way. (115)

Seeing clients in the broadest possible context generated a great deal of empathy for them, which was an important component of this strengths-based worker-client relationship. All the interviewees who described this approach talked of putting themselves in the shoes of their clients and feeling how hard it was to be involved in the child protection system and to parent well. With little comments like "I understand that all families struggle, I certainly struggled, I'm a parent with two kids" (116), they drew parallels between their own lives and those of their clients. The empathy helped sustain them in the ongoing pursuit of the clients' strengths and goals.

Particular activities supported this version of strengths-based practice. Workers talked of asking solution-focused questions to elicit clients' hopes and resources and using compliments as an empowerment strategy. One worker held family meetings, another accompanied clients as they connected to community agencies, and another spent a great deal of time listening. These activities were seen as both eliciting therapeutic change and supporting the construction of family-led child protection plans. Being strengths-based was not, however, determined by whether or not workers performed these activities. It was determined by the extent to which workers maintained their pursuit of a balanced understanding.

This version of strengths-based practice was similar to Saleebey's strengths perspective (Saleebey, 2012). This has been described as a "both, and" perspective, in that it attends to both strengths and challenges (Blundo, 2012; Kisthardt, 2012; Saleebey, 2012). It is a way of balancing a focus on problems with their solutions, recognizing that maintaining the latter requires a great deal more work. "Pursuing a balanced understanding" also had much in common with strengths-based child protection approaches like Signs of Safety (Turnell & Edwards, 1999) and safety-oriented practice (Berg & Kelly, 2000). They too call for curiosity, openness, and continual questioning to broaden the range of possible storylines through which collaboration with clients might be built. Unlike those child protection approaches, however, it included no mechanism for workers to act against the will of a client. Workers found it difficult to maintain a balanced perspective, and they were forced to abandon this approach altogether when they felt that something other than a balanced perspective was required.

Narrowing the Perspective

Remaining open to the big picture was all very well and was often enough to generate a collaborative worker-client relationship and a pool of strengths and resources from which a plan to address child safety issues could be built. However, there were times when a position of curiosity elicited neither the strengths nor the consensus to keep a child safe. Despite the workers' best efforts, being strengths-based did not always lead to a workable balance between concerns about the child and the resources needed to address them. As one worker described it, "overwhelming deficits" (115) could carry the day.

In moments like these, it was necessary for workers to temporarily narrow their perspective and set aside the perspectives of others. They might need to mandate clients to comply, to withdraw ineffective services, or to forcibly remove a child to safety. Interviewees had no problem with this idea. They all had a clear sense of their mandated purpose; as two workers said, "At the end of the day ... I've got a job to do" (236; 86). This job was to ensure child safety, and it involved setting firm boundaries and taking protective action when required.

The problem was making sense of where these actions fit within a "pursuing a balanced understanding" approach. Interviewees described "hav[ing] to walk a very thin line between being ... strengths-based and having expectations or needing to draw a firm line" (115). Drawing a firm line was inconsistent with the open, enquiring stance this version of strengths-based practice required. Mandated authority was either described as a barrier or left out of the discussion altogether. It was certainly not integrated into the approach in a way that allowed workers to consistently see themselves as strengths-based whether they were acting for or against a client. It was extremely hard for them to maintain a philosophical position of curiosity while simultaneously taking the kind of overtly authoritative action that suggested, at least in the moment of that action, a mind made up.

The difficulty these interviewees faced is that the principles of non-judgmentality, acceptance, and client self-determination, which underpinned their approach, have typically been framed as incompatible with the use of professional power (Healy, 1998). These principles have often been interpreted in simplistic ways, far removed from the intentions of mid-century theorists like Felix Biestek and Carl Rogers, who most influenced their adoption as core social work values. They were never meant to prevent the worker from evaluating behaviour and taking action. Biestek's principle of non-judgmentality, for instance, was

based on a conviction that the casework function excludes assigning guilt or innocence, or degree of client responsibility for causation of the problems or needs, but does include making evaluative judgements about the attitudes, standards, or actions of the client. (Biestek, 1957, p. 90)

Likewise, the principle of acceptance did not exclude constraint of unacceptable behaviour. It simply meant that workers "must perceive, acknowledge, receive and establish a relationship with the individual client as he actually is, not as we wish him to be or think he should be" (Biestek, 1957, p. 69). Client self-determination was always intended to be "to the greatest extent possible" rather than unfettered by constraints (Woods & Hollis, 1990). The point was to avoid assigning blame rather than to avoid judgment.

It is easy to lose sight of these subtleties, particularly when so little has been written to help practitioners maintain a strengths perspective from a position of power. Child protection strengths-based approaches like Signs of Safety directly tackle this question, and Turnell has made a strong pitch to acknowledge

the daily reality for child protection professionals ... that they must con-stantly make judgments ... The whole notion of being non-judgmental is a problematic professional aspiration since human beings, whether profes-sional or otherwise, cannot, not have opinions. In aspiring to the cher-ished goal of being non-judgmental, professionals potentially distance themselves from part of what it is to be human. I would want to propose a vigorous campaign ... to reclaim and re-energise judgment making as a vital and integral aspect of good human service practice generally and constructive child protection practice in particular. (Turnell, 2004, p. 8)

The interviewees who described strengths-based practice as "pursu-ing a balanced understanding" did not see it as incorporating the full extent of their authority to make and act on their professional judg-ments. They had no clear permission within the approach to act against the client's will. Coercive action temporarily superseded the pursuit of a balanced perspective. It was the point at which they needed to set strengths-based practice aside, if only briefly, to use a different approach.

Balancing the Perspective

Even within the context of a collaborative worker-client relationship, interviewees found it hard to focus on both the strengths within a fam-ily and the risks to a child. As one worker commented,

What do I struggle with when I do strengths-based practice? ... weighing the strength versus the risks. I mean, ultimately, I mean we still have to do our job which is to ensure the safety of the kid so, you know, I think it's always sort of like we want to look at strengths but that's not completely disregard the risks as well ... So like it's just balancing that with the risks I think. Talking about the risk and not sort of letting that slide at the same time, I think that's been, that's sometimes a challenging part. (86)

Maintaining this balance so as to accurately assess and respond to the child's needs required ongoing reflection and a great deal of clinical support and consultation. One interviewee talked of having an "internal thermometer" (116) by which she measured the strengths and risks pertaining to a child. It was only regular discussion with her supervisor and team that provided her with the necessary "checks and balances" (116) to calibrate her thermometer accurately. Another worker said,

I think that in order to do good strengths-based work with families we need to be in constant learning and training ... Whenever I'm too sure of myself I always step back and ask myself: wait a minute, what am I forgetting? (115).

All who subscribed to this approach talked of their openness to learning from clients, colleagues, and their own experiences. The feedback provided through reflection and consultation enabled workers to keep looking for the big (balanced) picture. The problem they faced was that child protection settings are not known as environments in which reflection and consultation are well supported. It is hard, emotional work to risk being uncertain and vulnerable in agencies that tend to prize certainty and predicting and managing all risks (Parton, 1998). Workers need to feel a sense of psychological containment if they are to do this kind of reflective relational practice (Beddoe, 2010; Ruch, 2007; Trevithick, 2003). It is this that enables them to lower defences, honestly share experiences, and open themselves up to learning from their mistakes and from the perspectives of others.

In the past, practitioners recommended that "weekly conferences of several hours were held regularly for discussion of complicated or baffling cases" (Woods & Hollis, 1990, p. 16) and that social workers have both personal therapy and skilled supervision (Smalley, 1967; Woods & Hollis, 1990). Today the primary forum for child protection consultation in the countries we are discussing is individual supervision from the person to whom the worker directly reports. This is problematic; workers can find it hard to disclose their challenges to these direct superiors (Beddoe, 2010, 2012; Bradley et al., 2010; Dill & Bogo, 2009; Hair, 2013). Their reluctance is partly due to the fact that supervision is often used as a means to monitor and prescribe practice rather than to support it. There are strong pressures on line supervisors to focus on administrative tasks and the management of risk and supervisee behaviour, and "for many practitioners supervision is an occasional event which has been reduced from a holistic support mechanism, addressing management, educational and support needs, to a purely managerial tool for accountability in practice" (Richards, Ruch, & Trevithick, 2005, p. 416).

This administrative focus and the fact that supervisors hold significant information about, and power over, supervisees tends to decrease trust, the perception of confidentiality, and practitioners' willingness to disclose their struggles (Beddoe, 2012). In one Canadian study, over a quarter of social workers surveyed said that their supervisor's role in appraising their performance made it difficult for them to discuss their practice challenges (Hair, 2013). In an Australian study in which social workers were asked to identify an ethical dilemma in their practice, fewer than half had discussed that dilemma with their line supervisor, due to concerns about privacy and their supervisor's authority, administrative focus, and availability (McAuliffe & Sudbery, 2005). Child welfare supervisors themselves describe the problem as worse when they have an authoritarian style or poor conflict-resolution skills (Dill & Bogo, 2009).

To sustain ethical engagement with clients, workers need to be able to discuss their work as the complex mix of emotional, moral, legal, psychological, and practical issues it is (Oliver, 2013). In this study, workers frequently called for "CLINICAL supervision: meaning supervision that is not simply focused on the day-to-day tasks and documentation but is about doing the work and its impact on both worker and client" (390). When asked what was needed to implement a "pursuing a balanced understanding" approach, one interviewee responded,

> We'd start with that real clinical supervision. I mean we'd start with training our managers or team leaders to have those skills and to have that ... philosophy, those attitudes that allow them to get the growth and skills that they are intended to model. (86)

However, child protection agencies do not tend to have organizational climates in which workers can safely share their challenges, voice their non-mainstream views, and constructively critique their own practice. This makes sustaining the effort to pursue a balanced understanding, and calibrating that balance in a way that works for the child, very hard indeed.

Pursuing a Balanced Understanding

Founded on: curiosity.
Characterized by: belief in client strengths, a drive to understand the big picture, the worker's persistence.
Undermined by: difficulties balancing strengths and risks, taking decisive action against parental wishes.
Achieves child safety through: changes in parental insight, motivation and capacity; client-determined plans using strengths and community resources; worker authority and resources.

Reflective Questions

1 How is your definition of strengths-based child protection practice similar or different from "pursuing a balanced understanding?"
2 Some people tend to see the glass as half empty. Some see it as half full.
   a) Do you naturally focus more on people's strengths or problems?
   b) Why do you think this is?
   c) What implications do your answers have for your child protection work?
3 To what extent do you agree with the position that "everybody has strengths"? Are there limits to this position?
4 Think of the interactions you have had today with the significant people in your life. These could be clients, colleagues, partners, family members, or friends. To what extent did these actions take their strengths into account? How do you feel about this?
5 When are you least likely to be balanced in your assessments? When are you most likely? Explain with reference to your theoretical knowledge and/or your personal experience.

6 What values and beliefs motivate you to continue to engage curiously with clients, even when this is difficult?

7 Think of Joe, the grandfather and sole caregiver of three-year-old Sam. Joe has cared for Sam since his daughter asked him to babysit for the child two years ago. She has not been seen since. Joe hates child protection workers, having had his own children permanently removed from his care due to his long history of problematic alcohol use and violence towards their mother. He knows that his drinking has gotten out of hand again recently and that is not good for Sam, whom he loves fiercely. He messed up last night, can't remember a lot of the details, and doesn't know what to do next. He was expecting this visit from the social workers, and he has no intention of cooperating in their plans. Joe sees social workers as agents of a shadowy and corrupt state, and he will not make their life easy or work with them on plans he knows are designed to subjugate him.

You are the child protection worker who has been tasked with making a plan with Joe. His grandson was brought to an emergency foster home last night, after police were called to the home due to a noise complaint and found Joe and another man intoxicated and engaged in a fist fight. Sam appears healthy and well-cared for. As far as you know, there have been no previous reports about Joe's care of Sam, but Joe's drinking is a long-standing concern.

   a) Create a list of strengths or potential strengths you would want to explore with Joe.
   b) How might you probe for these strengths in your first meeting with Joe? What, specifically, might you say?
   c) If you are "pursuing a balanced understanding," how might you contextualize the concerns and explore them with curiosity?
   d) How might you use the strengths to address the concerns?

About ten minutes into the meeting, Joe suddenly becomes very angry when you tell him that Sam is not coming home today. He springs to his feet, overturns the table separating you, and yells "Get the hell out of my life or I'll kill you." He is a big man and is bearing down on you with raised fists.

   e) How might you feel?
   f) What would you do?
   g) Is there any way to keep "pursuing a balanced understanding"? Explain your answer.

Section Two Summary

Twenty of the twenty-four child protection workers interviewed for the study described versions of strengths-based practice that allowed little room for the overt use of their authority. Strengths-based practice supported them to perform their "caring" responsibilities but not the "controlling" responsibilities that are equally important when child safety is a concern. Presenting workers with considerable challenges in managing their time, emotions, and judgments, these versions of strengths-based practice had to be suspended when the moment came to take decisive action against clients' wishes.

The list of scenarios for which workers deemed strengths-based practice inapplicable (see Table 1 on page 65) made a lot more sense when strengths-based practice was interpreted as "relating therapeutically," "supporting client self-determination," "connecting to internal and external resources," or "pursuing a balanced understanding." These versions of the approach were poor choices for front-line child protection practice when ...

- clients were not willing to work collaboratively or faced long-standing, complex challenges. When strengths-based practice excludes the ability to be directive and relies on more time or support than is available, it will achieve child safety only with clients who are more cooperative, motivated, or well-resourced.
- clients had untreated mental health difficulties, substance use issues, or limited cognitive capacity. When strengths-based practice requires productive participation in a therapeutic relationship or in the development and implementation of a safety plan, it can ask too much of clients whose thinking or behaviour is significantly impaired.

- clients were hostile or violent. When strengths-based practice does not give workers latitude to assertively set boundaries or dictate the terms of the interaction, its open, collaborative stance can feel unsafe.
- clients deliberately or severely harmed their children, committed crimes, or were sociopathic or psychopathic. When strengths-based practice asks workers to make close, supportive relationships with clients whose behaviour triggers strong emotions or requires authority-based responses, it can feel emotionally and ethically problematic.
- workers needed to take immediate action to secure a child's safety. When strengths-based practice relies on suspending judgment or proceeding by agreement, definitive authoritative action like removing a child from its mother's arms will fall well outside its reach.

Clearly, a different interpretation of strengths-based practice was needed if workers were to use the approach with all clients at all times in support of their professional mandate to keep children safe.

That interpretation was "firm, fair, and friendly practice."

SECTION THREE

Firm, Fair, and Friendly Practice

"Firm, fair, and friendly practice" was the one version of strengths-based practice that interviewees said could be used with all clients at all times. It was a way of working that enabled practitioners to operationalize the key principles of strengths-based practice even when clients were not on board. It supported practitioners to work primarily with the client's perspective, goals, and strengths in the belief that clients were experts on their own experience. However, it also supported workers to use their mandated authority, to be directive, and to act against the clients' will when they assessed this to be necessary. It pushed workers to go beyond pursuing a balanced understanding to take balanced action in which the clients' expertise and authority was continually weighed against their own.

"Firm, fair, and friendly practice" meant starting from a particular way of thinking about the client and the relationship. Like "pursuing a balanced understanding," it was a philosophy about how to do the work. As one interviewee said,

> Strengths-based practice is an orientation, it's an ideology, it's a way of thinking, conceptualizing clients and the work we do with them and the approach we take when we interact with them. You can have a client who's completely remorseful for what's happened, fully engaged, you know, really buying into the collaborative plan to help bring strength to their family unit and really wanting to see where the relationship between them and the [agency] can bring them in the future, and you can have a client that comes in and says: "F... you I'm not gonna work with you, I'm gonna kill your kids and burn down your house." I mean, I've had both. That doesn't change [strengths-based practice], it changes what you can do with them but it should never change how you engage with them. (254)

The philosophy informed particular strategies for the worker-client interaction. Taken together, these comprised the elements of "firm, fair, and friendly practice" illustrated in Figure 2.

In this version of strengths-based practice, workers continually sought to maximize their collaboration with clients. They acted on the assumption that clients were capable of exercising their self-determination and sought to use clients' strengths both to build the collaborative relationship and to resource child protection plans. However, when there was evidence that clients were unable to lead the work in a way that increased child safety, practitioners temporarily became more directive and interpreted this as being within the boundaries of a strengths-based approach. In these moments, worker authority and expertise supplemented client authority and expertise. Clients were still seen as people with capacity and self-determination, but the arena within which they could exercise these was temporarily reduced.

Figure 2. Firm, fair, and friendly practice

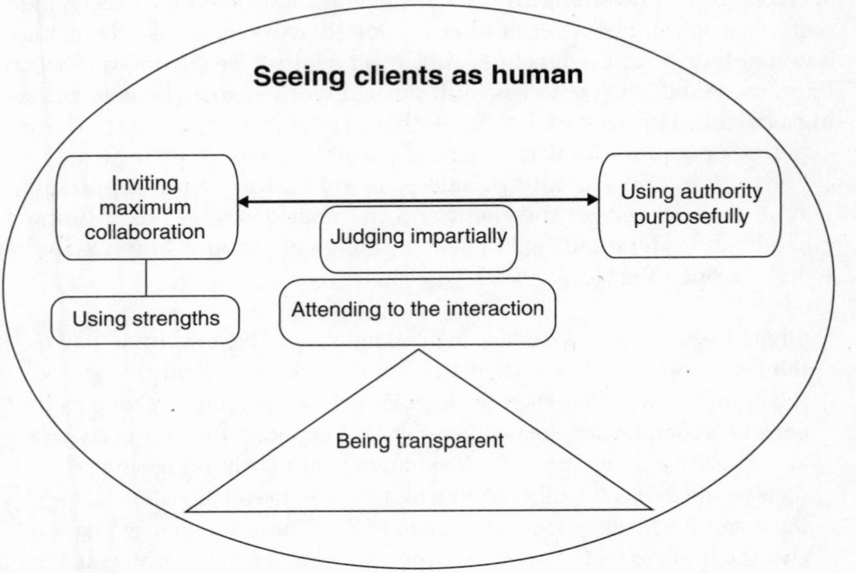

From Oliver, C., & Charles, G. (2015a). Enacting firm, fair and friendly practice: A model for strengths-based child protection relationships? *British Journal of Social Work*, bcv015. Reproduced courtesy of Oxford University Press.

For the workers implementing "firm, fair, and friendly practice," the extremes of paternalism and partnership, and care and control, were easily reconciled through the very explicit position that both were necessary to perform their child protection role. Saleebey (2012) talked of a strengths perspective replacing an "either/or" position with a "both/ and" position. Clients did not have either strengths or challenges; they had both strengths and challenges. "Firm, fair, and friendly practice" extended that idea to the coexistence of worker and client power. It framed both clients and workers as having authority and expertise.

Workers could only navigate this fluid relationship of partnership and paternalism successfully with certain other conditions in place. It relied on workers making the shifting relational dynamics transparent, seeing the humanity of their clients, making judgments impartially, and attending carefully to every interaction. These were the core components of a strengths-based practice that never needed to be switched off or end in accusations of betrayal and disappointment. This approach reflected key messages about what constitutes effective relationships in social work and in other fields that involve working with involuntary clients. It also harmonized well with strengths-based solution-focused child protection approaches like Signs of Safety. Indeed, "firm, fair, and friendly practice" might be seen as a description of what needs to happen within the worker-client relationship for these approaches to be sustained.

Chapter Ten

Inviting Maximum Collaboration and Using Strengths

"Inviting maximum collaboration" and "using strengths" are probably the elements of "firm, fair, and friendly practice" with which readers are most familiar. These activities are normally front and centre in any presentation of a strengths-based approach. In this study, eighty-five per cent of survey respondents who proposed their own definition of strengths-based practice said the approach meant using client strengths, and nearly a third talked of client collaboration or partnership. In "firm, fair, and friendly practice," workers considered using strengths to be an important strategy for inviting client collaboration, and they saw inviting maximum collaboration as a core component of the approach.

"Firm, fair, and friendly" (102; 176) workers continually invited clients to work collaboratively with them in relationships in which clients took the lead to the greatest possible extent. However, in contrast to colleagues who interpreted strengths-based practice in other ways, they did not attempt to deny their own power as they strove to increase clients' power. They were clear that their professional obligation to intervene in the lives of others meant that what they had with their clients could hardly be characterized as a relationship of equals. As one worker put it,

> What I notice is that the social worker's making efforts and, it's never gonna be equalized, but to create a safe environment where that person can feel a bit more equal and neutralizing that power dynamic. Not erasing it, 'cos you can never take that away, but giving the client a voice and acknowledging what they're saying and then, you know, doing their job respectfully. (176)

The extent of the collaboration was always contingent on the client's capacity, the worker's own needs for safety, and the demands of the child protection worker's mandate to safeguard the child. Any sense of equality was the product of continual renegotiation and a great deal of hard work.

The extent of possible collaboration shifted over the course of the worker-client relationship in response to changes in the level of client engagement and risk to the child. The focus of the collaboration was sometimes on forming and executing a plan to increase child safety. If clients were unable or unwilling to identify solutions and strategies for a safety plan, however, it did not mean that collaboration and the client self-determination it supports were beyond reach. The focus of the collaboration became the child protection *process* rather than the plan. Workers became more directive about arrangements for the child while inviting clients to collaborate on the small decisions about how they were to engage with those arrangements or with the worker. Expectations of collaboration were downsized but still important. Some level of meaningful collaboration was always possible.

Clients might have little choice about meeting with a worker, but they could be invited to control where and when that meeting took place. Workers might be clear that a child protection investigation was needed, but they could immediately ask the client to determine how frequently they would like to be informed of its progress. Collaboration was sometimes built through client participation in these small decisions about the ways in which they engaged with the work. The key was to remain open to, and actively solicit, the client's presence and perspective. But what if the only thing offered by a client was a damning critique of the worker's actions? The client's expression of this critique, and the worker's acceptance of it as one of many valid perspectives, was a collaborative act. Each time the worker supported the client's choices and perspectives in these small questions of process, the potential for greater collaboration increased. It built the trust that enabled clients to engage more extensively in a plan for their child, allowing workers to move into a position in which they were more of a resource to, rather than authority over, the clients.

One interviewee's story illustrated this ongoing commitment to inviting collaboration. She was in the process of bringing into care the children of a man with whom all attempts to develop a more collaborative safety plan had failed. She described this man as much larger than herself and physically very intimidating. The removal was very much against his will, which was why the police attended, and the situation was extremely volatile. As she described it,

> He was clearly intoxicated when I arrived at the house and, it's funny because at one point he gave me a great big bear hug and lifted my feet off the ground and the police are looking horrified and I'm just talking him down, "Put me back down." But as we're leaving I'm trying to be really clear about, "I'm gonna call you tomorrow. And we're gonna go to court because of your kids." And the police were like, "Stop talking, stop talking." And I'm thinking I don't want this man to wake up tomorrow morning and wonder where his kids are and what's happening with them. (176)

In a tense moment when many workers would have taken the police officers' advice and left as quickly as possible, this worker continued to reach out by attempting to contract about next steps. During the act of wielding the full extent of her mandated authority, she sought to facilitate this client's continued collaboration and to give him the information he needed to remain engaged in the child protection process. During the following day's phone call, she invited him to work with her to make contact with the children and to devise a plan for their return. Due to her perseverance in reaching out to him today, he would be prepared with the information on which a more collaborative relationship might be built tomorrow.

An important part of the next day's phone call would be to acknowledge the man for caring so much about his children that he had not let them go into care without a fight, for having the self-control to put the worker down rather than squeeze her to death, and for being willing to communicate with her despite recent events. Identifying and complimenting clients' strengths in this way were important strategies to facilitate a shift towards greater collaboration. "Firm, fair, and friendly" interviewees described these strategies as having a therapeutic effect and increasing client motivation, self-esteem, and agency. As one worker said,

> I start to build on that strength, it brings a sense, you know, and I'll use a social-worky word, you know, it brings empowerment, right? And so people get this natural, you know, endorphin release like, "Wow gee, I can do good things, I can do this." (102)

Comments like this echoed an idea that is central to constructivist and narrative theories and common to all strengths-based and solution-focused approaches: The stories we tell ourselves about the world govern the range of choices we have for acting in it. They were also informed by the idea that believing in your capacity to achieve a goal makes it more likely you will achieve it. One interviewee explicitly related this to social cognitive theory (Bandura, 1977, 1991). Social cognitive theory so accurately explains the motivational potential of strengths-based practice, and is so rarely considered in relation to the approach, that it is worth pausing for a moment to consider its relevance. It describes a three-way reciprocal relationship between cognition, behaviour, and the environment. It proposes, in general terms, that what we believe influences how we act. In more particular terms, it holds that what we believe we can do influences what we do. Having high self-efficacy, or believing strongly that we can do something, leads us to set higher goals and be more committed to those goals. The belief in the likelihood of a successful performance provides a positive guide for that performance, enabling us to evaluate progress towards it and learn from failed attempts. It makes it more likely that we will sustain the effort required for success. Every experience of success thereby builds self-efficacy.

What does this mean for the worker in our bear hug story? Framing the previous day's events as evidence that this man is a good father who cares deeply about his children and is capable of exercising great self-control helps him see himself this way. The strengths-based narrative opens up more possibilities for him to act as a good father, to demonstrate his caring, and to act with constraint. Knowing that he did this once makes him more likely to believe he can do it again and to sustain his efforts in pursuit of that goal. It opens up space for client and worker to collaborate as two people with something to offer each other. It does not ignore the facts of his intoxication and the children's removal. It does, however, lead to a very different set of possibilities than the problem-soaked narrative that might be more commonly constructed. "This man is a bad father who lost his kids, got drunk, and assaulted the worker" is not a story on which a collaborative relationship is easily built.

"Firm, fair, and friendly" interviewees also talked of using clients' strengths to develop collaborative safety plans. Clients contributed to the plan in the areas in which they felt most motivated or competent or with the resources to which they already had access. Workers described clients taking the lead in setting goals and in crafting strategies to meet these goals. One talked of a father who expressed a goal to re-establish a relationship with his son who was living elsewhere. He had his own car, something the boy's caregiver did not have. He offered to drive the boy to and from sports matches, thereby meeting his own goal by his own strategy that used his own resources. Another worker said,

> I start to build on things they're good at, you know. Mum might be really good at organizing. Dad is good at doing tasks, you know, like going to an appointment, or, you know, making sure to pick the kids up. Dad might be good at carrying out Mum's organized list. (102)

This version of strengths-based practice included encouraging clients to pursue their solutions to the child protection problem and, often, linking to supportive people in their broader family and community network. One interviewee, for instance, discussed his recent work with a mother who determined who should be at a family conference and called the family members herself to invite them. Another commented that

> you hold in your heart and soul that you wanna work with parents collaboratively, that you wanna manage risk in the community, and that you wanna focus on strengths, and not ignoring worries and concerns but you wanna focus on strengths, resilience, and building capacity and finding those protective factors from within the family system as a whole. (248)

Of course, many clients needed little encouragement to collaborate. From the beginning they had the capacity and willingness to become active partners in identifying and resourcing a plan for their child. For those who were less engaged, solution-focused questions provided a way to elicit the client's strengths, hopes, and motivation. These exceptions, scaling, relationship, coping, and miracle questions were a very small part of the picture of "firm, fair and, friendly practice," but they were nevertheless an important way for workers to shift the conversation to strengths and continually invite the client to collaborate. The skilled "firm, fair, and friendly" worker might build collaboration with our bear-hugging father without them. It might be enough to acknowledge that he felt passionately about his children and had the inner strength to engage in a productive phone conversation, which many in his situation would have found impossible to do. From this acknowledgment might spring a plan for him to call his children that day and to let the worker know his assessment of what they needed while they were away from home. From that conversation might spring the foundation of a plan that included the client's ideas as to how he might best manage his drinking and get himself into a situation in which he could parent safely. If his goals, ideas, and strengths did not flow quite so easily, solution-focused questions were there to help.

It should come as no surprise that practitioners of this approach found using client strengths and inviting maximum client collaboration to be helpful to maintaining strengths-based relationships. These are core ideas in any rendering of strengths-based practice. Although often expressed in a different theoretical language, they are also core ideas in research exploring effective relationships with mandated clients in other fields of practice. Take, for example, the evidence supporting pro-social modelling in criminal justice (Trotter, 1997, 2006; Trotter & Ward, 2013). Pro-social modelling has been found to reduce offender recidivism and increase offender satisfaction with their interactions with corrections officers. It appears to be particularly effective with people who experience psychopathy (Ross, Polaschek, & Ward, 2008), depression, avoidant behaviour, multiple interpersonal problems, and difficulties establishing relationships (Orsi, Lafortune, & Brochu, 2010). It is worth noting that these clients are common in child protection work.

Pro-social modelling means the modelling and reinforcement of pro-social values and behaviours in interactions with clients. It includes searching for what is going right and giving praise and positive reinforcement for these strengths and successes – exactly the same processes that strengths-based practice describes. In essence, it involves workers acting towards clients in the way they wish clients to act towards them and others. In the criminal justice field, this means probation officers modelling, expressing, and supporting views that support the value of a crime-free lifestyle. In child protection settings, workers might model behaviour that is open, collaborative, and respects the feelings and needs of others. Client success in replicating this behaviour, whether that is with the worker, with family members, or with the child, is reinforced or rewarded. For clients on probation, one of the most valuable rewards offered is reducing the frequency of expected contact with the probation officer (Trotter, 2009). In "firm, fair, and friendly practice," the reward discussed by interviewees was to invite clients to exercise more self-determination and to take a greater role in determining the nature of the worker-client interaction or the plan to which it led.

With some clients, inviting maximum collaboration resulted in the kind of relationship envisaged by strengths-based writers from the Kansas tradition. It was a matter of supporting families to identify what they wanted for their children and helping them connect with the resources they needed to achieve those goals. With these clients, workers could sit happily at the partnership end of the partnership-paternalism continuum (Turnell & Edwards, 1999), and strengths-based practice could feel like a supportive endeavour to both parties. With other clients, collaboration on some elements of the process might coexist with coercion on other elements or on the broader child protection plan. There was never a time, however, when collaboration was impossible or workers stopped inviting clients to move with them towards greater partnership.

Reflective Questions

1 Brainstorm ways in which clients might collaborate ...
   a) in the child protection process.
   b) in a child safety plan.
2 There are five types of solution-focused questions described in this chapter.
   a) Name each type.
   b) Describe the particular purpose of each.
   c) Join with a partner. You have ten minutes to interview your partner to elicit the most comprehensive picture possible of his or her strengths, resources, and goals. You can only use solution-focused questioning.
3 Think of a time when you felt you were engaged in a truly collaborative process with someone.
   a) What made you feel that way?
   b) What impact did the collaborative process have on you?
4 What would tell you that your client was participating in the work to the fullest extent possible?
5 Think of the least collaborative person you know.
   a) What feelings or responses does he or she trigger in you?
   b) Draw on your experiences and/or your theoretical knowledge to describe what you could do to keep inviting his or her collaboration in an open and authentic way.
   c) What would help you do this?

Role Play: Shauna

Divide into groups of three. One person will be the observer, one the client, and one the worker.

Only the observer and the client should read the "Client's Information" on page 205. Decide which of the two scenarios your group will play.

Only the worker should read the "Worker's Information" on page 206.

The observer's role is to notice the specific comments, questions, or actions that move the conversation forward and those that get in the way.

Start the role play at the point in the interview when the worker starts exploring for strengths and resources.

After fifteen minutes take turns to debrief, starting with the role players and addressing:

1 How did you feel?
2 What worked well?
3 What did not work well?
4 What did you learn about inviting maximum collaboration and using strengths from this role play?

Chapter Eleven

Using Authority Purposefully

"Firm, fair, and friendly practice" was most clearly distinguished from the other versions of strengths-based practice by the fact that it incorporated workers using their authority. Interviewees started their very definitions of this approach by talking about their authority. As one said, "I can't think of [strengths-based practice] as the softer, collaborative, voluntary approach because ultimately I work under the legislation and that's really clear what our mandate is" (176). "Firm, fair, and friendly practice" allowed workers to purposefully use their authority without abandoning a strengths-based approach. It represented the adaptation of traditional strengths-based ideas to the context of the child protection role. As another interviewee said,

> We do, I think, completely want to adopt tools and principles from strengths-based practice with how we engage our clients, but those tools and principles have to respect the legal obligation that we're under, that the client is under, and the laws that govern child protection. (254)

This approach enabled workers to assume whatever level of authority was necessary to meet the goal of child safety. It framed the acts of "leading" (102), "guiding" (176), and being "cut and dried" (254) as necessary when there was evidence that in any particular moment full collaboration could not be achieved without them. One worker described moving into a more authoritative position in this way:

> After trying to de-escalate things, keep things on a calm, thoughtful level, there are still times when my assertive presence emerges. It's not aggressive, it just then moves into the "y'know, there's some things I have to

do." And we can, you know, I often say, "We can do it the easy way or the hard way. I'm always up for doing things the easy way. What about you guys?" (248)

When clients "resisted" workers' efforts to engage, workers needed to persist and exercise their authority even about the need for client contact. This was because effective collaborative work required that both parties participate. As one interviewee described in her account of doing strengths-based practice with a client who had rejected social work intervention for several years: "I've forced a meeting every other week with Mum, to check in and she just sort of broke down and was, 'OK, I guess I'm gonna have to tell you about my life'" (176). Coercion was used to create the conditions for a more collaborative interaction.

The first key point about this use of authority is that the ability to assertively set and maintain clear boundaries was described by workers as a supportive, strengths-based act. It made the worker-client relationship fair and one in which clients always knew where they stood and could trust that workers would follow through on their clear commitments to child safety. It kept the relationship purposeful, goal oriented, and focused on the child's needs. One worker said of the relationship,

> I'm there to praise and encourage and stuff like that, all the while I'm toeing a very solid line, right? Like, I mean, I'm not here to be your buddy, I'm not your friend at the door, you know, I am a child protection worker who's responding to a valid child protection concern, y'know? This is not a voluntary service. This is an involuntary service, and so I'm not there to be your bestie. I'm there to make sure that the children's needs are met. (102)

The second key point was that it framed the use of authority as a temporary act, as a tool for specific, time-limited purposes. As one interviewee said, "I don't shy away from the fact that I come from a position of authority, but I don't necessarily have to use it, like the police don't have to use their gun, but you know that they have authority" (102). The purposeful use of authority was always immediately followed by efforts to invite greater client self-determination. The level of authority was constantly adjusted to match and reward client insight, capacity, and engagement in the process. As soon as they could, workers looked to dial back their level of directiveness to establish a more collaborative relationship. As one worker said,

> Just because I would need to be really sort of heavy handed, maybe that's a poor word, but sort of rigid and directive at the beginning doesn't mean I'm always gonna have to be that. The goal is that they're gonna start to engage with it and start to see what we see to some degree. I don't need them to take on my perspective but to at least see the protection concerns and then I'm gonna sort of step out and let them work with it and then they're gonna tell me what they need to change more, or feel supported and it's this, a lot of evolution with strengths-based practice. (176)

This constantly shifting balance of strategies of care and control created the kind of microclimate of sanctions and rewards that has been recommended in work with involuntary clients (P. Harris, 2008). Clients were "rewarded" for their collaborative efforts to increase child safety with greater control over their case, compliments, and expressions of concern and support. When workers assessed clients to be engaging in ways that did not promote the needs of their child, they responded with a more assertive position in which the scope for client self-determination became more limited. Behaviour that appeared to undermine efforts to increase child safety was confronted. In this strengths-based approach, the obligation to understand the client's perspective and behaviour as a valid reflection of their experience did not always extend to the obligation to accept it.

This careful calibration of positive and negative reinforcement of client behaviour has been found to be particularly effective with mandated clients (Rooney, 2009), including those in child protection (Trotter, 2002), addictions (P. Harris, 2008), and criminal justice services (Kennealy, Skeem, Manchak, & Eno Louden, 2012; Trotter, 2009). Its effectiveness may be due to the fact that it offers workers a wider range of strategies with which to influence the client's behaviour than if they were to attempt to be supportive or directive only (Kennealy et al., 2012). It also offers clients a wider range of acceptable ways to respond. As the researchers who proposed this theory put it,

> [Workers] achieve a much broader base of power for changing behavior in the prosocial direction than when they act exclusively as cop or counselor. When supervised by a balanced officer, offenders may realize that what they cannot achieve by complying perfectly with the rules may be

achieved by disclosing these problems to the officer and appealing to him or her for help. (Kennealy et al., 2012, p. 8)

What is clear is that effective work with mandated clients sometimes requires more than an empathetic and supportive relationship. Empathy is an important ingredient of any working relationship, but when used as the primary relational tool, it can overwhelm and alienate some mandated clients (Ivanoff, Blythe, & Tripodi, 1994) and at the very least be ineffective (Trotter, 2006). It seems that for some mandated clients in the early stages of the change process, the overt use of power may be more effective in motivating participation than persuasion or relying on the relational bond (De Leon, 1988; P. Harris, 2008). Using strategies of control can allow time for the client to develop the insight necessary to engage in voluntary treatment and to develop intrinsic motivation to collaborate (Morgan & Hemming, 1999). Coercion might be needed at first in order to create the conditions for an honest, productive, and more reciprocal exchange.

There has been scant acknowledgment of this need for coercion in recent child protection policy and academic literature (Tuck, 2013). Perhaps it is hard to see where "authoritative child protection" (Sidebotham, 2013) might fit within the contemporary discourse, which is focused on partnership as the cornerstone of good practice (Tuck, 2013). Perhaps identifying that some clients are unable to work within a purely supportive relationship feels unnecessarily stigmatizing and raises the spectre of the kind of intrusive, punitive practice described by past clients as alienating and harmful (Cleaver & Freeman, 1995; Davies, 2011; Mayer & Timms, 1970). The social work profession as a whole has tended to characterize the overt use of power as being opposed to the ideals of client self-determination and empowerment (Bar-On, 2002). We are supposed to proceed on gentler terms, through persuasion and support.

The Kansas tradition of strengths-based practice has certainly reinforced the idea that worker authority and client empowerment are mutually exclusive. As one article put it, "The strengths approach to social work practice values empowerment of individuals seeking services and advocates *a relationship of collaboration as opposed to one of authority* [emphasis added]" (Grant & Cadell, 2009). The strengths perspective frames power as a relatively static and unidirectional entity; the worker's process goal is to shift as much power as possible into the client's hands and to keep it there. In line with the early days of strengths-based case management, when workers were "pre-professionals," the client is the only one supported to claim an expert position. Professional expertise is criticized for impeding the genuine appreciation of client capacity required for strengths-based work (Blundo, 2001; Grant & Cadell, 2009).

The problem with this perception of power is that it reflects neither the worker's nor the client's reality in child protection settings. Even in apparently collaborative relationships, child protection clients experience power being used hierarchically over them and reciprocally with them *at the same time* (Bundy-Fazioli et al., 2009; Dumbrill, 2006). The domain in which they can self-determine is always limited, at the very least by the expectation that they comply in cooperative work to support their child's safety (Mirick, 2013). Any sharing of power is temporary and the product of an active process of negotiation and renegotiation (Bundy-Fazioli et al., 2009). Successive enquiries into the failings of child protection systems have called for workers to develop their abilities to intervene authoritatively because "work with resistant, hostile, non-compliant (including disguised non-compliant) parents and dealing with manipulation and deception is a significant feature of everyday child protection practice" (Tuck, 2013, p. 5).

The workers who described "firm, fair, and friendly practice" were very clear that sometimes parents were simply not able or willing to hold the best interests of their children to heart. They framed this as a temporary parental stance rather than a permanent parental trait, but it was a stance that needed to be managed using their professional authority. Their view of how to do this fits with a move over the last decade to rethink power in social work (Bundy-Fazioli et al., 2009; Bundy-Fazioli et al., 2013; Sidebotham, 2013; Tew, 2006; Tuck, 2013). This has reframed power as neither inherently good nor bad and as having the potential to be used both productively and oppressively (Tew, 2006). Rather than denying or trying to invert the hierarchical power they held over clients, these workers acknowledged its important protective function while focusing on creating opportunities to invite "co-operative power" (Tew, 2006) or "power with" as well as "power over" the parents with whom they worked (Dumbrill, 2006).

To the "firm, fair, and friendly" interviewees, power was fluid, relational, constantly shifting, and the reason they could sustain a strengths-based approach. Knowing that they could legitimately use their statutory authority created the safety to engage in the whole-hearted and authentic stance of openness and collaboration that strengths-based practice required. It prevented workers from being harmed by their willingness to connect with clients, to receive parental feedback, and to be transparent. Interviewees were very clear that there were times when their own safety and well-being required them to disengage from the client, to back away from their position, or to limit their openness to abusive client behaviour. The purposeful use of their authority enabled them to do these things, even as they looked for opportunities to move back once again towards greater partnership. These workers had reconciled authority and collaboration within a strengths-based approach. The following chapters consider the components of the worker-client relationship that enabled them to move up and down the paternalism-partnership continuum without getting stuck.

Reflective Questions

1 Take two minutes to sketch a diagram that illustrates your beliefs about authority. Discuss your diagram with a partner. How did you develop these beliefs?
2 Think of a time when someone exercised his or her authority over you in a way that did not feel helpful.
    a) What impact did this have on the way you felt and acted at the time?
    b) What impact did this have on the way you felt and acted after the event?
    c) What was it about the way the person exercised his or her authority that did not work for you?
    d) What could the person have done differently to make your experience of his or her authority more helpful?
3 What theories, knowledge, or research throw light on how to exercise authority with child protection clients most effectively? Which of these resonate most with you?
4 In which situations are you most comfortable asserting your power? In which situations are you least comfortable? How do you account for the differences in your answers to these two questions?
5 On a scale of one to ten, where one is not comfortable at all and ten is totally comfortable, how comfortable are you with the authority you hold or will hold as a child protection worker? What would make you one point more comfortable?

Role Play: Ada

Divide into groups of three. One person will be the observer, one the client, and one the worker.

Only the observer and the client should read the "Client's Information" on page 207.

Only the worker should read the "Worker's Information" on page 208.

The observer's role is to notice when the worker is able to purposefully use his or her authority while inviting maximum collaboration.

Start the role play at the point when the worker knocks on the door for the home visit.

After fifteen minutes take turns to debrief, starting with the role players and addressing:

1 How did you feel?
2 What worked well?
3 What did not work well?
4 What did you learn about using authority purposefully from this role play?

Chapter Twelve

Being Transparent

The foundation of the "firm, fair, and friendly" strengths-based relationship was transparency. Transparency is the drive to make information accessible and understood – to make visible what is hidden. The interviewees who discussed other versions of strengths-based practice described transparency as supporting their strengths-based approach but not as part of it. For them, being clear about their role, concerns, expectations, and interventions helped keep their strengths-based approach aligned with their child protection role. It helped them navigate tensions between the supportive or enquiring stance of strengths-based practice and the more directive stance they might need to adopt if a strengths-based approach failed to promote sufficient child safety. However, in "firm, fair, and friendly practice" transparency was a core component of strengths-based practice itself.

Interviewees often used the word "honesty" to name this component. One described strengths-based practice as requiring he be "honest, brutally honest" (102). Another said,

> I think a fairly firm version of strengths-based practice [is] ... coming from a position of honesty and integrity and is values and morals that I hold personally about how I practice ... the way that I have the most productive relationships with my clients is to be really honest about where they stand ... I guess that goes back to creating honest relationships right? Like don't small-talk about things that aren't important to you. Don't pretend you're interested in that when it's not part of your life. (176)

What they went on to describe, however, went beyond the common definition of honesty as sticking to the facts and being free of deceit and pretence. It included a proactive commitment to be clear in their explanations, to be open with their information, to be upfront in their approach, and to keep nothing hidden. This broader concept is better known as transparency.

What were these strengths-based workers transparent about? As with those implementing other versions of strengths-based practice, they openly shared information about the child protection concerns, their role, their expectations, and the likely outcomes of clients' decisions. They were clear about what was negotiable and what was not. They also explained their authority and discussed the non-consensual nature of their contact. As one worker put it,

> When I meet with the family I try to acknowledge, "This is a difficult way to meet, you didn't ask me into your life ... so there I am, you have all kinds of feelings about that." I start from a place of acknowledging their feelings, and "I'm not here because you invited me here, I'm here because I have to be here" ... otherwise I'm at risk of misleading them about each of our conversations. (248)

These interviewees went considerably further than others in discussing with clients how they worked. In addition to being transparent about child protection processes in general, they gave a great deal of information about their personal approach. They might tell a client, "If I need to make a decision with a small amount of time and a small amount of information, I'm gonna be really cautious in my decision-making" (176), or

> say right up front, "you know I've got really strong biases and you'll learn them really quickly and you all get to toss them out if you don't feel comfortable with them ... when I'm talking to you and I'm going on and on too much, shut me up." (248)

The intent was to give clients information that would help them navigate the working relationship. It was part of an active and open negotiation of the terms of engagement. As one worker commented,

> I kind of say, "We're in this relationship whether we like it or not, so let's set some ground rules so we can both feel safe and we both feel heard and we both feel respected ... and then I kind of open it to them, "What do you want from me?" (176)

"Firm, fair, and friendly practice" also involved going further than is typically described in using immediacy to track and discuss the changing nature of the worker-client relationship. Workers were open about the limits of this relationship, the likelihood of disagreement, and the ways in which the relationship changed over time. They did not belabour these discussions, and they tried as soon as possible to move the focus to client strengths. However, they returned to them often enough that both worker and client had a clear understanding of the purpose and nature of their work together, the legal context in which it occurred, and their mutual expectations. On a regular basis they reviewed with clients the ways in which they were working together, starting with

> "here's the information we understood or understand. And here's my experience of how we're working together and how we're processing things." You're being very blunt about it ... they have a right to know what we're thinking and why we're thinking it, and what our responsibility is moving forward with that. (254)

Workers openly addressed the existence, impact, and parental perceptions of their power. The worker-client relationship was not simply the power-house of strengths-based practice. It was also the subject of constant scrutiny and open discussion.

This transparency was an ongoing requirement. Workers holding one of the more limited definitions of strengths-based practice would lay out their concerns and discuss their role in the first meeting but only revisit this conversation in the event of a significant change in circumstance. Having set the stage for the work to be done, they shifted the focus to the family's solutions and strategies. "Firm, fair, and friendly" interviewees practised transparency throughout the life of a case.

Transparency was achieved by discussing matters that often go undiscussed. It was also achieved by speaking about them in a particular way. Being strengths-based meant using simple, "crystal clear" (176) language to facilitate understanding. Technical jargon or terms that might evoke emotional reactions or be hard to understand were out. Also out was "fluffy" (254) language that glossed over concerns. Down-to-earth language that conveyed meaning bluntly and clearly was in. It often mirrored the words used by clients; as one worker commented, "I'm saying to them in their words so that I understand ... I use their language back" (102).

This level of transparency served three main functions. The first was to support the development of a trusting working relationship. In "relating therapeutically" and "supporting client self-determination," workers' primary tool for building this relationship was their focus on the client's strengths and respect for the client's position. In "connecting to internal and external resources," it was their reliable, supportive presence, and in "pursuing a balanced understanding" it was their curiosity. In "firm, fair, and friendly practice," the trusting worker-client relationship was built through transparency.

Research with both workers and parents engaged with child protection services has revealed this connection between transparency and trust (Gallagher et al., 2011; Ghaffar et al., 2012). As one researcher commented, "Whilst service users might not like *what* was being said, they tended to appreciate that it was being said to them" (Gallagher et al., 2011, p. 125). Clients want to know that workers will do as they say, and the precondition for this is that workers say what they will do. The very explicit process of sharing information and following through with promised consequences helps establish trust, enabling clients to get on with the work in the knowledge that there will be no surprises. One worker described this process with a mother whose child she had brought into care:

I laid it out for her exactly why her child was gonna be in care, how long I could see her child being in care, without giving a date but ... what's her life going to look like when she gets her child back? And that was like the first little sort of nugget of trust that she had with me. Then I could come back the next day and we could talk about that again, and by the time we got to court she felt confident that I was gonna do my job and say what I needed to say and that she was gonna concentrate on what she needed to concentrate on and that she was gonna get her son back. She actually believed that she could work towards this goal. And it happened and we did it together and it was all about being really, really honest about the concerns. (176)

Being transparent had a second function in that it supported client self-determination. When workers were crystal clear about their thinking and possible consequences, it enabled clients to make informed choices about their response. It helped clients to engage in a series of cost-benefit analyses when they were faced with the prospect of working with professionals they did not choose on plans they did not want.

This idea of informed choice underpins much of the work exploring effective relationships with clients of mandated services. It has led to the advice that workers explain to clients the details of the techniques used to shape their behaviour so they might make fully informed choices and because "they have a right to know about a process whereby their attitudes and actions may be influenced or changed" (Trotter & Ward, 2013, p. 10). This work has often drawn on social exchange theory (Cook & Rice, 2006), in which clients are framed as rational decision-makers who will change their behaviour if that change is in their interests. It proposes that clients repeatedly calculate whether the rewards of collaboration at any particular moment outweigh the risks. However, clients need reliable information to make these calculations. This makes transparent discussion of the nature, purpose, and process of the worker-client relationship one of their most important requirements, and negotiation of how their interests are to be met one of the most important tasks.

This focus on the negotiation of interests is evident in many approaches developed specifically for mandated clients. Workers are advised to engage with clients with the expectation that they share no common ground (Barber, 1991; Cingolani, 1984) and that it will only be through an explicit process of negotiation that they will develop the shared goals and tasks long deemed necessary for an effective working alliance (Bordin, 1979). Research with child protection clients has reinforced the dangers of assuming a shared perspective on the work; clients' understanding of the nature and reason for child protection intervention can be profoundly different from that of their worker (Gallagher et al., 2011). This means workers must be clear about their own expectations and seek out the client's interests and goals to develop a negotiated plan to which both parties are motivated to commit (Rooney, 2009; Trotter, 2006). It is skills in negotiation and conflict management that are most needed when assessing or making demands of mandated clients with whom there is little trust (Ferguson, 2005).

Transparency not only supports the negotiation of goals and tasks, it enables clients to make informed choices as to whether and how they will perform their role (Barber, 1991; Ivanoff et al., 1994; Rooney, 2009; Trotter, 2006). This is important in child protection work, where the roles of worker and client are often unclear. One of the most common complaints from child protection clients is that they do not know what is expected of them (Berg & Kelly, 2000). Clients tend to see their worker as a friend and helper or as a supervisor and investigator but rarely as both (Trotter, 2004). It can be hard to know how to respond to the worker's dual surveillance and helping role (Regehr & Antle, 1997;

Trotter, 2004). The refocusing on family support over investigation has arguably left both worker and client with more ambiguous roles and increased uncertainty about power (Littlechild, 2008). Transparency is desperately needed if everyone is to know where they stand.

The third function of transparency in "firm, fair, and friendly practice" was to help workers move between different levels of directiveness without undermining their working alliance with clients. Talking openly about the dual legal and therapeutic nature of the relationship prepared both workers and clients to navigate the relational dynamics as they moved between collaborative and directive positions. Naming these shifts as they occurred made it easier to address their effects. As one worker said,

> For me, strengths-based is honest. It's very honest, it's very transparent, it's very open about the [agency], about the process, about the tendencies of what might happen in a file, about the shared desired outcome ... And for me, it's like, "here's the chain of how it works. If you do this and this is the outcome, here's what happens next. And if you don't do this, then here's the next step that the [agency] usually takes, and it might not happen with you and you need ... here's how we tend to do things. Second step, third step, fourth step, fifth step based on the contingencies ... So it's not when these things happen, it's because I changed my mind and I don't care about you anymore and don't care about your family anymore and I'm thinking bad thoughts, it's because as we talked about this, these are just the kinds of things that need to happen. I don't want them to happen, but they have to happen." (254)

Ongoing transparent communication enabled workers and clients to continually adjust their expectations of each other as the power between them shifted. Without this kind of openness, it is easy to see why parents might resort to common defensive strategies like resistance or false compliance in the face of child protection workers' demands (Dumbrill, 2006). Yet if both worker and client can develop a shared understanding of how the other will behave, clients are more likely to feel satisfied (Trotter, 2006) and to perceive the power exercised over them as caring rather than controlling (Svensson, 2003). When it comes to involuntary clients, this alignment of roles and expectations cannot be left to chance. It requires explicit and detailed negotiation.

Most strengths-based child protection texts urge workers to be honest and open about the nature of the child protection concerns, the

worker's role, and the goals and expectations of the working relationship. They encourage workers to be clear about what is negotiable and
non-negotiable and to provide enough information to ensure that the
choices clients make are fully informed. This transparency has tended
to be framed, however, as a strategy for the initial engagement process
or for the breaking of important news. There has been little detailed
exploration of its continued use through the life of a case to make visible the changing dynamics of the worker-client relationship. In "firm,
fair, and friendly practice," transparency was an ongoing obligation.
When interviewees made comments like, "I don't lie, I don't stretch the
truth, I don't not play all my cards, I'm very transparent" (102), they
were speaking of transparency not only as a strategy but as a value
informing every interaction.

Reflective Questions

1 Rearrange the list below to reflect how easy you think it is (or
  would be) to be transparent with clients about each issue.
  Start with the easiest issue and work your way down to the
  least easy. Then, explain why you ordered the list the way
  you did.
    a) The child protection concerns
    b) The child protection process
    c) The choices available to parents
    d) The consequences of the choices available to parents
    e) The involuntary nature of parental involvement
    f) Your power
    g) Parental power
    h) How you like to work
    i) Disagreement, frustration, or conflict in the working
       relationship
    j) Changes in the dynamics of the working relationship
2 With whom is it easy to be transparent and with whom is it
  difficult?
3 "Saying what you see can lead to trouble." Make links between
  this idea and the idea that transparency should only be used in
  conjunction with inviting maximum collaboration and the
  purposeful use of authority within this strengths-based
  approach.

4 Think of the last time you had to have a difficult conversation, i.e., to transparently address with someone an issue that you found hard to talk about.
   a) How did you react?
   b) How would you like to have reacted?
   c) What got in the way of you being able to say what you wanted to say?
   d) What theories, values, and experiences are most helpful for you to remember when you are faced with the need to have a difficult transparent conversation?
5 Working in pairs, brainstorm what you might say in the early stages of meeting with a new client that will help you establish conditions supporting transparency throughout your working relationship. Look at the list in Question 1 to ensure you set up conditions that support transparency about the range of issues. In a mini role play, practise using the suggested words, phrases, and explanations.

Role Play: Rob

Divide into groups of three. One person will be the observer, one the client, and one the worker.

Only the observer and the client should read the "Client's Information" on page 209.

Only the worker should read the "Worker's Information" on page 210.

The observer's role is to notice when the worker is able to effectively use transparency to move the relationship forward.

Start the role play at the point when the worker knocks on the door for the home visit.

After fifteen minutes take turns to debrief, starting with the role players and addressing:

1 How did you feel?
2 What worked well?
3 What did not work well?
4 What did you learn about being transparent from this role play?

Chapter Thirteen

Attending to the Interaction

The next component of "firm, fair, and friendly practice" was an ongoing attentiveness to the worker-client interaction. This strengths-based approach required workers to be highly sensitive to the conditions for productive communication. Attending to the minutiae of their interactions with clients helped workers to continually transmit their caring and supportive presence. It served to keep workers attuned to the shifts in the relationship about which they were to be transparent. It kept them on the alert for opportunities to invite more collaboration and adjust their behaviour in response to changes in client engagement. It softened the impact of their blunt transparency and made the purposeful use of their authority more palatable. It was part of a continual process of checking and correcting their communication in order to support understanding and collaboration.

Workers who described their strengths-based approach as "firm, fair, and friendly practice" were very mindful of the subtle ways in which they could support or undermine the relationship with their clients. One way of doing this was through their movement in, and manipulation of, their physical space. Child protection is embodied work; how workers move through a client's house, or whether and when they become physically immobilized, has a profound influence on whether they are able to connect with their clients in a way that enables them to do their job (Ferguson, 2009). To the "firm, fair, and friendly" interviewees, sitting alongside clients on a couch was a way to signal that they viewed those clients as equal partners. It contrasted starkly with the position of detached expertise implied by sitting behind a desk or on the other side of the boardroom table. Taking off shoes on entering a client's house indicated the worker's respectful willingness to follow the client's way of walking through the world. These details mattered. As one worker said, "My physical presence, where I talk to people, the difference between me meeting clients in my office as opposed to the bloody boardroom; all of that then reinforces every day the relationships that I have" (248).

Another way to attend to the interaction with clients was through careful choice of language and voice tone. As one interviewee commented,

> Right from the get-go the language you're using, and the tone of your voice and the body language that you're using, exudes connectivity and relationship and you're saying to clients directly my intention is good. (254)

While it was important to use down-to-earth and clear language to support transparency, workers also had to take care to choose words that did not demean or alienate. Their choice of language was mindful and oriented towards tending to their relationship. One worker said of himself,

> I am calm and I'm grounded and I'm really thoughtful about the language, again that sounds silly but choosing the words. How many times I've had people and things begin to go sideways because of a misunderstanding, because the language, my choice of words, triggered. So it wasn't helpful. (248)

These workers repeatedly checked to ensure that they and their clients were on the same page. They talked of using therapeutic techniques like tracking the client's meaning and checking their understanding by using reflective statements. As one said,

> I'm extremely strengths-based above and beyond the physical because I bring a lot of counselling to my approach with clients and how I engage them and how I talk to them, how I attend to them and track with them where they're at. And for me that's an important part of my practice to be intentional about. (254)

They needed to maintain the responsivity that enabled them to notice and honour clients' needs, like the need to take a break during an interview. Attending to these small details carried powerful messages about how clients were seen.

"Firm, fair, and friendly" interviewees also talked of taking care of the interaction through a more explicit process of negotiation. The transparent discussion of the relationship described in the previous chapter enabled them to align expectations about the smallest details of the interaction:

> I kind of open it up to them: "What do you want from me? What do you think is an appropriate time for me to return your call? Are you expecting me to return it in 24 hours? In 48 hours? Longer than that?" ... setting up ground rules with my clients around what feels safe for them and what feels safe for me, and what we do when we're not feeling safe anymore and how we can work through that. (176)

They openly negotiated their commitments to the client and then took care to honour these commitments, no matter how trivial they might seem. One interviewee explained this in relation to meeting times. When he agreed to meet a client at one o'clock,

> I'll be there at one o'clock, not 12:50, not 1:05, and I'm there at one o'clock. And if I'm not gonna be there at one o'clock I will phone and I will apologize, y'know, I'll explain why I'm late and I will, if it's my fault, "Will you forgive me?" (102)

This focus on the minutiae of the worker-client interaction should come as no surprise. Strengths-based child protection approaches developed from solution-focused therapists working primarily through the worker-client interaction. Published accounts of approaches like Signs of Safety have tended to emphasize the use of therapeutic techniques like solution-focused questions and to provide extensive case examples of the therapeutic dialogue between worker and client. They focus on the worker-client relationship as the key vehicle of change. As Turnell & Edwards (1999) state, "It is the small increments of careful interaction that are the fundamental building blocks of creating cooperation between worker and family" (p. 137).

Perhaps one reason for the popularity of strengths-based practice is that it aligns with the broader movement in social work over the last decade to embrace relational or relationship-based practices. This movement is a direct challenge to the managerial and administrative agendas that have come to dominate public service work. It can be seen as part of an attempt to reclaim care and caretaking as central to the social work mission (Weick, 2000). Informed by attachment theory (Howe, 1998), feminist relational theory (Freedberg, 2009), and the relational psychodynamic paradigm (Borden, 2000; Ornstein & Ganzer, 2005), relational social work is grounded in the idea that humans develop in relationship to others and to their environment. It frames the worker-client interview as a therapeutic space in which clients can learn experientially through an accepting, nurturing, and empathic relationship with their worker. The creation of a healing relationship is an end in itself. It is also the means to better assessments and more effective client connections with the broader social environment (Trevithick, 2003).

Within a relational perspective, both worker and client are active participants in an intimate bidirectional relationship (Alexander & Charles, 2009; O'Leary, Tsui, & Ruch, 2013). Each influences and is influenced by the other (Freedberg, 2009). Workers do not try to contain their emotional reactions or those of their clients by setting rigid interpersonal boundaries but rather engage with, interrogate, and learn from them (Freedberg, 2009; Ornstein & Ganzer, 2005). Indeed, they may intentionally seek intense emotional attunement to make themselves vulnerable and open to the clients' experiences (Freedberg, 2009).

There are significant tensions between approaches deemed to work well with mandated clients and the relational social work perspective. "Firm, fair, and friendly practice" has more in common with the former than the latter. It fully embraces the reality of the worker's power, while relational approaches have tended to avoid this problematic issue. It emphasizes transparent negotiations, a clear delineation of roles, purposeful use of authority, and careful manipulation of negative and positive reinforcement. This contrasts starkly with the porous boundaries and assumption of commonality between worker and client that is so important to relational practice. However, there are two areas in which "firm, fair, and friendly practice" does pick up on relational social work ideas. One is its emphasis on the humanity of clients, discussed in Chapter 15. The other is the way it focuses on the worker-client interaction.

The good news is that the strategies interviewees described for attending to that interaction are not advanced therapeutic techniques. It is true that three of those who discussed this approach had received education in counselling and advanced communication skills, which they credited for helping them attend to the interactional details. However, the skills they described are those that any social work student might learn. The influence of humanistic psychology and counselling theory in social work (Forrester et al., 2008) means that tracking client meaning, making reflective statements, and being mindful of language and physical presence are common interpersonal communication strategies. Active listening, paying attention to understand, making use of self, and techniques to demonstrate empathy, genuineness, and respect are taught as basic tools of the trade (Richards et al., 2005). This does not always result in relational competence; one UK-based study to assess communication skills with a simulated client found child protection workers using few reflections, many closed questions, and little empathy (Forrester et al., 2008). However, attending to the interaction is a component of the "firm, fair, and friendly" strengths-based relationship that average child protection workers should see as within their reach.

Reflective Questions

1 How do you know when you are being attended to? How do you know when you are not?
2 Think of a person in your life who attends carefully to interaction with you. What, specifically, does this person do that makes you feel attended to?
3 Reflective statements can be a powerful way to track and reflect a speaker's meaning and feelings.
   a) What is a reflective statement?
   b) Working with a partner, talk about the part of your day so far today that has elicited in you the strongest emotions. Your partner's task is to help you feel fully understood and to encourage you to go into more depth and detail by using reflective statements.
4 Being thoughtful about the language you use is one way of tending to your interaction.
   a) What "trigger words" have you learnt to avoid in child protection work?
   b) How did you learn this?
   c) What might you use instead of these "trigger words" to enable you to remain transparent?
5 In child protection work it can be challenging to be emotionally present and attentive to interactions with clients.
   a) Based on your own experiences and/or theoretical knowledge, what gets in the way of attending to interactions with clients or with others?

b) How would you ideally interact with your clients? Describe in detail what would you do, say, and feel that is different from what you do, say, and feel now.
c) What could help you move one step closer to the ideal interactions you have just described?

Role Play: Ada

Divide into groups of three. One person will be the observer, one the client, and one the worker.

Only the observer and the client should read the "Client's Information" on page 207.

Only the worker should read the "Worker's Information" on page 208. Knowing that Ada will be upset with you, make sure your use of physical space, language, and communication skills show that you care about her and about your relationship.

The observer's role is to notice when the worker is able to effectively attend to the interaction in order to move the relationship forward.

Start the role play at the point when the worker knocks on the door for the home visit.

After fifteen minutes take turns to debrief, starting with the role players and addressing:

1 How did you feel?
2 What worked well?
3 What did not work well?
4 What did you learn about attending to the interaction from this role play?

Chapter Fourteen

Judging Impartially

The fourth component of a "firm, fair, and friendly" strengths-based approach was impartial judgment. This required workers to look past their assumptions and emotional reactions to come to judgments that were balanced, fair, and based on the broadest possible understanding of the client's situation. As one worker said, with strengths-based practice "my job is to have open ears and an open mind" (176). Another would tell clients, "It's imperative that you felt that I was objective and impartial" (248).

All those who described this version of strengths-based practice acknowledged that they were in a position of judgment with respect to their clients. They did not seek to deny that they had opinions and feelings about those with whom they worked. As one interviewee said, "I'd like to say that I go in there without being judgmental but that's not true. I mean, we all have our own judgments" (176). All subscribed to the idea that judging was an inescapable part of being human. They echoed the sentiment that

> the whole notion of being non-judgmental is a problematic professional aspiration since human beings, whether professional or otherwise, cannot, not have opinions. In aspiring to the cherished goal of being non-judgmental, professionals potentially distance themselves from part of what it is to be human." (Turnell, 2004, p. 8)

These interviewees were also clear that they were in a position of judgment because they were being paid to evaluate the quality of the care provided by the parents with whom they worked. For them, the social work principle of non-judgmentality meant that they should accept their clients' weaknesses as part of their humanity, but it did not prevent them from identifying, evaluating, and acting on those weaknesses. The challenge was to "suspend your frame of reference while holding on to your responsibility and the reason that you're there" (254). It can be hard to draw a clear line between assessing responsibility for problems and casting blame, but for these workers, their conviction that their professional role required them to make judgments helped. Doing this in a strengths-based way meant that they had to be transparent about this role and the nature and basis for their judgments. It also meant that they had to come to these judgments in a fair, balanced, and non-reactive way. These judgments had to be impartial, so

> you're not going to approach [clients] like you're angry with them or there's a vendetta or they're a bad, evil person, or as if they're less than human ... that's strengths-based when they know at the end of the day that can be repaired ... you can work with that person because you didn't inject something into that relationship that poisons it for future collaboration. (254)

Impartiality for these workers had both a cognitive and an emotional component. The cognitive component involved seeing all sides of the story and compiling a picture of clients that included both their strengths and their challenges. As one worker said,

> I want to build on the good things and I'm not only gonna shine the light on the good things, I'm gonna shine the light on the things that aren't working very well because, after all, that's why I'm there. (102)

It meant approaching clients from a position of curiosity and remaining open to revising assessments in light of new information. It meant continually seeking to explain clients' behaviour with reference to the broader context. This was particularly important with client behaviour that was otherwise difficult to accept. Anger towards workers was reframed as the result of fear or anxiety, and abusive acts towards children were seen as the result of learned behaviour or past victimization. Judging impartially involved

> looking past the cover of the book and look[ing] at the content of the book ... We're all victims of circumstance in some way, shape, or form.

Maybe not victims but we're all products of circumstance, and perhaps there's a reason why this person acts the way they do. (102)

This component of "firm, fair, and friendly practice" was very similar to the approach described by those who saw strengths-based practice as "pursuing a balanced understanding." It was a matter of developing a holistic view based on the ability to accept and sort through different perspectives in a thoughtful and non-reactive way. It meant adopting the stance of enquiry that has always been an important part of solution-focused child protection practice. From the beginning, workers have been advised to understand the position of each family member (Turnell & Edwards, 1999) and to elicit multiple perspectives in order to "hold at least five different stories in their head at one time" (Turnell & Essex, 2006, p. 38). They have been urged to

> become more curious in their perceptions. In other words, listening to a family requires the ability to set aside one's judgment until further conversation takes place. For example, when a client says, "[child protection] workers only wreck families, they don't help" the curious practitioner might ask "what's happened that tells you they wreck families?" (Berg & De Jong, 2004)

Workers are encouraged to suspend their judgments for as long as possible in order to maximize their openness to the perspectives of others. Once they come to judgment, they must let it go if a competing perspective makes more sense. For "firm, fair, and friendly" workers, this ability to look at child protection situations holistically and to remain as open as possible to new information underpinned the cognitive element of impartiality.

There was also an emotional element to judging impartially. For workers who described "firm, fair, and friendly practice," an important part of being strengths-based was to be calm and grounded. They needed to regulate their emotions in order to remain "emotionally available" (254) and "present in the moment" (248). Managing their emotional reactivity enabled them to remain open to hearing and analysing different perspectives fairly. It meant that they avoided becoming caught up in their own feelings, and it allowed them to fully attend to the worker-client interaction. As one interviewee said, strengths-based workers had to be "capable of self-regulating and managing themselves and really empathizing and understanding where somebody else is at, while being able to separate that from what they still need to do" (254).

It is not only child protection workers who recognize the value of this kind of emotional self-regulation. The parents with whom they work have also talked of their appreciation for workers who demonstrate impartiality in their judgments and are calm, non-anxious, and non-reactive (B. Drake, 1996; Schreiber et al., 2013). Child protection intervention tends to provoke high levels of parental anxiety and fear. As one parent said of the arrival of the child protection worker,

> Holy, man I was scared! I didn't know where to go or what to do. I kept saying to her "oh here we go again." She said, "I'm not here to scare you." "Well you are because you are scaring me right now you're in my house!" (Dumbrill, 2006, p. 30)

It is hard to think clearly when experiencing this level of emotional arousal. "In the heat of the moment, strong feelings outbid thought and they dim the ability to reflect and analyse" (Howe, 2010, p. 330). Yet child protection intervention places high demands on parents to think about the needs of their child, to reflect on their behaviour, to engage their creativity so they can come to new solutions, and to deal rationally with unfamiliar people and systems. To be most helpful, workers need to be able to contain, calm, and process parental emotions rather than fan them with their own reactivity. As one "firm, fair, and friendly" worker said,

> I'm emotionally invested in my cases and I have opinions about the children and families, but it's not my job to put my emotional opinion in my work. My job is to guide the child and the parents through the work. And it's really emotional for them, and I need to be strong and regulate my emotion, to always be calm and hear their concerns and respond back, and if you can't do that, I think is where you actually, you can't do strengths-based practice, and in fact I think you probably end up doing damaging practice. (176)

Strong negative emotions like fear, anxiety, and stress impair the worker's ability to come to impartial judgments. They can get in the way of workers being able to accurately interpret ambiguous information (LeBlanc, Regehr, Shlonsky, & Bogo, 2012) and to read social cues like facial expressions (Williams et al., 2007). They can lead to memory impairments, selective attention, and change the way workers rate risk (LeBlanc et al., 2012). They can make workers less likely to reappraise their own beliefs (Gross, 2013), less able to use their knowledge in practice (Bogo et al., 2013), and less able to relate to parents empathetically (Howe, 2010).

These links between emotional regulation, better decision-making, and more collaborative practice have led to a recent interest in mindfulness and self-regulation strategies in professional training (Berceli & Napoli, 2006; Bogo et al., 2013; Mullins, 2011; Schreiber et al., 2013). One UK study, for example, recommended child protection workers be trained in "anxiety-reduction techniques such as relaxation techniques (focusing on reducing muscle tension), visualization and imagery, diaphragmatic breathing, stress inoculation (functional patterns of self-talk), and meditation" (Schreiber et al., 2013, p. 713). While the links are also being made to self-care (McGarrigle & Walsh, 2011), these recommendations are not simply so workers can relax after a hard day. There is a growing awareness that workers need to know how to manage their own emotions effectively if they are to assume the attentive, open, and curious stance required to come to decisions that are impartial and fair.

Why is this so important? Beyond the moral arguments, fairness is emerging as an important factor in effective work with mandated clients. Research in community criminal justice has found that when officer-offender relationships are assessed by offenders to be "firm, fair, and caring," they result in lower recidivism rates (Kennealy et al., 2012; Skeem, Louden, Polaschek, & Camp, 2007). It seems that clients are more likely to collaborate and follow the rules when they feel that neutral, fair, and respectful processes are being applied. A core principle of work with mandated clients is to strive for this kind of consistency and fairness in the management of rules and decisions (Calder, 2008b). This is at least as important as empathy and positive feelings when it comes to making working relationships with people who would rather not reciprocate.

In "firm, fair, and friendly practice," the drive to judge impartially was not simply motivated by a wish to better understand clients and to come to more appropriate and informed decisions. It was a relational tool. It helped workers engage and remain engaged with their clients. Judging impartially helped workers navigate the shifts between collaborative and more authoritative stances. These shifts were more manageable because the judgments that informed them were felt to be fair.

Workers could be more transparent about their decisions because they felt able to stand behind the processes they had gone through to make them. They were better able to attend to their interactions with clients because they had their emotional responses under control. And as they sought to revise and expand their understanding in order to come to impartial judgments, they sustained the search for strengths and ways to invite collaboration.

Reflective Questions

1 How comfortable do you feel with your judgment role as a child protection worker?
2 How do you reconcile this role with professional values like non-judgmentality and acceptance?
3 An important part of impartiality is managing your emotional reactions.
   a) How good are you at doing this with the people in your life?
   b) Which situations most easily dysregulate you emotionally?
   c) Based on your personal experience and/or theoretical knowledge, what effect does emotional dysregulation have on your ability to think things through clearly?
   d) Based on your personal experience and/or theoretical knowledge, what strategies are most effective to help you become and remain emotionally regulated?
4 Think back to Mike, Ada's partner. You believe he has seriously physically and sexually abused his daughter, Katy, over an extended period. When you made your last home visit, he was in the house, violating the safety plan and a legal order to stay away. Imagine you insisted on checking all the rooms for him and have just come upon him in the bedroom.
   a) What might you be feeling?
   b) What might you be thinking? Speak your internal self-talk out loud as you enter the room.
   Here is Mike's reaction: You have been "caught" in the house by the social worker. In a way it's a relief, as you were done with all the hiding and pretending. It actually might make sense to talk to her to try to get this thing sorted out. You know that you've got to come clean eventually if you have any hope of salvaging your relationship with Ada and Katy. It's better now. They seem to be keeping in line and giving you the respect you deserve. You can't

forgive yourself for what you did to Katy. You still have trouble understanding your feelings towards her. You were sexually abused yourself as a kid, so you know how bad it feels. You never meant it to go as far as it did – a little touching seemed OK, but you're upset it progressed to full sex. You blame Katy for that though. Katy is such a precocious kid; she didn't stop you, and the way she was always strutting around, she seemed ready.

  c) What feelings does this elicit?
  d) What strategies might help you in the moment to manage these feelings so as to stay impartial in your judgment?
  e) How does Mike's reaction change the initial story you had constructed about the situation (look back to Question 4b)?
  f) Where are the openings in Mike's story to explore for context and to connect with him as a person with strengths and weaknesses?
5 How do you stay curious about your clients in child protection work? What gets in the way of this, and how can you overcome these barriers?

Role Play: Joe

Divide into groups of three. One person will be the observer, one the client, and one the worker.

Only the observer and the client should read the "Client's Information" on page 211.

Only the worker should read the "Worker's Information" on page 212. Find ways to show Joe that you are judging him impartially, so you can hopefully build a relationship with him that is different from the ones he has had with previous workers.

The observer's role is to notice when the worker is able to demonstrate his or her impartial judgment.

Start the role play at the point when the worker knocks on the door for the home visit.

After fifteen minutes take turns to debrief, starting with the role players and addressing:

1 How did you feel?
2 What worked well?
3 What did not work well?

4 Was there ever a time when the worker's safety appeared to be at risk? If yes, did the worker take action (through the purposeful use of authority, inviting more collaboration, being transparent, or attending to the interaction) to secure their safety and preserve their ability to judge impartially?

5 What did you learn about judging impartially from this role play?

Chapter Fifteen

Seeing Clients as Human

"Firm, fair, and friendly practice" was a value-based approach. This should come as no surprise; strengths-based practice has always been embedded in the values of partnership and respect. In this version, however, the core value that underlay the strengths-based relationship and informed all work with clients was not quite as expected. It was not that clients were experts or equals, it was that they were fellow human beings.

This version of strengths-based practice required workers to see their clients – all of their clients – as human. The moral imperative to treat fellow humans well *because they are human* was the driving force in keeping the strengths-based relationship honest and authentic. It helped workers respect, accept, and connect with their clients. It supported them to act in ways that demonstrated that clients were experts, equals, or people with inherent strengths, and it was far more meaningful than direct exhortations to hold these values. The moral foundation of the approach was simple: as one worker put it, "I go back to my version of strengths-based, which is honouring the other human life in the room" (176). Another said,

> The way that you [act] has to always be respectful of the humanity of the person that you're working with. And, therefore, if it is, it's going to be strengths-based, right? I don't view them as a monster through a lens, I actually, yes, so you busted somebody's head open and you then blew up a house; none of that stuff is excusable, but that doesn't mean you're not a human being anymore. And so how do we connect with you as a human being while still doing the stuff that we need to do in response to the behaviours that you demonstrated? (254)

It might seem strange to need to affirm clients' humanity. Why would this ever be in doubt in a human services profession? The child protection literature over the last twenty years, however, contains plenty of evidence that workers struggle to relate to their clients as fellow humans. They have been found to experience high rates of burnout (McFadden et al., 2015), a condition characterized by the emotional distancing and cynicism of "depersonalisation" (Maslach, 2003). Managerial categorization and control strategies intended to increase the efficiency of child welfare agencies have been blamed for reducing clients to little more than a set of problems or needs (Rogowski, 2012). Technology-based client-management systems can leave workers piecing together their clients' human stories from fragmented information scattered across computer screens, actuarial checkboxes, and dichotomous categories (Hall, Parton, Peckover, & White, 2010; Huuskonen & Vakkari, 2011; Parton, 2008; White, Wastell, Broadhurst, & Hall, 2010). When child welfare decision-making relies so heavily on disembodied information passed around professional networks (Parton, 2008), it becomes easy to lose sight of the fundamental humanity of the people with whom we work.

To the interviewees describing this version of strengths-based practice, seeing clients as human necessarily meant seeing them as worthy of respect. Workers talked of treating clients "like a human being, like a human being should be treated, with respect and kindness" (102) and sharing an "innate belief in the goodness of humankind" (248). When telling stories of their work with clients, they made comments like "that's another human being and that's precious and valuable" (176) and "the client needs to feel right that there's some positive regard for them in their humanity" (254). Doing strengths-based practice meant responding to each client as human, and seeing them as human meant seeing them as people with value and capacity.

For these workers, referencing a client's humanity was another way to say they were "people worth doing business with" (Turnell & Edwards, 1999, p. 30) or that they were "a repository of resources, not a pool of pathology and deficits" (Berg & Kelly, 2000, p. 17). It acted as a powerful shortcut to the core professional and strengths-based value that clients should be treated with respect. It also sustained hope and encouraged workers to keep searching for strengths and collaborative intent, even with people who appeared non-collaborative or unlikeable or presented great risk to their child. This was because the capacity for growth, resilience, and change were seen as part of the human condition. As one worker said,

> You're hopeful in humanity and in the humanity of this person that they can achieve something better and grow. Because I think that a big part of life is about process and growing and expanding to something beyond what you were. (254)

This comes very close to the reason for hope offered by Saleebey (2012): "The natural state of affairs for human beings, evolved over eons of times and at every level of organization from cell to self-image, is the repair of one's mind and body" (p. 15).

Keeping the clients' essential humanity in mind also helped workers be more accepting. As one worker said, "We're all human, we'll both make mistakes" (176). Clients' difficulties were normalized as part of the human condition. Indeed, seeing clients as human might be framed as the end point of the contextualization process previously described as supporting impartial judgment. Workers sought to understand client behaviour in the broadest possible context, and this was the context of the shared human experience. The idea of the humanity of clients was an integrative one in that it helped workers accept clients as people with both negative and positive qualities and to view them holistically as people who "experience life and have likes and dislikes and feelings" (176).

Seeing clients as having a shared humanity also created a sense of connection. As one worker said, "I am a human being just like them, we are joined in that" (102). The power of this human connection has been noted before in writing about strengths-based practice. As Kisthardt (2012) states,

> By realizing that there is more in our shared experience as human beings that makes providers more like participants than different from them, we gain the courage to be warm, caring, empathic, and genuinely affirming of people's own visions. (p. 66)

Others have suggested that by normalizing their own pain and struggle as part of the human condition, workers might reduce their distance from clients to better enact strengths-based practice (Grant & Cadell, 2009). When they acknowledge and accept their own human weaknesses, they become less able to assume a position of objective, detached expertise. The pay-off can be great, as

> allowing the worker their own humanity, history and emotionality in the work alongside that of family members arguably allows for mutuality of engagement, empathy, empowerment and self-development, and may give added vitality to the work." (Lefevre, 2008, p. 81)

In this study, drawing on their shared human experience enabled workers to stay engaged with clients even in the face of hostility. It encouraged workers to keep trying to connect and supported feelings of caring and compassion that were very motivating. As one worker said,

> I care about people in general ... I care about my clients in the sense of, probably more from a therapeutic lens, in the sense of, in the humanity of, who we are as human beings. We want, you want positive outcomes for all human beings that exist. Negative things happen, that doesn't mean you want negative things [to] happen, so you care for them in that sense, you will good things, you know, to materialize in people's lives and their experiences. (254)

Seeing clients as human was a way to spark authentic feelings of respect, caring, acceptance, and mutuality. It was extremely important that these feelings were authentic. If they were not, the focus on strengths could easily become a cynical exercise in manipulation. As one worker said,

> On the surface someone looking in can say, "Oh well, it's like putting icing on a cake but the cake is actually made with cow-pies" ... if the intent is to deceive and try to make it easier for you to then talk about difficult things, folks will see through that and, and they won't be able to stay with you in the course of the conversation. So there has to be a true sense of genuineness, and the clients we're sitting with, whether it's just in your office or around the table, they need to feel, I believe, the compassion in your language, they need to see it on your face, they need to see it in the way you sit with them. (248)

There was little doubt that clients would detect inauthentic feelings and that this would undermine the entire strengths-based relationship.

Interviewees were not, however, driven by these pragmatic considerations. At the suggestion that strengths-based practice could be used manipulatively by workers who did not subscribe to its values, one interviewee responded,

> That's a really ignorant, dishonest, disrespectful marionette way of looking at someone, like they're just an object and I completely devalue them as a human being and as a worthy relationship by treating them so poorly. And I couldn't live with myself. I would be gutted, like I would just be, I mean, my stomach is turning right now just thinking about it. Just not cool. (102)

It was the moral imperative to treat their fellow humans with respect and caring that kept the strengths-based relationship honest.

Strengths-based child protection approaches have tended not to make much of the idea that clients and workers share a common humanity. These approaches have a humanistic orientation, and some draw on the theme within the Kansas strengths perspective that resilience and the capacity for growth are inherently human qualities. They make occasional reference to activities like "honouring the strengths and humanity of the parents" (Turnell et al., 2008, p. 114) and avoiding "dehumanizing or demonizing" clients (Turnell & Edwards, 1999, p. 158). However, the theme of their shared humanity is rarely used overtly to promote worker-client collaboration.

One has to look beyond the strengths-based practice literature, to writings about relational social work (Freedberg, 2009; Maidment, 2006; Mandell, 2008; Ornstein & Ganzer, 2005; Ruch, 2005), to find authors emphasizing the humanity of clients in the same way as "firm, fair, and friendly" interviewees. From a relational social work perspective, it is neither possible nor desirable for workers to separate their personal selves from their professional selves (Mandell, 2008). Workers respond to clients in ways that were authentic, honour the emotional content of the relationship, and acknowledge their shared humanity. They must "lay aside professional masks, to be human and down-to-earth" (De Boer & Coady, 2007, p. 41). There is no expectation that workers maintain a neutral detachment from the clients in the name of professional objectivity. Deep emotional empathy, compassion, and even love for clients are seen as acceptable so long as they are used in a therapeutic way (Maidment, 2006). Rather than denying their human reactions, workers engage with, interrogate, and learn from them.

Emphasizing our very human connection to the people with whom we work does not mean we should abandon the concept of professional boundaries. On the contrary, it makes those boundaries more important than ever, albeit in urgent need of an update. If we can no longer rely on emotional distance to protect clients from the harms that can come from inappropriate worker-client relationships, then we must turn instead to a very clear understanding of the relationship's professional purpose (O'Leary et al., 2013). The benchmark for whether a worker-client relationship is ethical becomes the extent to which it enables workers to meet their professional obligations and realize their professional values. For the social worker, greater latitude to connect in a way that feels natural and intuitive comes at the price of greater vigilance as to whether that connection is in the client's best interests and demonstrates respect for the client's intrinsic worth. The only way of ensuring this is to explicitly negotiate the conditions of the relationship with each client while acknowledging that some behaviours will always clash with our values and purpose and so will always lie beyond the boundaries of a professional relationship (O'Leary et al., 2013). This gives us a clear mandate to avoid abusive, exploitative, or otherwise confusing or demeaning behaviour while holding open the possibility of feeling deeply with our clients, gaining deep gratification from our interactions, and being more truly ourselves.

Research with clients suggests this kind of connectedness is preferable to emotional detachment. It has led to calls for workers to demonstrate their "compassionate ordinariness" (Huxley, Evans, Beresford, Davidson, & King, 2009) and their "human qualities of kindness, warmth, compassion, caring, sensitivity, empathy and thoughtfulness" (Beresford, Croft, & Adshead, 2008). Workers have been asked to show their humanity by being honest, down to earth, sharing their emotions, and disclosing information about their lives (Beresford et al., 2008; De Boer & Coady, 2007; Schreiber et al., 2013). Some clients have even talked of forging friendships with their workers that are characterized by mutual affection, informality, reciprocity, and strong emotional bonds (Beresford et al., 2008; De Boer & Coady, 2007). Parents within the child protection system have called for comfortable and friendly working relationships that make them feel listened to and cared about (Ghaffar et al., 2012; Schreiber et al., 2013).

This kind of informal, reciprocal, and deeply human relationship is an important element of strengths-based child protection approaches. "Firm, fair, and friendly" workers strived for it, not hiding behind their professional persona or pretending to be other than they were. They went further than is common with most approaches, however, in describing faith in the humanity of their clients as a guiding value. Seeing their clients as fellow humans kept workers reaching for collaboration. It kept them in touch with genuine feelings of respect for, acceptance of, and connection with their clients. It kept their authority in check. Their wholehearted commitment to seeing their clients as human made the "firm, fair, and friendly" strengths-based relationship work.

Reflective Questions

1 What beliefs, experiences, and people motivated you to enter the helping professions?
2 If there were no limitations on your practice and you could be exactly the worker you want to be, what values would drive your practice? What makes these particular values important to you?
3 Describe a time, either in your child protection work or in your interactions with others, when you were able to put into practice the values identified in Question 2. What happened? How did it feel?
4 To what extent does the idea that clients are human resonate with the guiding values you described in Question 2? In what ways can this idea help support and sustain these values?
5 Make a list of areas of struggle and pain in your life. Now make a list of your strengths, talents, and resources. Repeat the exercise for a client or someone whom you tend to see as very different from you. What conclusions do you draw about your shared humanity?
6 Think of a time when you have felt that someone truly believed in and valued you.
    a) What effect did this have on you?
    b) What did this person do to show you this?
    c) How did you know he or she was "for real"?
    d) What conclusions do you draw for your interaction with clients?

Role Play

Choose one of the four role-play scenarios in the Appendix. This is your opportunity to demonstrate that you see all of the clients involved in your chosen scenario as human and to convey what this means to you.

Practise using all components of the "firm, fair, and friendly practice" approach.

Divide into groups of three. One person will be the observer, one the client, and one the worker.

Only the observer and the client should read the "Client's Information." Only the worker should read the "Worker's Information." Before you attempt the role play, take some time to reflect on the idea that those involved in the scenario are human, just like you. Reflect on the ways in which this might help you respect, accept, and connect with them.

The observer's role is to notice what the worker does that demonstrates the perception that the client is a fellow human as well as what is said or done to move the relationship forward.

After fifteen minutes take turns to debrief, starting with the role players and addressing:

1 How did you feel?
2 What worked well?
3 What did not work well?
4 What did you learn from this role play?

Section Three Summary

Many parents involved in the child protection system are unwilling participants. This makes for a very different worker-client relationship than is commonly described in generalist social work texts. As Ferguson (2005) writes, "Empathy, sensitivity, warmth and Rogerian 'unconditional positive regard' are still consistently identified as what social work should be about. But these are deeply problematic in work with involuntary clients" (p. 793).

Workers who interpreted strengths-based practice to mean "firm, fair, and friendly practice" appeared to have found an approach that included but did not rely on these "deeply problematic" qualities. They joined solution-focused child protection theorists and the growing number of contemporary social work authors who suggest that partnership and paternalism need to go hand in hand in child protection work (Barber, 1991; Berg & Kelly, 2000; Ivanoff et al., 1994; Rooney, 2009; Sidebotham, 2013; Trotter, 1997, 2006; Tuck, 2013; Turnell & Edwards, 1999; Turnell et al., 2008). They described a model for the worker-client relationship that drew on ideas from relational social work and the Kansas tradition of strengths-based practice but that was most clearly informed by the solution-focused therapy developed in work with mandated clients. In doing so, they echoed messages from researchers from a variety of mandated practice fields about how to work effectively with clients who do not want to work with you.

"Firm, fair, and friendly practice" was an approach that workers could implement with all clients in all situations. The approach enabled them to use their authority purposefully while searching at all times to maximize the potential for collaboration. It required them to use family strengths to empower clients, develop sustainable child protection plans, and nurture the worker-client relationship. It included a transparency that went beyond the usual openness about child protection concerns, the worker's role, and the consequences of parental decisions to include a willingness to speak about the shifting relational dynamics on an ongoing basis. It required impartial judgment, which relied both on the ability to work with the broadest possible perspective and on the ability to emotionally self-regulate. It incorporated an extraordinary attentiveness to the worker-client interaction and was driven by the belief that clients are human, which makes them worthy of respect, acceptance, and connection. "Firm, fair, and friendly practice" described how to remain true to the principles of strengths-based practice while carrying out the full range of mandated responsibilities in child protection work.

SECTION FOUR

Becoming a Strengths-Based Child Protection Practitioner

"It's just kind of a way of being I guess. Becomes intrinsic after a while." (216)

"It becomes part of your being, it becomes who you are ... it's not just about the techniques that you use when you're working with people, it's also about how you conduct yourself, in your work setting and in your personal life." (72)

Chapter Sixteen

Identifying as a Strengths-Based Child Protection Practitioner

It is all too easy to pay lip service to strengths-based practice. Talk of client self-determination can be used to justify poor service, and lists of strengths can disarm clients before hitting them over the head with news of their inadequacies. There are plenty of examples of workers claiming to be strengths-based while continuing to focus on problems and pathology (Berg & De Jong, 2004; Blundo, 2001, 2012; Grant & Cadell, 2009; Lietz, 2011; C. Rapp et al., 2005). Workers might ask solution-focused questions, hold family meetings, and complete strengths assessments, but these are empty exercises when done without an authentic commitment to see clients as fellow humans with strengths, to engage collaboratively, and to enact good decisions. As Saleebey (2012) advocates,

> Practicing from a strengths orientation means this – *everything* you do as a social worker will be predicated, in some way, on helping to discover and embellish, explore and exploit clients' strengths and resources in the service of assisting them to achieve their goals, realize their dreams, and shed the irons of their own inhibitions and misgivings. (p. 3)

If workers are to implement strengths-based practice authentically, effectively, and consistently, they must work from strengths-based values. Values are the principles we live by and the means by which we judge what is important and good. Some have described the process of reorienting to strengths-based values as adopting a new paradigm or world view (Blundo, 2001, 2012; Corcoran, 2005; Grant & Cadell, 2009; Graybeal, 2001). In this chapter, I consider it as a matter of professional identity development, as we move from *doing* strengths-based practice to *becoming* strengths-based practitioners.

Professional Identity and Values

Professional identity comprises the values, beliefs, and attitudes that define the ways in which we perceive and carry out our work (Adams, Hean, Sturgis, & Clark, 2006). It denotes how we see ourselves in the workplace – *who* we see ourselves as. It is frequently understood using social identity theory (Tajfel, 1978, 2010). This suggests that identity is not static; we don't choose the professional identity we like best and move on to other things. We are constantly sorting through messages from the environment and our own history to define our professional selves. Developing a professional identity involves a process of filtering through a range of different possibilities for what kind of worker we can be, should be, and want to be at any given time. In child protection work, we might choose to see ourselves as an investigator, a child advocate, a parental ally, a strengths-based practitioner, or any number of other possibilities. Having mentally categorized ourselves into the group that fits best, we will, until such time that it makes sense to identify in a different way, attribute emotional significance to that categorization, integrate it into our self-concept, and compare ourselves to others in ways that support our chosen identity.

To negotiate our professional identity, we draw on our personal values, prior experiences, and messages from peers, educators, colleagues, the media, and the broader culture (Hotho, 2008; Osteen, 2011). These provide "identity scripts" (Hotho, 2008) that guide our perception of what being a child protection worker entails. We are more likely to choose identities that are supported by unambiguous and accessible identity scripts, fit well with our professional self-concept, and support professional self-esteem (Hogg & McGarty, 1990). A professional identity is more likely to hold sway if it is highly valued by others and agrees with our understanding of our professional role and the tasks we are asked to perform in our daily work.

There is little question that being a strengths-based practitioner is an identity likely to support professional esteem. Strengths-based practice is now commonly portrayed as the way both social workers and child protection workers *should* be doing business. In the study on which this book is based, eighty-nine per cent of respondents saw strengths-based practice as a good approach for child protection work, and eighty-five per cent thought it increased the chances of success. It was hard to find any worker who did not want to practise in a strengths-based way.

This leaves the question of whether being a strengths-based practitioner fits with the professional self-concept of child protection workers. They are only likely to see themselves as strengths-based practitioners if that identity aligns with their day-to-day activities. The participants in this study described five different versions of strengths-based practice, and four of those did not fit when workers had to assume a more authoritative stance. When it came to acting against parental will, they had to suspend their strengths-based approach. Workers who define strengths-based practice as a purely supportive approach will find it very hard to develop a sustained commitment to strengths-based values or to see themselves as strengths-based child protection practitioners. Too much of their daily work simply does not support this identity. The child protection worker identity is likely to be most salient, leaving strengths-based practice as a set of activities to be applied in limited situations rather than an all-embracing philosophy or professional identity.

In the study, only those workers who framed strengths-based practice as incorporating both the care and the control functions of the child protection role could see themselves as being strengths-based at all times. These workers had most clearly internalized the values on which strengths-based practice is built. One described the approach as "intuitive and innate" (248), commenting that "it's not that somebody taught me as such to work in this way ... there's beliefs I have about humanity, there's values I have about humanity and the culture and the society I live in" (248). They emphasized the philosophy underpinning the approach and described their heartfelt commitment to its values. As two workers said, strengths-based was "just who I am" (254; 102). It is likely that these workers experienced a mutually enforcing process whereby their strengths-based values helped them enact strengths-based practice, which supported their identification as strengths-based practitioners enacting strengths-based values in their work.

Professional Identity and Dissonance

At this point it is worth pausing to ask why it is necessary to identify as a strengths-based child protection practitioner. Is there anything wrong with seeing strengths-based practice as something you do at some times and not at others? Why not assume a professional identity as a collaborative and respectful social worker who picks from a range of possible approaches, including strengths-based practice, as required? Workers could implement strengths-based practice as a supportive approach in the Kansas tradition and switch to a more directive or problem-based approach when needed. Saleebey (2012) himself has said that there is nothing in the strengths perspective that prevents it from being used with other frameworks and that "I don't think it is prudent to give up the deficit model of the human condition or the problem-based approach to helping" (p. 290).

The problem is that workers in this study appeared to dichotomize strengths-based practice and its alternatives, making it hard to shift smoothly between the different approaches. Study interviewees rarely described alternatives to strengths-based practice in positive or even neutral terms. The alternatives were synonymous with bad practice; they were "wagging the finger" (323), "bullying" (236), being "accusatory and black and white" (115), "coming down with the hammer all the time" (216), being "very rude to clients, very harsh" (254), "oppressive" (115), "hard-handed" (266), "heavy-handed" (248), and engaging in "police-dominated practice" (999). Strengths-based practice was contrasted with examples of social work practice that few would condone, like telling a parent "Mum, you're out of the house because of the sexual abuse and you'll see your kids in eighteen months when everyone's through therapy" (73), "removing and just saying: 'you have to do as I say and jump through these hoops'" (407), and "scooping the kids out of Aboriginal communities" (189). One worker said, "If you weren't practising from strengths-based ... you were just downtrodden and yelling at people all day long and being the heavy" (216). For another, non-strengths-based practice meant

> a negative, finger pointing dictatorial attitude that says I'm holier than thou and, you know, you're gonna, I'm the mighty child protection worker and you're scum ... other social workers, they just go in there and they bring the hammer down. Bang. (102)

Few workers offered an alternative to strengths-based practice that might be recognized as respectful, compassionate, and supportive of client autonomy. This is understandable in light of the way that strengths-based practice and directive ways of working have often been framed as opposites. Person-centred strengths-based approaches have been deemed to be theoretically incompatible with statutory work (Mirick, 2013; Murphy, Duggan, & Joseph, 2013). Kansas strengths-based theorists have criticized the pursuit of facts, characterized worker scepticism as unhelpful (Saleebey, 2012), and attributed power conflicts to worker intransigence (Kisthardt, 2012). It is easy to see this tradition of strengths-based practice as diametrically opposed to child protection approaches requiring the careful evaluation of evidence, the rational calculation of probabilities, and the judicious use of authority. There is little question that the latter is sometimes necessary to protect children (Laming, 2009; Munro, 1999, 2011; Sidebotham, 2013). The problem is that workers have had very little guidance as to how they might switch deftly between approaches framed as being so very different.

Two of the best supported theories in social psychology alert us to the fact that workers are likely to have a great deal of trouble switching between strengths-based and more directive approaches when they are cast as opposites. The first is the theory of cognitive dissonance (Festinger, 1962; Harmon-Jones, Amodio, & Harmon-Jones, 2009). This proposes that when people hold conflicting cognitions they will typically reject one in favour of the other or attempt to reframe them to make them consistent. We seek consistency in our beliefs, to the extent that holding conflicting cognitions creates the discomfort known as cognitive dissonance. When we reject one of the beliefs to resolve our cognitive dissonance, we often disparage the rejected choice in order to justify its rejection. This re-evaluation makes it harder to access the rejected cognition in the future. The second theory is social identity theory (Tajfel, 1978, 2010). This describes a process similar to the one described by cognitive dissonance theory, but in relation to social identity. When our chosen identity is threatened we will abandon it, cling more tightly to it, or redefine it to accommodate the threat.

What does this have to do with reconciling strengths-based and other approaches in child protection work? Most study participants dealt with the dissonance between supportive strengths-based practice and authority-based child protection work by rejecting one of the approaches. They could not identify as strengths-based child protection workers because they saw being a child protection worker as incompatible with being a strengths-based practitioner.

Most abandoned any nascent identity as a strengths-based practitioner when it did not fit with their statutory child protection role. They rejected the possibility of using a strengths-based approach with clients with whom a directive stance was or might become necessary. This removed the need to wrestle with the discomfort of reconciling an entirely supportive strengths-based stance with an authority-based stance. Their rejection of strengths-based practice was codified in a set of rules about when strengths-based practice was inapplicable. By generalizing their rejection of strengths-based practice to broad categories of clients like those with mental health problems or "resistant" clients, they reinforced their own belief that strengths-based practice was only for limited situations. It was for certain clients in certain situations, not a way of being in the workplace. Having defined it in this way, they were less likely to apply the approach broadly in the future.

An alternative strategy in the face of the dissonance between strengths-based and authoritative stances is to hold on as long as possible to a purely supportive frame. Some workers who described strengths-based practice as "relating therapeutically," "supporting client self-determination," and "connecting internal and external resources" were very slow to abandon their self-perception as a strengths-based practitioner, even when it disagreed with their identity as a competent child protection practitioner. They described glossing over risks in conversations with clients, avoiding management oversight, dismissing the opinions of others as risk averse, and supporting unsafe safety plans in the name of strengths-based practice. Having invested so much in the supportive relationship, it was hard for them to switch to a more critical or directive stance, even when they believed it was necessary. In defending their identity as strengths-based practitioners, they abandoned core elements of the child protection role.

This tendency to under-identify risk, to suspend scepticism, and to elevate the goal of preserving the worker-client relationship above the goal of child safety has been described as symptomatic of "professional dangerousness" (Calder, 2008a; Dale, Davies, Morrison, & Waters, 1986). This is "the process whereby professionals involved in Child Protection work can behave in a way which either colludes with or increases the dangerous dynamics of the abusing family" (Morrison, 1990, p. 262). It typifies the over-investment in one identity and the failure to integrate dissonant information predicted by social identity and cognitive dissonance theories.

It is easy to see how workers who identify as strengths-based and define strengths-based practice as an entirely collaborative approach might discount information indicating a need to act against a client's wishes. To protect their strengths-based identity, they can become stuck in what Calder (2008b) calls the strengths "track." However, sticking in a strengths "track" will only work until the needs of the child, courts, supervisors, or managers force them to shift to a risk "track." The lack of integration of these two tracks means that such a shift is likely to feel abrupt, prompting feelings of betrayal and confusion when the basis of the worker-client relationship changes midstream.

To develop an identity as a strengths-based child protection practitioner, workers need to find a way to integrate the identity of strengths-based practitioner with the identity of child protection practitioner. They need to make being strengths-based and being directive less dissonant. It is hard to redefine the child protection role – this is entrenched in child protection legislation, policy, and systems. The only option then is to (re)define strengths-based practice to accommodate the child protection role.

"Firm, fair, and friendly" workers had aligned their definition of strengths-based practice to fit their image of good protection work. They had rejected definitions that they felt left children at risk and confused clients. Their identity as strengths-based child protection practitioners was not repeatedly threatened by the need to exercise their mandated authority. Their version of strengths-based practice enabled them to move smoothly between strengths and risks tracks – between supportive and directive stances – as motivation and capacity changed from client to client and throughout the life of a case. Indeed, they saw everything they did at work as an expression of that identity, including resorting to coercive measures and removing children from parental care. This supported them to make a considerable emotional investment in that identity, incorporating strengths-based values into both their personal value system and their professional self-concept.

This process of forging a strong identity as a strengths-based child protection practitioner does not happen overnight, and "firm, fair, and friendly" workers attributed it neither to their training nor to their knowledge of the literature. It was the end point in a difficult process of redefining strengths-based practice to fit the limits of their child protection role. As one worker said of strengths-based practice,

> Before, you know, I thought it was useless because I'd go out there with the "it's collaborative" and I'd just kind of feel like "alright this is not working" ... if you interviewed me four years ago I would have said "I don't like strengths-based practice, I like my practice," but now I can see what I was trying to create for myself and the clients is strengths-based. (176)

Starting with an appropriate identity script for "strengths-based child protection practitioner" should reduce the need for workers to struggle to reconcile the dichotomized identities of strengths-based practitioner and child protection practitioner while they go about their difficult business. The details of "firm, fair, and friendly practice" and solution-focused child protection approaches like Signs of Safety provide these identity scripts. They can act as blueprints for how to do strengths-based practice in such a way that workers can remain committed to the values of strengths-based practice even when acting against clients' wishes. Starting with these blueprints may reduce the number of workers who, committed to being strengths-based but without a means to reconcile this with saying "no," find themselves sacrificing their responsibilities to the child so as to keep a connection with the parents. It may reduce the number of workers who give up on the approach because the strengths-based practice they learnt in school does not help them with clients who do not exercise their self-determination to achieve child safety. It may reduce the number of workers who reject strengths-based practice as "coming out of university-based therapists who have no concept of what some of our clients are truly like ... look[ing] at people through rose coloured glasses" (336). If they have, from the start, an identity script that allows for the exercise of authority and is applicable throughout their day, workers may be less likely to define strengths-based as something they do with select clients in select situations and more likely to see strengths-based child protection practitioner as something they can *be*.

Reflective Questions

1 Take three minutes to draw a visual representation of your professional identity. Describe what you have drawn and why.
2 How has your professional identity changed over time?
3 From your personal experience and knowledge of the literature, explain what influences how you choose to identify at work.
4 Imagine you are retiring from a long and successful career in child protection work, during which you were able to grow into the kind of worker you always wanted to be.
   a) How would people describe you at your retirement party?
   b) What qualities would they comment on?
   c) What kind of relationships would they say you had with your clients and colleagues?

5 Now imagine it is many years later, and there is room on your headstone or a commemorative plaque for seven words to sum up the kind of worker you were.
    a) What seven words would you want to be remembered with?
    b) What stands in the way of you being that worker now?
6 What actions can you take in the next three months to help you identify as a strengths-based child protection practitioner?

Chapter Seventeen

Educating the Strengths-Based Child Protection Practitioner

How do we go about educating for strengths-based child protection practice? The first step is helping learners understand the differences between strengths-based approaches for generalist practice and those for child protection practice. The second step is teaching a child protection–specific approach, using a model like "firm, fair, and friendly practice," to show the kind of worker-client relationship to aim for. This is not a one-shot deal. The fact that all study participants said they knew about and used strengths-based practice did not stop twenty per cent of them from calling for more training in the approach. Education needs to be ongoing, practical, and focused on building skills to navigate tensions between authoritative and collaborative practice and between problem-focused and strengths-focused work. As one child protection worker said, the need was for "more training in 'real' social work, i.e., how can protection really use [strengths-based practice] while still being faced with a deficit-based model, where faults are pointed out, and we still have the power to remove someone's children?" (142).

This call for practice applying strengths-based ideas to the real situations faced by front-line workers matches what we know about how people learn (Dreyfus & Dreyfus, 2005). When they begin to learn a new skill, novices focus on learning the concrete facts and rules about what to do. As learning progresses, they begin to integrate important situational information, mentally noting how the skill worked in one situation as opposed to another. This leads them to develop their own rules not only about what to do, but about how and when to do it. More experience in applying the skills brings more learning if learners are emotionally engaged enough to reflect on their practice. The combination of experience and reflection on that experience helps strengthen successful responses and inhibit unsuccessful ones. Learners develop a range of mini models about how to use the skill in different situations. These come to form the equivalent of a personal database of ways to perform the skill with different people in different contexts. By the time they master the skill, learners are expert practitioners who will have stored multiple context-specific models in their memory. Experts no longer draw explicitly on the original rules about how to perform the skills and, indeed, often forget what these rules even are. They rely increasingly on an intuitive sense of how to enact the approach, informed by their complex web of situational cognitive models.

This learning process is the result of experience and reflection. Practitioners can earn the experience the hard way, through trial and error with their clients. They can also gain this experience vicariously, with the support of educators and supervisors. Through discussions, reflective exercises, role plays, and simulations, learners can add more about applying a child protection–applicable model of strengths-based practice in tricky situations to their cognitive database. This is the kind of supported learning that front-line workers in the study called for.

Learning as a Process

One way of looking at the five versions of strengths-based practice described in this book is that they are different points in the developmental process of becoming a strengths-based child protection practitioner (see Figure 3).

Workers who subscribed to the "relating therapeutically," "supporting client self-determination," and "connecting to internal and external resources" versions of strengths-based practice can be considered as being in the earliest stages of the learning process. These interviewees were focused on the approach as a set of skills and actions to be performed. They had not yet developed a rich database of situational models that could help them generalize their practice. They were able to apply the approach in only a limited number of situations and had developed clear rules about when strengths-based practice was not applicable.

Those in the "pursuing a balanced understanding" group appeared to be at a later stage in the learning process. They were more flexible in their application of strengths-based practice and could see themselves as being strengths-based in far more situations. They drew on the practices of the first three groups, but they talked less about the mechanics

Figure 3. Learning to be a strengths-based child protection practitioner

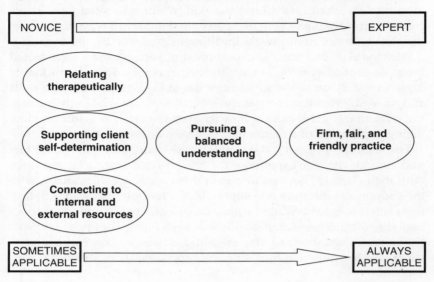

of what to do and more about how and why to do it. The stories of their practice showed that they performed the same basic strengths-based activities as their colleagues, but their descriptions of the approach were more focused on its values and philosophy rather than the activities themselves. The fact that human capacity to integrate new information is limited means that an important part of the learning process is automatizing basic skills so we no longer have to think about them (Moulton et al., 2007). This frees up cognitive space to learn more complex applications of the skill. That is what these interviewees appeared to have done. Basic strengths-based skills and activities were no longer the subject of a great deal of conscious deliberation, as the approach had started to feel more natural and intuitive for them.

Those who subscribed to "firm, fair, and friendly practice" expanded their description of the approach to incorporate their use of authority. The pursuit of a balanced understanding was extended to the pursuit of balanced action. Situational information about how to make a "pursuing a balanced understanding" approach work, like the shared view that it was easier to do when transparent about conflict, was incorporated into the very definition of "firm, fair, and friendly practice." These interviewees had redefined the approach to include transparency about conflict as they turned their minds to how to be strengths-based in highly conflictual situations. They each appeared to have developed an extensive cognitive database of models about how to perform strengths-based practice in different contexts. This supported them as they applied the approach with all clients. The basic skills and activities of strengths-based practice came so naturally that they often forgot to mention them. They rarely explicitly talked of the use of solution-focused questions and ideas like drawing on clients' strengths in their definitions of strengths-based practice. However, these were easily detectable in the descriptions of their strengths-based work with clients and clearly remained part of their approach.

Workers sometimes talked explicitly about the developmental process of becoming a strengths-based child protection practitioner. Fourteen interviewees described themselves as being in the process of moving towards a belief that strengths-based practice can be done in different ways with different clients and broadening from a focus on particular techniques to a more flexible approach in which values were more important. Some talked of integrating attention to risks and attention to strengths, and some spoke of seeing the approach as relevant to more and more clients. As one "firm, fair, and friendly" interviewee said,

> I suppose at a point in time I would have said that [strengths-based practice was inapplicable] with domestic violence, with people who are violent, working with those parents who live with mental disorders or live with the disease of addiction ... But I wouldn't even say that now. (248)

"Firm, fair, and friendly" interviewees all described redefining strengths-based practice over the course of their careers, with a key point of realization being that the approach had to include their mandated authority. One said,

> I've had the job of mentoring two new workers and ... they come back with "it's cooperative and voluntary and, you know, we're just gonna take a whole softer approach." And it only takes them a few intakes to realize that it can't actually work that way. (176)

The idea of this developmental process in becoming strengths-based appears supported by the numbers. The survey respondents who said the approach was always applicable had considerably more years of experience using the approach (Mdn = 10) than those who said it was only sometimes applicable (Mdn = 5). The "relating therapeutically," "supporting client self-determination," and "connecting to internal and external resources" interviewees had an average of eight years using strengths-based practice, the "pursuing a balanced understanding" interviewees had an average of 10.25 years, and the "firm, fair, and friendly practice" interviewees an average of 16.5 years. The small sample size makes any interpretation of these numbers speculative at best, but they are congruent with interviewee descriptions of coming to the more inclusive definitions later in their experience with strengths-based practice. All of the "firm, fair, and friendly" interviewees saw the approach as requiring a high degree of skill and emotional maturity.

Only a few learners will progress on their own from understanding generalist models of strengths-based practice to seeing themselves as "firm, fair, and friendly" strengths-based practitioners in all situations. In the study, a more common developmental trajectory was for experience to help clarify the risks to children and to reduce the number of times workers deemed strengths-based practice appropriate. Instead of generalizing their learning about strengths-based practice, workers developed rules about when the approach could not be used. In following these rules, they inhibited their ability to experiment with the different ways in which they might apply strengths-based practice. Their cognitive database of strengths-based practice could not expand.

Learning to be "firm, fair, and friendly" is a process that needs support. Teaching a model of strengths-based practice that is easily generalizable because it applies to more than just the well-resourced, collaborative clients is a good start. Framing achieving competence in strengths-based practice as a developmental process can also help. It might make workers less likely to stop their learning at an early stage. They might be more willing to perceive challenges as a predictable feature of the learning process rather than reasons to create rules about categories of clients or situations for which the approach will always be inapplicable.

Training can make a difference. A study into the implementation of an American strengths-based child protection model concluded that a team receiving five days of training and twenty-four monthly consultations used the model significantly more than a team in which the supervisor received only one day of training (Antle et al., 2008).

The trained team saw greater cooperation from families, more goals achieved, and fewer child removals and referrals to court. However, there is now a great deal of evidence that one-off education sessions rarely succeed in securing behavioural change or in empowering learners to deal with future problems (Barbee et al., 2011; Collins-Camargo & Millar, 2010; Mildon & Shlonsky, 2011; Nadeem, Gleacher, & Beidas, 2013). It is as learners are supported to work through the challenges of applying a particular approach to their daily practice that they begin to integrate their new knowledge and skills into their work. Learners need ongoing opportunities to reflect on and rehearse strengths-based practice if they are to lay down useful cognitive models for how to apply the approach in real-world situations. These opportunities will be most effective if they match the learner's developmental trajectory. Novices need to start by learning the core strengths-based skills, the how-to of conducting strengths-based questions, and implementing strengths-based interventions. As they master these skills, learners can be supported to apply their learning to increasingly challenging situations. The list of situations for which study respondents said strengths-based practice was inapplicable (see Table 1) provides a starting point for considering where they are likely to need help.

Learning Humility and Power

The workers who talked of making "firm, fair, and friendly" relationships shared two characteristics. The first is humility. These workers frequently second-guessed themselves in the interviews. They commented on their own lack of sophistication and competence, like "I'm a real simple fella" (102), "I'm a slow learner" (176), "I look back and see times when I lost my way" (248), and "I don't speak social work speak very well" (254). They talked of constantly learning from their clients, their colleagues, their families, and their mistakes. When asked what makes those who are strengths-based different from those who are not, one worker simply said, "Humility. I'm humble, I'm a human being just like they are and human beings are prone to mistakes. We're not perfect" (102).

The second characteristic is comfort with their mandated role and authority. These workers saw their mandate as important and necessary and their authority as a helpful tool. As one worker said, "I don't apologize about the work I do" (254). The resolve to use their power when necessary is illustrated in another's description of practice with a young mother in

> a situation that was really unsafe, where things were being thrown and the police were called, and she was clearly not in control of herself or her thinking. And everyone wanted a Voluntary Agreement, and I said "I can't. This woman can't sign. And I don't want her to regret that. I'll take the heat for this, this is my choice, there's no way that she can parent right now" ... everyone was dancing around her, and I said, "It's not her choice." (176)

There seems to be an important connection between humility, comfort with power, and the ability to do strengths-based practice. Indeed, the combination of appropriate authority and humility has been identified as central to good child protection practice no matter what the approach (Sidebotham, 2013; Turnell, 2004). We know that when people perceive themselves to be lacking power they tend to become more controlling (Bugental & Lewis, 1999). This phenomenon was first explored with teachers and parents who believed they had little control over the outcomes of their own actions (Bugental & Lewis, 1999). When compared to adults who felt more powerful, they were more sensitive to threats to their authority and responded to these threats more coercively. When challenged, they showed disrupted speech patterns and information-processing difficulties that impeded their communication and set the scene for "an escalating pattern of misunderstanding and conflict" (Bugental & Lewis, 1999, p. 62). These conditions are not conducive to humility, nor to the attentiveness to the worker-client interaction, the impartial judgment, and the careful calibration of authority and collaboration necessary for "firm, fair, and friendly practice."

A self-perceived lack of power can sabotage workers' ability to be strengths-based because it leaves them less open to hearing others' feedback. This feedback is rarely experienced as emotionally neutral; they need to feel confident enough to risk engaging with it (Eva et al., 2012). There is a "sweet spot" when it comes to the level of confidence required to be open to critique. Too little or too much confidence, and we are likely to avoid the input of others, discount negative feedback, or attribute our mistakes to external factors (Eva et al., 2012). These psychological defence mechanisms undermine collaboration and contribute to errors in reasoning (Gambrill, 2006). In child protection practice, "the single most important factor in minimizing error is to admit that you may be wrong" (Munro, 2008, p. 141).

The trouble is that many child protection workers feel powerless (Bar-On, 2002; Bundy-Fazioli et al., 2009). Despite holding nominally powerful positions, they tend to feel uncomfortable about their authority and vulnerable to attack. It is easy to see how these feelings might result in reactivity and difficulty embracing the different perspectives that are so important to strengths-based practice. It can be hard to accept the views of clients when these are perceived to be an assault on the worker's precarious power. In child protection work, client feedback is often a critique of the worker's performance and perspective. As one "firm, fair, and friendly" worker commented, "Clients have been some of my best teachers. Particularly when I screw up and they let me know" (248). It takes a great deal of self-possession to continue to be open to dissenting views when

> the courts don't like your action, the [police] doesn't like your action ... and you just have to be really calm and take in their concern ... Because you're inviting criticism right? You're inviting, I mean, it's not necessarily always criticism, but you're inviting your clients to feel like they have, well, not feel, but to give them a voice and give them an opportunity to talk about what in the intervention or the relationship isn't working. (176)

Workers need to be helped to that sweet spot of confidence, to skilfully and confidently exercise their authority without clinging to the need to be right. This is a difficult prospect when working in settings often characterized by a high degree of anxiety, distrust, and violence – conditions that might make any worker feel powerless. It is likely no coincidence that three of the four interviewees who described "firm, fair, and friendly practice" were men. The same reproduction of structural power relations that sees a disproportionate number of men achieve senior positions in social work (Pease, 2011) may well have helped them feel comfortable with their authority. They had also previously worked in jobs in which they carried considerable power. They had had a great deal of practice outside of their social work training in getting to the position described by one as,

> You've got to be comfortable with your authority, I mean that's one thing ... You can't do this work if you're not comfortable holding authority in relationship to other people. And for me having worked in the [criminal justice system] I mean, I've spent most of my career working, you know, percentagewise, as an agent of social control. (248)

The importance of humility and comfort with power creates a problem for educators. Professional education has been criticized for reinforcing a sense of expertise at odds with the humility and genuine appreciation of client capacity required for strengths-based work (Blundo, 2001; Grant & Cadell, 2009). Humility is now finding its way into curricula in the health and social care professions as educators consider how best to teach competencies like cultural humility and reflexive and reflective practice (Butler et al., 2011; Chang, Simon, & Dong, 2012; Fisher-Borne, Cain, & Martin, 2015; Juarez et al., 2006; McCoyd & Kerson, 2013; Ortega & Faller, 2010). There is increasing interest in teaching methods that help learners reflect on the limitations of their perspective and to recognize it as only one among many possible ways of looking at the world. While not always linked to overt teaching about the value of humility in practice, these are likely to promote a more humble approach. However, child protection educators clearly have some way to go in wrestling with the paradox of teaching humility as a core professional value and sign of competent practice when a practitioner can comment that

> the whole goal of university is to be right 'cos you can't write a paper and be wrong ... [New workers] carry that sense of having to be right into the workplace ... My experience says just be humble, say "look it you're right, I'm wrong. Totally missed it, sorry. I didn't mean to disrespect you and can we move forward from this? ... What can we do to fix what I just broke?" ... Newbies don't get that. (102)

As Turnell and Essex (2006) comment, "The skilful use of leverage is often not part of the helping professionals' usual toolkit" (p. 46). Of the 152 core competencies identified by the Council of Social Work Regulators for entry-level social workers in Canada in 2012, only two spoke, with little specificity, to competence in the use of authority. This reflects a deeply entrenched ambivalence about power within the social work profession (Bar-On, 2002; Bundy-Fazioli et al., 2013). The operation of professional power has often been framed as inherently opposed to the ideals of self-determination and empowerment (Bar-On, 2002). The overt use of authority has traditionally been seen as the product of failure – the failure of collaboration, persuasion, and education. The profession has preferred to focus on these as the tools of its trade.

Child protection practitioners and would-be child protection practitioners need opportunities to acknowledge without shame the social control element of the role and to explore how to exercise this control compassionately. The reconceptualization of power in recent social work literature might well help (Bundy-Fazioli et al., 2009; Bundy-Fazioli et al., 2013; Tew, 2006). This moves learners away from the idea that power is a unidirectional and stable force operating upon a particular party labelled as powerless. It presents it instead as an interactional, negotiated, and multidimensional experience that can be used both productively and oppressively. The operation of professional power is no longer a "zero-sum game" in which possession of power by one party means the removal of power from the other (Tew, 2006). Seeing the authority of the child protection worker as neither inherently good nor bad opens up the discussion as to how, when, and why that authority should be used in daily practice. Simply helping students and practitioners talk about the complexities of their professional power is likely to help them better come to terms with it (Bundy-Fazioli et al., 2013).

Learners can benefit from practice in openly negotiating the terms of engagement in unequal power relationships (Trotter, 2006; Rooney, 2009). Case-based cognitive rehearsal, role plays, simulations, and opportunities to practise and reflect on real-life experiences of the productive use of power can help. Such learning opportunities need not be limited to considering how to manage power with clients. "If social workers are to help their clients, then they must master the discourse of power and use it effectively" (Bar-On, 2002, p. 998). There is room for a great deal of creativity in supporting learners to safely negotiate, experience, and reflect on their power vis-à-vis their peers, practicum supervisors, faculty, colleagues, supervisors, managers, and the systems in which they operate. It is through safe experimentation and reflection that learners can come to "master the discourse of power" and find the sweet spot of humility and confidence that will support them to be "firm, fair, and friendly."

Reflective Questions

1 Take an inventory of your current learning needs in relation to strengths-based child protection practice. On a scale of one to ten, where one is "not at all" and ten is "completely":
   a) How knowledgeable do you feel about strengths-based child protection practice?
   b) How confident are you that you can take a strengths-based approach at all times with every client?

    c) What would help you move one point higher on each rating scale? Be specific about the actions you might take or the supports you might access.

2 In what situations or with what clients do you think taking a strengths-based approach is particularly difficult? Brainstorm ways to stay strengths-based in these situations or with these clients.

3 What are the pros and cons of being humble in the workplace?

4 Think of when you feel most open to the input of others. What helps you feel this way?

5 Think of a relationship in your life in which there is a notable power difference. This might be with your child, your parent, your supervisor, your instructor, your student, etc. Track how power shifts in this relationship by identifying specific situations when you felt you held power over that person, when you felt you shared power with that person, and when you felt that person held power over you.

6 Imagine you are responsible for teaching trainee child protection workers about the relationship between humility and comfort with power.

    a) What personal experiences and/or theory would you draw on?

    b) What messages would you give?

Chapter Eighteen

Supporting the Strengths-Based Child Protection Practitioner

Assuming a professional identity as a strengths-based child protection practitioner is not simply a matter of individual choice. Identity is profoundly shaped by the environments in which we operate. Unless workers feel that their identity as a strengths-based child protection practitioner is both valued and supported in their workplace, they are likely to abandon that identity in favour of one that is more accessible. As they do so, they may well misattribute the challenges they faced in being strengths-based. Nearly a third of study participants blamed their clients for their inability to be strengths-based. Without the right organizational foundation for strengths-based practice, training in the approach will be less effective and workers will be tempted to see their clients' behaviours or attitudes as the cause of their difficulties enacting the approach (Maybery & Reupert, 2006, 2009). This makes the attention now being paid to the structural changes needed for implementation of strengths-based approaches of paramount importance (Barbee et al., 2011; Idzelis Rothe et al., 2013; Maybery & Reupert, 2006, 2009; Pipkin et al., 2013; Turnell, 2012).

Being a strengths-based child protection practitioner is not easy. One survey respondent wrote that "strengths-based practice requires constant effort ... a constant 'presence of mind,' in order to be genuine and effective" (133). It can be hard to continually search for the positive, reach for collaboration, and maintain the bottom line. When practitioners are afraid, it can be impossible.

Feeling fearful was repeatedly identified by study participants as distinguishing those who could do strengths-based practice from those who could not. Workers who described themselves as always doing strengths-based practice made comments like "I always feel safe in myself" (176) and "I'm not afraid to meet clients, I don't feel like I have to constantly put up barriers ... I don't wanna be that person who's afraid of every little thing" (86). In contrast, all interviewees who talked of feeling scared or anxious with clients described this as inhibiting their attempts to establish strengths-based relationships. As one said,

> I find in child protection, when you're out there doing these investigations, you're not received with arms open, "Come on in" kind of thing, right? So if you come into a family's home and they do not want you there, it's really hard to say, "OK let's talk about your strengths." ... People say "No, no, no you can do that anywhere and everywhere," and I don't believe that. When somebody has a gun collection sitting right there, it's not gonna happen. At that point you're thinking "Something shitty's about to happen and I need to get out of here." (323)

Many workers described responding to fear with the psychologically protective strategies that have been well documented in child protection literature (Calder, 2008a; Ferguson, 2009; Goddard & Tucci, 1991; Stanley, Goddard, & Sanders, 2002). Some resorted to avoidance. They became more guarded and wary of connecting with their clients. Rather than getting to know them as individuals, they relied on stereotypes and avoided or abandoned contact altogether. Others managed their fear by trying to please their clients, to "kill them with kindness" (216; 243). They tried to be friendly and positive and to keep all conversation focused on clients' strengths. However, this strategy often failed as "strengths-based to a parent who's very angry ... can come across as condescending. They don't want to have you smile, they don't want empathy, they just want you to ask your questions and get back out of there" (216). This strategy often resulted in important information being left unsaid. As one worker who frequently felt fearful said,

> I'm not communicating the protection concerns as clearly, because I feel afraid of how the client's going to react. So I often really, really soften it. So I think I tend to maybe be strengths-based to a fault in a way. Where I'm dancing around what really the issue is and not quite being clear about it. (203)

The fact that fear and anxiety interfered with establishing strengths-based relationships with clients is important because, as one worker said, "Everybody works under fear" (72). A "pervasive sense of powerlessness and fear" (Barter, 2008, p. 94) is said to be endemic to contemporary child protection systems (Barter, 2008; Morrison, 1990; Ruch, 2007; Stanford, 2010). This sense has frequently been linked to the failure of child protection workers to carry out their role (Calder, 2008a; Ferguson, 2009; Ruch & Murray, 2011). Practitioners feel unprepared to manage angry, aggressive, and involuntary clients (Healy et al., 2009). Of all social workers, those who typically work alone, like child protection workers, have been found to feel most vulnerable (B. Harris & Leather, 2012).

There are good reasons for this sense of vulnerability. Child protection workers face a real risk of verbal and physical violence from their clients (Ferguson, 2005; B. Harris & Leather, 2012; Littlechild, 2008). One Canadian study found over half of the front-line workers studied had received threats of violence and almost a quarter had been assaulted by a client (Regehr et al., 2004). Paradoxically, the shift to emphasize family support over investigation may increase the risk of violence, as it leaves both worker and client with more ambiguous roles and increased uncertainty about power (Littlechild, 2008).

Many workers in the study spoke of frightening behaviour from clients. This included

- "yelling and screaming" (243);
- "calling names and swearing" (999);
- being "volatile and out of control" (254);
- making death threats;
- physically assaulting workers;
- having and using firearms.

Their descriptions were vivid. One talked of a client who was "in everyone's face, he's got this hair-trigger temper" (89) and another of being "out on an intake call, the [police] were with us, there were gunshots going off, it was just crazy" (156). These are frightening scenarios for anyone, especially as child protection work tends to happen in the isolating and unfamiliar territory of the client's home (Ferguson, 2005, 2009). And they may be particularly frightening for the young female graduates who disproportionately staff the child protection front lines (Healy et al., 2009). In the face of these threats, coercive, collusive, and avoidant responses make sense. It is hard not to sympathize with the young worker who said of two clients, "I want to tell them that I will call the cops and I will throw them in jail if they threaten me one more time" (216).

What do workers need in order to move from fear to feeling sufficiently secure in their own power to exercise their authority purposefully and compassionately? How do they come to feel confident enough to abandon defensive strategies and demonstrate the openness and humility required to engage in true collaboration? If child protection agencies expect their workers to be strengths-based practitioners, they need to provide them with both the tools and the organizational culture to support that identity.

The Tools of Strengths-Based Child Protection Practice

One of the assumptions underpinning solution-focused approaches is that "most people can change their behavior when provided with support and adequate resources" (Berg & Kelly, 2000, p. 63). There has been little discussion of the fate of these approaches when support and resources are inadequate. Many child safety concerns spring from problems that are not easily resolved even in the context of a positive working relationship. Their resolution relies on workers being free to invest their time and energy in the family. Resolution also typically relies on people outside the worker-client dyad, sometimes on specialist help for which there are long wait lists. Without this, workers navigating the fine balance between inviting collaboration and exercising their authority purposefully will be forced towards the authority end of the partnership-paternalism spectrum. This does not make the strengths-based worker-client relationship impossible, but it does make it more difficult.

A "firm, fair, and friendly" strengths-based relationship is based on the idea that both client and worker have expertise and resources to bring to the table. This idea rests on the assumption that workers have time to come to the table at all. In the study, however, the most common barrier to doing strengths-based practice was a lack of time; thirty-six per cent of survey respondents said they needed more of it. They frequently attributed the lack of time to build relationships to excessive caseloads and overwhelming administrative demands. It takes time to build and tend to a trusting relationship with a client, to invite their collaboration, to understand their story, to support their strengths, and to negotiate power. As one worker put it, "Relationships and trust aren't built overnight" (132). It takes even longer to build this trust with multiple members of a client's network. This is why lack of time for family meetings has been identified elsewhere as a barrier to strengths-based child protection (Bunn, 2013). As one study participant said, "It is a lot easier to tell a client what they need to do as opposed to taking the time to involve the family and extended family. Strength-based work can be very time-consuming" (232).

Assuming workers have the time to engage with their clients, they need to offer at least some of the practical services and resources required to support client-led plans. Without this, there is danger that strengths-based practice becomes little more than a "false front" (266) or, as another worker put it,

> The best way to save a buck ... an ideological investment in the form of cost saving that allows influential state agents to offload care responsibilities, which the state or the community should shoulder, to family members (usually women) who do not receive the training or economic compensation to sustain themselves or their dependents. (281)

For many clients, an important marker of social worker helpfulness is the ability to provide resources and offer very concrete, practical help (Schreiber et al., 2013). When workers show up empty-handed to the relationship, they start at a disadvantage:

> The fact that we have no services for our clients, it's super, it's super hard to be strengths-based with your clients when you remove a child and then you tell a parent, "We're sorry you're on a waiting list for supervised access, and it could be up to a month, or longer." ... So I mean it's hard to be strengths-based in the [agency] they've created, but I think you do try your best but you're always saying sorry. (999)

Survey respondents called for flexible, responsive resources to support family goals and plans. They called for greater access to family support, mental health, addiction, parent-teen mediation, family violence, and homemaker services. They wanted to be able to give clients fuel vouchers and bus passes. They talked of strengthening supports for placements offered by extended family members and developing a safety net of respite services. They talked of forging better links with public health, education, and legal aid programs. They sought money to support parent-child activities and provide honorariums to Elders. Some wanted better access to specialist knowledge and support in the form of psychologists, psychiatrists, and family meeting facilitators. While recognizing that strengths-based practice required them to tap into informal family and community resources, they called for the addition of formal services and funding so that creative plans that met the unique needs of each family could be effective.

It is hard to argue with the claim that greater access to time and resources would increase the capacity of front-line workers to practise in a strengths-based way. It is, however, important to note that many study participants asking for these tools are likely to have seen strengths-based practice as relying exclusively on client collaboration. If workers are armed only with their powers of persuasion, some clients will inevitably need a great deal more time and support than any one worker is able to give. The interviewees who described "pursuing a balanced understanding" and "firm, fair, and friendly practice" focused less on these tools and more on the organizational culture needed to support strengths-based practice. They saw themselves as succeeding in enacting strengths-based practice *despite* not having the time and resources they desired. What they needed was an organization that shared their goals, helped them think through the complexities of the approach, and inspired them to keep going. They needed to work in an environment in which strengths-based child protection practice was part of the organizational culture.

The Culture of Strengths-Based Child Protection Practice

When the agency in which you work neither values strengths-based practice nor sees it as consistent with your child protection duties, it is hard to identify as a strengths-based child protection worker. When there is confusion as to what strengths-based practice even means, the challenge increases. We choose identities that support a professional self-esteem and self-concept and for which there are unambiguous and accessible identity scripts. This makes the organizational culture a key factor in the way in which workers will choose to identify and practice.

The agency hosting the study on which this book is based had written strengths-based practice into policy, had invested heavily in its training, and had many champions of the approach. Yet for most study participants, the identity script of strengths-based child protection practitioner was ambiguous and unsupported by organizational values. There was no common understanding of what strengths-based child protection practice meant. Disagreements over its definition kept conversations about the approach at such an abstract level that it was hard for workers to engage with its complexities or to consider the details of its application to specific cases. This impeded workers' ability to develop their cognitive database of models about how to be strengths-based in different situations. As a result, they could not develop the expertise needed to implement the approach at all points during their working day. As one worker said,

> Maybe part of the problem on an [agency] wide level is strengths-based has just become a buzzword and it's kind of vague and I don't think people, like everyone's going to define it their own way ... so it's hard to really say, "Is it working?" And then, "How do we get better at it?" Because that's going to look different for everybody, so I guess it's tough for me to say is it, the approach itself, doesn't just, simply doesn't work, or is it just we're not doing it the right way 'cos there's no right way of strengths-based practice, so I don't know, it's sort of a conundrum. (203)

The identity script of strengths-based child protection practitioner was not simply vague. It was actively sabotaged by conflicting messages given by educators, colleagues, supervisors, and managers. Widespread confusion about the meaning and value of strengths-based practice meant that regardless of how they defined the approach, practitioners felt at odds with their colleagues in their attempts to enact it. There were many stories about the problems created when others within the organization had an understanding of strengths-based practice that conflicted with the worker's own. As one worker said,

> When we're trained in strengths-based practice, the information coming from the trainers, from one trainer to the other, is different about what that looks like ... I find that how people interpret and teach strength-based practice to be inconsistent and often inaccurate. I have been taught that it is a practice that does not say the bad stuff and only speaks in positive terms. This is not strengths-based practice. But there are many workers who are confused. (254)

Workers clearly needed the agency to commit to a shared vision of what strengths-based child protection meant in practice. They wanted this commitment to start at the top, with senior management providing strong leadership for the approach. Workers called for "leadership to not just give lip service to these ideals but to actually support workers in their practice" (184). Many study participants cared that their senior managers not only knew about strengths-based practice, but that they knew the details of how it played out in their daily work. It was only by understanding these details that managers could fully understand what supports their workers needed to make it happen. In this, workers echoed comments made by evaluators of a solution-focused model in Washington state:

> Leadership may assume that this is not something they need to be trained on, that others can learn the details of the model and they can just manage. However, when senior leadership is not expert in the model, critical decisions in the life of the system that affect practice are not noticed as critical. (Pipkin et al., 2013, p. 1931)

It is increasingly recognized that "any meaningful long-term implementation must be driven by an agency's executive and by leaders who understand the approach well" (Turnell, 2012, p. 50); leadership buy-in is one of the most basic building blocks of a strengths-based organizational culture (Barbee et al., 2011; Idzelis Rothe et al., 2013; Pipkin et al., 2013; Turnell, 2012).

While agency leaders are tasked with driving and resourcing a common vision of strengths-based practice, it is supervisors who exercise the most influence on the ways in which front-line practitioners enact that vision with clients (Bundy-Fazioli et al., 2013; Gibbs, 2001; Lietz, 2009, 2013; Lietz & Rounds, 2009; Munro, 2005; Ruch, 2007). Mediating between the front lines of practice and higher levels of management within child protection bureaucracies, supervisors carry a great deal of power to determine case planning, the allocation of the time and resources to support it, and the ways in which child protection workers perform their role (Bogo & McKnight, 2006; Bundy-Fazioli et al., 2013; Dill & Bogo, 2009; Gibbs, 2001; Lietz, 2013; Munro, 2005; Ruch, 2007). Twenty per cent of survey respondents said that in order to do strengths-based practice, they needed more support from their direct supervisors, while an additional sixteen per cent called more generally for better management support. Workers wanted their supervisors to be schooled in the philosophy of strengths-based practice and to demonstrate their support for that philosophy by backing creative family plans, assuming calculated risks, and understanding how hard it can be to enact the approach. Supervisors needed to be "truly strengths-based minded, to support and understand the time and energy that goes into strengths-based practice" (386).

There was a common call for regular skilled clinical supervision "that is not simply focused on the day-to-day tasks and documentation but is about doing the work and its impact on both worker and client" (390). This was needed because doing strengths-based practice in a way that attended adequately to both strengths and risks was difficult work. One interviewee said,

> I always try to discuss the family situation first and foremost with my supervisor or with my team members and having that trust in their opinion as well as in the feedback that I'm getting back. So for me as a social worker, my internal thermometer, I try to keep that balance by relying heavily on my team as well as on my supervisor. And this is where … the team dynamics and the relationships in the workplace become really, really important because it's very hard to do strengths-based social work when you don't have that trust or that relationship with your team and with your supervisor because you might be thinking one thing and there's nobody to provide those checks and balances to you. (116)

Good supervisors offering quality clinical support were needed "to remind me, mentor me and inspire me to stay on the positive thought process and not get bogged down in negativity" (138).

It is hard to overestimate the importance of clinical supervision in child protection work. Clinical supervision is one of the few venues for workers to process emotions elicited by the work and to find a way through the uncertainty inherent to it (Ruch, 2007). It can help workers retain critical control of their practice by allowing them to reflect on the many intuitive, in-the-moment decisions they made over the course of their busy working day (Eraut, 2000). It supports workers so they can use their professional judgment (Munro, 2011). This judgment is crucial to responsive relational approaches, like strengths-based practice, which cannot be implemented by simply following procedures.

Clinical consultation can also help workers get in touch with the values driving their practice. It can provide a venue for reconnecting with what it means to be strengths-based. As one interviewee said,

> Sitting with you last week, one of the things that I probably didn't think about at the time is it would cause to come into the conscious present all that I value and believe in. And so when I was sitting talking with [name] yesterday, all of that was so much more available to me in my language and in my conversation. And so this, these two conversations, have

definitely provided that opportunity to remind me of first principles and my own journey and that will of course serve to reinforce my passion for this way of working. (248)

This matters because these values, and the sense that they were doing what was morally right, helped interviewees remain firm, open, and engaged with clients, even in the face of a threat. It acted against the fear and anxiety that got in the way of building strengths-based relationships.

There is a clear moral dimension to the ability to "talk back to fear" (Stanford, 2010) and take the risk to engage in open, non-defensive practice. Research in the field of nursing suggests that this kind of courageous practice can be supported by helping practitioners reflect on the ethical nature of their daily interactions and to explicitly connect practice challenges to their guiding values (Rodney, Doane, Storch, & Varcoe, 2006; Storch et al., 2009). This can be done alone; all "firm, fair, and friendly" interviewees said they prepared themselves for client contact by reflecting privately on their purpose and their core values. It is best achieved, however, within agencies that provide workers with "safe spaces" to openly discuss the challenges they face (Austin, 2007; Corley, Minick, Elswick, & Jacobs, 2005; Pauly, Varcoe, Storch, & Newton, 2009). This is one reason why those considering what is needed for successful implementation of strengths-based child protection approaches have recommended that agencies provide ongoing opportunities for workers to talk about what it means to enact such approaches in daily practice (Idzelis Rothe et al., 2013; Lietz & Rounds, 2009; Michalopoulos, Ahn, Shaw, & O'Connor, 2012; Turnell, 2012).

It does not always follow that asking workers to discuss their cases will lead to them doing so in an open and honest way. It is often difficult for workers to engage in the kind of reflection they need with their line supervisors (Beddoe, 2010; Bradley et al., 2010; Dill & Bogo, 2009; Hair, 2013; Lietz, 2009). A significant amount of trust is needed to discuss what is most troubling in child protection work. Willingness to disclose practice struggles can be undermined by knowing that the person with whom you consult holds power to discipline or fire you or is more focused on managing your behaviour, risk to the organization, and administrative tasks than your professional development (Beddoe, 2012). In one Canadian study, over a quarter of workers surveyed said that their supervisor's role in appraising their performance made it difficult for them to discuss their practice challenges (Hair, 2013).

In an Australian study in which social workers were asked to identify an ethical dilemma in their practice, fewer than half had discussed the dilemma with their internal supervisor, due to concerns about privacy and their supervisor's authority, administrative focus, and availability (McAuliffe & Sudbery, 2005). It seems that it is not enough for supervisors and managers to be open to talking about the challenges of strengths-based practice; they need to be open to doing it in a particular way.

When study participants talked of the support they needed, from direct supervisors all the way up to senior management, they described a non-blaming climate of encouragement and empowerment, with trust and support for their judgment as the default setting, in contrast to the "culture of suspicion" (226) that typically prevailed. They called for respect for their strengths as workers, trust in their perspectives and goals, honest feedback on their work and their limitations, attention to the feelings triggered by the work, and a willingness to provide them with the resources to meet their goals. They were, in effect, asking that strengths-based practice be used with them. "Everybody in line, from director, manager, everybody down, needs to be doing strengths-based practice, needs to be showing us, dealing with us, in a strengths-based manner" (999). The call was for strengths-based management at all levels of the organization.

The core values and strategies of the strengths-based management described by study participants are summarized in the text box below.

Values

- Workers are valuable partners in a shared mission to promote child and family well-being.
- Workers are people with strengths and the capacity to work effectively when provided with adequate support.

Strategies

- Establish a partnership with the worker based on the goal of supporting child and family well-being through strengths-based practice. Ensure all case discussions are oriented to this goal.

- Hold a definition of strengths-based practice that is appropriate to child protection work and consistent with the worker's definition.
- Have regular contact with the worker to develop a relationship of compassion and respect, in which the worker feels known and supported. Respond quickly to requests for support.
- Trust that each worker knows most about what they need to do their job well and support them to describe this fully.
- Develop a deep understanding of the worker's experience, needs, and perspective by listening, asking questions, and showing genuine curiosity.
- Model strengths-based practice in all interactions by using strengths-based questions, acknowledging workers' strengths, and paying equal attention to strengths and challenges.
- Provide leadership by bringing expertise, clinical skills, and hope.
- Expand workers' perspectives by helping them think creatively and by providing honest and informed feedback.
- Be transparent about your own thinking and any limits on practice.
- Be open to a variety of creative strategies for pursuing the shared goal of child and family well-being, and support any ideas that workers generate from a strengths-based consultation process.
- Provide the time and resources necessary to support the worker's plan.
- Join with the worker to assume any risks inherent in an agreed plan.
- Accept that mistakes will be made and see them as opportunities for learning, not blame.
- Recognize the worker's self-care needs, and provide sufficient time and resources to enable workers to sustain a healthy level of functioning.

There are good reasons for workers to ask for this kind of management approach. The first is that it is likely to make them feel better and more effective. When strengths-based practice is used with workers, exactly the same motivational and capacity-building processes are activated in workers as they hope to activate in their clients. Being treated with caring and with respect for their strengths makes workers feel more valued and effective in their role (Gibbs, 2001). Receiving positive feedback builds self-efficacy, which motivates workers to keep setting and pursuing goals (Bandura, 1997). Workers who feel self-efficacious and valued are more likely to stay in front-line practice (Gibbs, 2001; Healy et al., 2009; Tham, 2007). They are also more likely to engage in the kind of collaborative relationships for which strengths-based practice is known (Bugental & Lewis, 1999; Tew, 2006). Strengths-based Leadership (Hodges & Clifton, 2004), a management approach incorporating many of the components summarized above, has been found to increase employee productivity, engagement, and self-efficacy (Rath & Conchie, 2009). Treating workers in a strengths-based way makes a tangible difference.

The second reason for workers to ask for strengths-based management is that it demonstrates that the values they are expected to apply in their work with clients are supported within the agency. Over the last twenty years, managerial and supervisory relationships with front-line workers have become dominated by administrative concerns (Beddoe, 2010; Bradley et al., 2010; Dill & Bogo, 2009; Hair, 2013; Lietz, 2009). Public service managerialism has increased the regulation of service delivery through procedures, performance indicators, targets, and audit processes (Harlow, 2003; Rogowski, 2012). In child protection services, the dominant ethos of family surveillance over family support, and the increasing power of the courts to judge good practice through family cases and legal enquiries, has seen much time devoted to packaging client information to be passed around professional networks (Parton, 2008). To stand up to the scrutiny of courts, management, and other professionals, workers need to ensure their i's are dotted and their t's are crossed. This can leave them in the position of spending more time reporting and accounting for their conversations with families than actually having them.

By taking a strengths-based approach to front-line workers, supervisors can start to correct the unhelpful focus on paperwork over people. They can demonstrate through their daily interactions that they value relational strengths-based work. It is important that this approach is not limited to the relationship between supervisor and front-line worker. If supervisors are to effectively practise and model strengths-based practice, it makes sense that they also need to experience it from those to whom they report. The requirement to engage relationally with others and support their unique strengths and individual, self-determined contributions to the agency's mandate extends up the organizational ranks.

The third reason for strengths-based management in agencies implementing strengths-based practice is that it models the strategies and techniques to be used with clients. One of the best ways for workers to understand what it means to implement strengths-based practice is for them to experience it in their relationship with their supervisor (Antle et al., 2012; Beckett et al., 2013; Frey et al., 2012; Kisthardt, 2012; Lietz & Rounds, 2009; Thomas & Davis, 2005; Turnell, 2012). Modelling is a powerful teaching tool, particularly when done by people who are seen as credible authorities (Bandura, 1986). When managers and supervisors employ strengths-based methods with their supervisees, they not only demonstrate their support for the approach, they show them very concretely how it can be done. This makes it more likely that those supervisees will replicate the approach in their relationships with clients and the people for whom they are responsible (Lietz, 2013; Lietz & Rounds, 2009).

This modelling effect suggests the value of going beyond strengths-based management to "firm, fair, and friendly" management if frontline workers are to make "firm, fair, and friendly" relationships with their clients. Aligning the agency's management and supervision model with the strengths-based practice model to which it subscribes not only promotes a common vision of strengths-based practice, it is also likely to lead to greater confidence and expertise in supervisors and supervisees (Frey et al., 2012). In the United States, problems with the implementation of the strength-based Family Centred Practice approach led to the re-design of supervision to replicate core components of the approach (Lietz, 2013; Lietz & Rounds, 2009). Supervisors were trained to systematically assess their workers' strengths and goals and to see their team as a community with inherent resources that can be identified and utilized through collaborative processes. Supervisors responded positively to its development (Lietz & Rounds, 2009), and the resulting approach, Strengths-Based Supervision, has now been implemented in three states (Lietz, 2013).

The advantage of modelling "firm, fair, and friendly" supervisory and managerial relationships is that this model specifically addresses the unequal power balance inherent to such relationships. It has been suggested that in child protection work, supervisors tend to feel uncomfortable exercising their authority with supervisees (Frey et al., 2012). Just as discomfort with their power is likely to make workers more reactive and less collaborative, so too will those higher up the organizational hierarchy. "Firm, fair, and friendly practice" can help those who seek to supervise collaboratively from a position of power to navigate the dual care and control relationships involved.

What does this mean in practice? Consider the case of a supervisor tasked with managing a recalcitrant worker who repeatedly arrives late for work, is non-communicative in team meetings, has several client complaints against him, and has responded with disgust to the initiation of disciplinary procedures. Assuming the supervisor is not tempted to avoid supervising this worker altogether, it is highly likely that a growing focus of their sessions will be on communicating and monitoring clear performance expectations. Alternatively, the supervisor might seek to align herself with the worker, listening to his complaints, empathizing with his position, and distancing herself from the concerns. Neither approach is likely to renew the worker's passion for his work nor motivate him to change his behaviour.

A "firm, fair, and friendly" approach would start with the clear acknowledgment that the worker is in a disciplinary process and en route to being fired. The supervisor would be open about her powerful role in this process, about the difficulties it will create in their relationship, and about any non-negotiable expectations. She would invite the worker to participate in determining how he might best be monitored and supported and how they might work together to turn things around. She might ask questions such as, "When do you feel most engaged at work? What work achievements make you most proud? When do you make the effort to be on time? What would your clients and colleagues say are your strong points? If a miracle happened and this team was one that excited and inspired you, what would be different?" Using a raft of solution-focused questions, the supervisor would dig for the worker's strengths and personal goals and explore with him how these might be hooked to the overall goal of demonstrating that he is a valuable and effective child protection practitioner who deserves to be treated differently.

The supervisor would offer the worker her support and resources to pursue these goals. "You take most pleasure out of doing direct work with children? How do we build more time for this into your working week? You led the union campaign for better working conditions and feel that your voice has been stifled since? What would be needed for you to become the team's representative to management?"

This is not about rewarding poor performance. It is about acknowledging and using what motivates each of us to do good work. During this and subsequent conversations, the supervisor would be careful to use her language and physical presence to nurture the relationship and her communication skills to track and acknowledge the worker's feelings and meaning. The supervisor would voice ongoing curiosity about small successes and about the changing relational dynamics.

She would keep in check her own frustration and perception of the worker as a troublemaker by seeking to understand life from his perspective and to acknowledge him as a person with strengths, challenges, and good reasons to act as he does. She would recognize that disengagement and anger are profoundly human responses to a difficult job and that human connection, authenticity, and kindness are often what is needed most. In the absence of sufficient change, she would proceed through the disciplinary process transparently and compassionately, seeing each demonstration of her authority as an opportunity to invite the worker into a more effective partnership.

This is not the easy option. The same perseverance needed to be strengths-based with hard-to-like clients is needed to be strengths-based with hard-to-like workers. This supervisor needs to know that her organization is behind her and to believe in the benefits of a strengths-based approach. She needs the skills to dig for the detail of strengths and the latitude from her superiors to support the supervisee's solutions. The pay-off is likely to go beyond knowing that this particular worker is getting his best shot at re-engaging with whatever attractions child protection holds for him. When, at every level of an agency, people establish "firm, fair, and friendly" relationships in pursuit of a common vision of strengths-based practice, the odds increase that "strengths-based child protection practitioner" will be taken up as an identity that fits for front-line work.

Reflective Questions

1 How do feelings of fear and safety impact the ability to do strengths-based practice?
2 Drawing on your own experiences and/or theoretical knowledge, what specific strategies can support workers to feel sufficiently safe to practise in a strengths-based way?
3 Create a map of the people in your life with whom you currently feel able to discuss troubling ethical and practical issues you might face at work.
   a) How might you add more people to this map?
   b) How might you strengthen your connection to these people so they can better perform this role?
4 Drawing on your own experiences and/or theoretical knowledge, brainstorm possible ways to advocate for the tools you need to do strengths-based practice.

5 Identify the person in your working life who has been most helpful to your professional development. This might be a supervisor, manager, teacher, or another person.
   a) What, specifically, has this person done that has been so helpful?
   b) What would he or she say are your best qualities?
   c) What would he or she say are your weaknesses?
6 Identify:
   a) Your professional goals over the next year.
   b) Your strengths that will help you achieve these goals.
   c) The areas in which you know you need to grow.
   d) The kind of relationship and help you need from your supervisor, manager, or teacher to help you move towards your goals.
   e) If you can, do this exercise with a partner or in front of a mirror. Imagine your supervisor, manager, or teacher is sitting in front of you. Practise telling your supervisor, manager, or instructor what you hope to achieve in your work over the next year, what strengths will help you, where you recognize you need to grow, and what you need from them to support you.
7 Design a structural intervention for your workplace or place of learning that will help promote a strengths-based organizational culture.

Section Four Summary:
Looking Back, Out, and Forward

Looking Back

What are the key messages to be taken from the practical wisdom and research on which this book stands? The first is that there is an important difference between supporting workers to *do* strengths-based child protection practice and supporting them to *be* strengths-based child protection practitioners. It takes a lot to view clients in terms of their capacity when the system in which you work categorizes them according to their failings and the risks they appear to pose. It takes a lot to continually strive for collaboration and connection with people whose first response is anger, suspicion, and a door shut very firmly in your face. To sustain any kind of authentic strengths-based approach requires a significant investment in the idea that this is how you wish to practise. Being strengths-based cannot be accomplished off the side of your desk.

This leads to the second key message. Front-line workers need to see "strengths-based child protection practitioner" as a valued and relevant professional identity if they are to commit to it wholeheartedly. As for the extent to which the identity is valued, I suspect few child protection workers would argue that working in partnership with parents and building on strengths is undesirable. As the evidence for strengths-based child protection approaches grows, and as these approaches become better defined and operationalized, it is likely that increasing numbers of child protection agencies will adopt strengths-based practice as their preferred approach. This leaves, then, the problem of how to ensure that the identity of strengths-based child protection practitioner is perceived to be relevant to daily practice.

It simply doesn't work in child protection to see strengths-based practice as a wholly collaborative approach and to attempt to use it with all clients. This ignores the reality that, with most families, there is a point at which the child protection worker must exercise the kind of purposeful authority that stretches well beyond any reasonable definition of collaboration. It also doesn't work to see strengths-based practice as a wholly collaborative approach and attempt to use it with only some clients at some times. It is too hard to switch between strengths-based practice and other approaches and too easy to get stuck in being supportive, being coercive, or being confusing. It is only by defining strengths-based child protection practice as incorporating partnership *and* paternalism that workers can see it as relevant at all times. "Firm, fair, and friendly practice" provides a way to remain in strengths-based relationships with clients while carrying out the full range of statutory child protection duties.

The "firm, fair, and friendly practice" model gives workers an accessible and well-supported identity script as a strengths-based child protection practitioner. Learning this script, however, is not enough. The next step is to master the how-to of strengths-based child protection practice. This means developing solution-focused questioning techniques, communication skills, and the ability to assess and address strengths and risks in the same breath. It means acquiring an array of strategies to systematically identify and build on strengths, to engage with the client's networks of supportive people and resources, to facilitate meetings in which families themselves generate solutions, and to write effective goal-oriented and safety-focused plans. Importantly, it means wrestling with the problems of power and humility to get to that sweet spot of confidence in which workers can be truly responsive to the family's perspectives and power and gently assert authority when needed. The final step in learning how to be a strengths-based child practitioner is to develop a personal database of examples of how to apply these skills and strategies in different situations with different clients. The third key message then is this: Mastery in this approach develops, like mastery in any approach, through ongoing training, practice, and reflection. Because we are as human as our clients, this includes learning from our mistakes.

The last key message echoes through every recent strengths-based practice implementation study: This cannot be done alone. It is an uphill struggle to define yourself as a strengths-based child protection practitioner in the absence of the people, tools, and organizational culture to support that identity. Fear gets in the way of making strengths-based relationships, and fear is endemic in child protection work. Attention to the conditions that create safety not only for clients but also for workers is needed. Both need real emotional and practical supports as well as the time and encouragement to pursue their goals. Both need to feel that they know where they stand and that there is a shared understanding of where they are heading. Both need to be acknowledged for their strengths and listened to and believed in by those exercising authority over them, even when that authority is used against them. Child protection management and staff might do worse than strive to treat each other, as well as their clients, in a "firm, fair, and friendly" way.

Looking Out

The danger of writing a book about the strengths-based worker-client relationship is that it leaves the impression that the worker-client relationship is really all that strengths-based practice is about. Let me be clear. Engaging effectively with our clients does not absolve us of responsibility to engage effectively with oppressive structures and social institutions. It does not replace change at the macro level; it enables it.

"Firm, fair, and friendly" working relationships offer a way to collaborate with families without constantly having to worry that fear, betrayal, unrealistic expectations, emotional reactivity, and narrow judgments will get in the way. They allow workers to listen to clients' experiences of structural oppression and to co-create the motivation and solidarity to take meaningful action. They allow workers to reach across the traditional boundaries that separate professionals from clients and to pool the resources and power each possesses. Rapp and Sullivan (2014) have said that "the strengths model puts the social squarely back in social work" (p. 137). You do not have to be a social worker to recognize that many of the problems faced by child protection clients are not individual problems but are located in the conditions in which we all live. If we are to have any hope of changing those conditions, we need to partner with our clients, deeply understand their experiences, make links with allies in the wider community, generate hope for a different future, and pursue shared solutions. This is exactly what strengths-based practice is intended to do.

It is not just in our work with clients that we must keep looking outward. One of the most consistent messages of recent studies is that when it comes to implementing strengths-based approaches, enthusiastic champions and training only get us so far (Sabalauskas, Ortolani, & McCall, 2014). For strengths-based practice to flourish, we need to turn our attention to creating relationships within and across our child-serving organizations that will enable us to act most powerfully for whole-systems change. Strengths-based practice models can provide a common framework for these relationships (Stanley & Mills, 2014). When all those who work with children and their families talk the same strengths-based language and share the same strengths-based vision, we increase our chances of joining to create real structural change.

Part of looking outward is recognizing that child protection is not the only field in which a "firm, fair, and friendly" approach might help. We are beginning to see strengths-based approaches implemented in authority-based fields like criminal justice (Hunter, Lanza, Lawlor, Dyson, & Gordon, 2016; Jones, Brown, Robinson, & Frey, 2015; Maruna & LeBel, 2015; Rex & Hosking, 2013). It is growing across the health and social care sectors, in professions like nursing (L. Gottlieb, 2012; L. N. Gottlieb, Gottlieb, & Shamian, 2012; Moyle, Parker, & Bramble, 2014; Wells, Shields, Hauck, & Bennett, 2014), psychiatric nursing (Beckett et al., 2013; Pearson, 2013), psychiatry (Ibrahim, Michail, & Callaghan, 2014), medicine (Sims-Gould, Byrne, Hicks, Khan, & Stolee, 2012), and child and youth care (Bertolino, 2014). In each of these fields, practitioners are expected to navigate relationships combining some degree of care and control. In some, like criminal justice work, the control is very explicit. In others, it comes in more subtle forms through professional control of information, expertise, time, and resources. In all, practitioners are asked to provide a caring human response that nurtures hope, trust, and resilience. It is not hard to see how those interacting with these professionals might appreciate being treated in a "firm, fair, and friendly" way.

Looking Forward

The evidence for strengths-based child protection practice continues to grow. In recent research, parents' perceptions of the use of strengths-based practice have been found to predict their level of engagement (Kemp, Marcenko, Lyons, & Kruzich, 2014), and strengths-based practice has been linked to closer team bonds, more professional collaboration, and fewer symptoms of burnout (Kemp et al., 2014; Medina & Beyebach, 2014a, 2014b). Young people in the United States have photographed representations of their strengths and goals to inform their case plans (Rice, Girvin, & Primak, 2014), and youth in care in New Zealand have used a solution-focused approach to incorporate a new sense of possibility into their life stories (Gibson, 2014). In the United Kingdom, practitioners have increased parental participation through "Strengthening Families conferences" (Appleton, Terlektsi, & Coombes, 2014), and in Canada, "mapping conferences" for complex cases have reduced the number of families re-referred (Lwin, Versanov, Cheung, Goodman, & Andrews, 2014).

These studies, and others like them, show the creativity with which strengths-based and solution-focused ideas are now being applied. They also demonstrate a commitment to rigorously examine the application of such ideas. This commitment is driving research to isolate the components and drivers of child protection–specific approaches (van Zyl et al., 2014) and to develop child protection–specific fidelity measures (Douglas, McCarthy, & Serino, 2014). We are building the knowledge base on which good strengths-based child protection can stand.

There is some way yet to go. Two of its founding fathers recently described the strengths approach as entering its "toddlerhood" (C. A. Rapp & Sullivan, 2014). By that measure, strengths-based child protection practice is still very much a babe in arms. The care and attention it is now receiving, however, suggests there is every reason to feel hopeful about its future. There are good reasons to want strengths-based child protection to grow up strong, and "firm, fair, and friendly practice" can help that to happen.

Appendix

Role Plays

Shauna: Client's Information

You, Shauna, are at a loss about how to deal with the social worker who is sitting in front of you. You called emergency social services last night because you really thought you were going to lose it with your baby. You've been feeling so down since he was born. You feel tired all the time, and sometimes you fantasize about just putting a pillow over his face to stop the crying. You know you probably have post-partum depression or something, but in your family people don't ask for help, especially not from social services. Your parents and friends would be horrified if they heard. That's the problem. You have tons of people who could help, but it would be so embarrassing for them to know how you are struggling with all of this. Like you, they think that at times like this you should quit complaining, stick a smile on your face, and keep going.

Your main goal is to get the social worker out of your house and your life with minimum fuss. Yes, it would be nice if you could get some help without being embarrassed in front of your family and friends, but that's not likely and you don't have the brainpower to figure any of that out right now.

Special Instructions for Chapter 10 Role Play Only

Scenario 1: If the worker asks effective solution-focused questions, respond in a way that identifies strengths and resources on which a safety plan can be built.

Scenario 2: Even if the worker asks effective solution-focused questions, do not identify strengths and resources on which a safety plan can be built. Respond in a way that makes the worker reach for collaboration in the process rather than a plan.

Shauna: Worker's Information

The report from emergency social services last night suggests that Shauna was extremely distressed when she called and workers really thought she would harm the baby. They assessed that it was not safe to leave mom and baby alone, so thank goodness Shauna's friend came over. You had been hoping this would be an easy case of asking the friend to stay for a few days until Shauna got the help she thought she needed and then case closed. But now Shauna tells you she needs nothing and is coping just fine without help – although you can see that she can scarcely think and is tired, flat, and very far from "all right." Her friend doesn't seem to think there's a problem either; she's left to go to work and is clearly not taking this seriously. You are worried that without some kind of help and safety plan in place, last night's crisis might happen again, and this time Shauna may not reach out. She said last night she was about to lose control – you dread to think what might happen to the baby if she does.

Your main goal is to ensure there is a safety plan for the baby in place, at least for the next week or so. You aim to use solution-focused questions to elicit Shauna's strengths, hopes, and strategies, on which you can build a collaborative strengths-based plan.

Ada: Client's Information

You, Ada, really do not want to see the worker right now. Mike, your partner or ex-partner (you're really not sure) is sleeping upstairs, and you're not going to have the worker snooping around to see that. You know she thinks Mike shouldn't be here at all, what with the court order that says he has to stay away and all that fuss about him touching Katy and getting handy with his fists last year. But Mike's changed. He's been home now for nearly a month, and nothing bad has happened. You're pretty sure you can handle his moods, so long as Katy doesn't antagonize him. She can be pretty antagonizing for a nine-year-old. And you'll just keep an eye on him and make sure he and Katy don't spend too much time together. You're still troubled by the sexual allegations, but you think it all got a bit blown out of proportion. Katy needs a dad around and seems really happy to have him back, which is the important thing. It feels like things are finally getting back to normal.

You really like the worker; she's helped you a lot, and you feel bad about lying to her, but you've managed to keep her in the dark about Mike for this long, and you intend to keep doing that. Besides, she's told you many times that she trusts you can protect your daughter. You'll throw that back in her face if she starts questioning your judgment – you thought you could rely on her.

Your goal is to keep the focus on the good stuff that has happened for you since the last visit. Hopefully you can prevent the worker from even coming in, but if she does make it past the front door, you want to ensure she leaves still ignorant that Mike is back in your life.

Ada: Worker's Information

After nine-year-old Katy disclosed sexual and physical abuse from her father, Mike, about a year ago, you feel you have done some great work with her and her mom, Ada. You really like them both and feel that you have been able to provide a lot of support for them. As a result of your work, Mike left the home and there is now a legal order ensuring he has no contact with Katy. There is pretty solid evidence that he was physically and sexually violent both to Ada and Katy, and while you are doubtful the case will ever go to a criminal conviction, you are pretty confident that Ada sees how dangerous he is and would let you and the police know if he contacted her.

Yesterday, a neighbour called anonymously to say Mike was back living in the home. You know you have to fully check out the situation. You want to do this in a way that doesn't totally wreck the relationship you and Ada have built.

Your primary goal on this visit is to fully assess the new report and ensure that Katy and Mike have no contact.

Rob: Client's Information

You, Rob, are the father of fourteen-year-old Craig. You think the worker is doing a good job at helping Craig. In a way it was good all that stuff happened with Craig saying he was suicidal. Craig needed someone to talk to, and the worker is really giving him a boost. Your wife is so happy the worker's around that she has taken the chance to go visit her mom for a few weeks to get a well-earned holiday.

You're not quite sure what the worker wants to talk to you about today, but so long as she keeps taking Craig to his group and giving him a bit of extra interest in his life then all is good. Craig's been a bit of a mystery to you recently, but you know that boys can go through strange stages and he'll grow out of it. You certainly had your own issues with feeling suicidal when you were his age, but you've never talked about any of that, and it's best not to dredge up the past. As far as you're concerned, everything is going well and you've been given a lucky break in getting this worker, and you want to keep her coming around until Craig's got himself sorted out.

Rob: Worker's Information

You find yourself in bit of a bind. After months and months, the work with this family feels as if it is going nowhere. Craig has started talking about wanting to kill himself again. A second emergency mental health assessment found him not to be in any immediate danger and suggested that he is "wanting attention." It did, however, recommend he get support from the mental health team. In order to access this, Craig needs to have an open file with your office. The trouble is, the family are taking up far more of your time than you can spare, and you're not sure they really fall within your mandate.

Although this came to you as referral for support, you think there is some low-level neglect going on. Certainly his parents have not been at all proactive about meeting Craig's mental health needs; they leave for work early and are often out socializing until late. Craig seems to be left largely to his own devices. You are still waiting for his parents to contact Aunt Helen to confirm she will be a safety contact for Craig in case he feels suicidal again. Somehow it is you who has ended up taking Craig to each session of the group for youth with depression. His parents say they can't take the time off work, and Craig says that he really enjoys it and won't go unless you take him. You managed to get him a skateboard through the school program – after a huge amount of work – and it had disappeared within weeks; you heard a rumour his mom gave it away.

You are being bugged by the thought that Craig's parents are taking advantage of you and not really stepping up. They are very cooperative and friendly, have told you that you are a great help to them, and are really pleased with your work. Craig's mom has just gone to stay with her own mother "for a while" – you're not sure why. His dad seems both to want you involved and to dismiss any concerns about Craig's mental health, which is confusing. You cannot keep this up.

Your goal at this meeting is to be transparent about *all* the necessary issues in order to get an effective strengths-based relationship back on track.

Joe: Client's Information

You, Joe, are the grandfather and sole caregiver of three-year-old Sam. You have cared for the boy since your daughter asked you to babysit for him two years ago and disappeared from the face of the earth. You don't know what happened to her, even whether she is dead or alive, and it breaks your heart. Her mom did a similar thing twenty years ago. You think that was your fault – all that drinking and beating up on each other. You were a very angry man back then, mostly because of the social workers. They took your daughter away too and stuck her in government care. The government is only interested in destroying you. They have spies everywhere, and they always seem to know when you slip up.

And now there's another government spy on your doorstep. You know you've got to let her in, but that's as far as it goes. You won't tell her anything or make her life easy or work with her in plans that you know full well are designed to subjugate you. You are angry and plan to quietly resist. You know your drinking's got a bit out of hand again recently and none of this is good for Sam, but you love the boy and you'll kill anyone who tries to stop you from raising him. You messed up last night, can't remember a lot of the details, and don't know what to do next.

Joe: Worker's Information

You are the child protection worker who has been tasked with making a plan with Joe. Joe's grandson was brought to an emergency foster home last night, after police were called to the home due to a noise complaint and found Joe and another man intoxicated and engaged in a fist fight. The foster mom says Sam appears healthy and well cared for. There have been no previous reports about Joe's care of Sam, but you know from police reports and a review of the old family files that Joe's drinking is a long-standing concern and that he has a history of violence. He is described in the old files as paranoid and delusional – lots of talk about shadowy government agents and conspiracies. The social worker involved with the family when Joe's own daughter was removed was clearly scared of Joe and talked of him making death threats.

Your goal is to complete as much of an assessment as possible and to make a plan with Joe about next steps.

References

Adams, K., Hean, S., Sturgis, P., & Clark, J. M. (2006). Investigating the factors influencing professional identity of first-year health and social care students. *Learning in Health and Social Care, 5*(2), 55–68. http://dx.doi.org/10.1111 /j.1473-6861.2006.00119.x

Alexander, C., & Charles, G. (2009). Caring, mutuality and reciprocity in social worker-client relationships. *Journal of Social Work, 9*(1), 5–22. http://dx.doi .org/10.1177/1468017308098420

Anderson, D. G. (2000). Coping strategies and burnout among veteran child protection workers. *Child Abuse & Neglect, 24*(6), 839–48. http://dx.doi .org/10.1016/S0145-2134(00)00143-5

Anderson, L. M., & Shafer, G. (1979). The character disordered family: A community treatment model for family sexual abuse. *American Journal of Orthopsychiatry, 49*(3), 436–45. http://dx.doi.org/10.1111/j.1939-0025.1979 .tb02626.x

André, D., & Fernand, G. (2008). Sherlock Holmes – an expert's view of expertise. *British Journal of Psychology, 99*(1), 109–25. http://dx.doi .org/10.1348/000712607X224469

Antle, B. F., Barbee, A. P., Christensen, D. N., & Martin, M. H. (2008). Solution-based casework in child welfare: Preliminary evaluation research. *Journal of Public Child Welfare, 2*(2), 197–227. http://dx.doi .org/10.1080/15548730802312891

Antle, B. F., Christensen, D. N., van Zyl, M. A., & Barbee, A. P. (2012). The impact of the Solution Based Casework (SBC) practice model on federal outcomes in public child welfare. *Child Abuse & Neglect, 36*(4), 342–53. http://dx.doi.org/10.1016/j.chiabu.2011.10.009

Appleton, J. V., Terlektsi, E., & Coombes, L. (2014). Implementing the Strengthening Families Approach to child protection conferences. *British Journal of Social Work*, bct211.

Armitage, A. (1995). *Comparing the policy of aboriginal assimilation: Australia, Canada, and New Zealand.* Vancouver: UBC Press.

Austin, W. (2007). The ethics of everyday practice: Healthcare environments as moral communities. *Advances in Nursing Science, 30*(1), 81–8. http://dx.doi .org/10.1097/00012272-200701000-00009

Ayre, P. (2001). Child protection and the media: Lessons from the last three decades. *British Journal of Social Work, 31*(6), 887–901. http://dx.doi.org /10.1093/bjsw/31.6.887

Bain, J. D., Ballantyne, R., Mills, C., & Lester, N. C. (2002). *Reflecting on practice: Student teachers' perspectives.* Flaxton, Australia: Post Pressed.

Bandura, A. (1977). Self-efficacy: Toward a unifying theory of behavioral change. *Psychological Review, 84*(2), 191–215. http://dx.doi.org/10.1037 /0033-295X.84.2.191

Bandura, A. (1986). *Social foundations of thought and action.* Englewood Cliffs, NJ: Prentice Hall.

Bandura, A. (1991). Social cognitive theory of self-regulation. *Organizational Behavior and Human Decision Processes, 50*(2), 248–87. http://dx.doi.org /10.1016/0749-5978(91)90022-L

Bandura, A. (1997). *Self-efficacy: The exercise of control.* New York, NY: Freeman.

Bar-On, A. A. (2002). Restoring power to social work practice. *British Journal of Social Work, 32*(8), 997–1014. http://dx.doi.org/10.1093/bjsw/32.8.997

Barbee, A. P., Christensen, D., Antle, B., Wandersman, A., & Cahn, K. (2011). Successful adoption and implementation of a comprehensive casework practice model in a public child welfare agency: Application of the Getting to Outcomes (GTO) model. *Children and Youth Services Review, 33*(5), 622–33. http://dx.doi.org/10.1016/j.childyouth.2010.11.008

Barber, J. (1991). *Beyond casework.* London: Macmillan. http://dx.doi.org /10.1007/978-1-349-21569-0

Barter, K. (2008). Building relationships with involuntary clients in child protection: Lessons from successful practice. In M. Calder (Ed.), *The carrot or the stick: Towards effective practice with involuntary clients in safeguarding children work* (pp. 93–103). Dorset, England: Russell House Publishing Limited.

Becker, D. R., & Drake, R. E. (2003). *A working life for people with severe mental illness.* New York, NY: Oxford University Press. http://dx.doi.org/10.1093 /acprof:oso/9780195131215.001.0001

Beckett, P., Field, J., Molloy, L., Yu, N., Holmes, D., & Pile, E. (2013). Practice what you preach: Developing person-centred culture in inpatient mental health settings through strengths-based, transformational leadership. *Issues in Mental Health Nursing, 34*(8), 595–601. http://dx.doi.org/10.3109 /01612840.2013.790524

Beddoe, L. (2010). Surveillance or reflection: Professional supervision in "the risk society". *British Journal of Social Work, 40*(4), 1279–96. http://dx.doi.org/10.1093/bjsw/bcq018

Beddoe, L. (2012). External supervision in social work: Power, space, risk, and the search for safety. *Australian Social Work, 65*(2), 197–213. http://dx.doi.org/10.1080/0312407X.2011.591187

Bennett, D., Sadrehashemi, L., Smith, C., Hehewerth, M., Sienema, L., & Makolewski, J. (2009). *Hands tied. Child protection workers talk about working in, and leaving, B.C.'s child welfare system.* Vancouver, BC: Pivot Legal Society.

Berceli, D., & Napoli, M. (2006). A proposal for a mindfulness-based trauma prevention program for social work professionals. *Complementary Health Practice Review, 11*(3), 153–65.

Beresford, P., Croft, S., & Adshead, L. (2008). "We don't see her as a social worker": A service user case study of the importance of the social worker's relationship and humanity. *British Journal of Social Work, 38*(7), 1388–407. http://dx.doi.org/10.1093/bjsw/bcm043

Berg, I. K. (1994). *Family-based services: A solution-focused approach.* New York, NY: W.W. Norton & Co.

Berg, I. K., & De Jong, P. (2004). Building solution-focused partnerships in children's protective and family services. *American Humane, 19*(2), 3–13.

Berg, I. K., & Kelly, S. (2000). *Building solutions in child protective services.* New York, NY: W.W. Norton & Co.

Berg, I. K., & Miller, S. D. (1992). *Working with the problem drinker: A solution-focused approach.* New York, NY: W.W. Norton & Co.

Bertolino, B. (2014). *Thriving on the front lines: A guide to strengths-based youth care work.* New York, NY: Routledge.

Besharov, D. J. (1985). Doing something about child abuse: The need to narrow the grounds for state intervention. *Harvard of Law and Public Policy, 8,* 539–89.

Biestek, F. P. (1957). *The casework relationship.* London, England: Loyola Press.

Blundo, R. (2001). Learning strengths-based practice: Challenging our personal and professional frames. *Families in Society, 82*(3), 296–304. http://dx.doi.org/10.1606/1044-3894.192

Blundo, R. (2012). Learning and practicing the strengths perspective: Stepping out of comfortable mind-sets. In D. Saleebey (Ed.), *The strengths perspective in social work practice* (pp. 25–52). Upper Saddle River, NJ: Pearson Education Inc.

Bogo, M., Katz, E., Regehr, C., Logie, C., Mylopoulos, M., & Tufford, L. (2013). Toward understanding meta-competence: An analysis of students' reflection on their simulated interviews. *Social Work Education, 32*(2), 259–73. http://dx.doi.org/10.1080/02615479.2012.738662

Bogo, M., & McKnight, K. (2006). Clinical supervision in social work: A review of the research literature. *Clinical Supervisor, 24*(1–2), 49–67. http://dx.doi.org /10.1300/J001v24n01_04

Bond, C., Woods, K., Humphrey, N., Symes, W., & Green, L. (2013). Practitioner review: The effectiveness of solution focused brief therapy with children and families: A systematic and critical evaluation of the literature from 1990–2010. *Journal of Child Psychology and Psychiatry, and Allied Disciplines, 54*(7), 707–23. http://dx.doi.org/10.1111/jcpp.12058

Borden, W. (2000). The relational paradigm in contemporary psychoanalysis: Toward a psychodynamically informed social work perspective. *The Social Service Review, 74*(3), 352–79.

Bordin, E. S. (1979). The generalizability of the psychoanalytic concept of the working alliance. *Psychotherapy, 16*(3), 252–60. http://dx.doi.org/10.1037 /h0085885

Boyas, J., Wind, L. H., & Kang, S.-Y. (2012). Exploring the relationship between employment-based social capital, job stress, burnout, and intent to leave among child protection workers: An age-based path analysis model. *Children and Youth Services Review, 34*(1), 50–62. http://dx.doi.org/10.1016 /j.childyouth.2011.08.033

Brace, I. (2008). *Questionnaire design: How to plan, structure and write survey material for effective market research.* London, England: Kogan Page Ltd.

Bradley, G., Engelbrecht, L., & Höjer, S. (2010). Supervision: A force for change? Three stories told. *International Social Work, 53*(6), 773–90. http://dx.doi.org/10.1177/0020872809358401

British Columbia Government and Employee Services Union (BCGEU). (2014). *Choose children: A case for reinvesting in child, youth and family services in British Columbia.* Victoria, BC: British Columbia Government and Employee Services Union.

Bugental, D. B., & Lewis, J. C. (1999). The paradoxical misuse of power by those who see themselves as powerless: How does it happen? *Journal of Social Issues, 55*(1), 51–64. http://dx.doi.org/10.1111/0022-4537.00104

Bundy-Fazioli, K., Briar-Lawson, K., & Hardiman, E. R. (2009). A qualitative examination of power between child welfare workers and parents. *British Journal of Social Work, 39*(8), 1447–64. http://dx.doi.org/10.1093/bjsw /bcn038

Bundy-Fazioli, K., Quijano, L., & Bubar, R. (2013). Graduate students' perceptions of professional power in social work practice. *Journal of Social Work Education, 49*(1), 108–21.

Bunn, A. (2013). *Signs of Safety in England: An NSPCC commissioned report on the Signs of Safety model in child protection.* London, England: NSPCC.

Burns, K., & MacCarthy, J. (2012). An impossible task? Implementing the recommendations of child abuse inquiry reports in a context of high workloads in child protection and welfare. *Irish Journal of Applied Social Studies, 12*(1), Article 3.

Butler, P. D., Swift, M., Kothari, S., Nazeeri-Simmons, I., Friel, C. M., Longaker, M. T., & Britt, L. (2011). Integrating cultural competency and humility training into clinical clerkships: Surgery as a model. *Journal of Surgical Education, 68*(3), 222–30. http://dx.doi.org/10.1016/j.jsurg.2011.01.002

Calder, M. (2008a). Professional dangerousness: Causes and contemporary features. In M. Calder (Ed.), *Contemporary risk assessment in safeguarding children* (pp. 61–96). Dorset, England: Russell House Publishing.

Calder, M. (Ed.). (2008b). *The carrot or the stick? Towards effective practice with involuntary clients in safeguarding children work.* Dorset, England: Russell House Publishing.

Chand, A. (2000). The over-representation of black children in the child protection system: Possible causes, consequences and solutions. *Child & Family Social Work, 5*(1), 67–77. http://dx.doi.org/10.1046/j.1365-2206.2000.00144.x

Chang, E., Simon, M., & Dong, X. (2012). Integrating cultural humility into health care professional education and training. *Advances in Health Sciences Education: Theory and Practice, 17*(2), 269–78. http://dx.doi.org/10.1007/s10459-010-9264-1

Choate, P. W., & Engstrom, S. (2014). The "good enough" parent: Implications for child protection. *Child Care in Practice, 20*(4), 368–82. http://dx.doi.org/10.1080/13575279.2014.915794

Christenson, B., Curran, S., DeCook, K., Maloney, S., & Merkel-Holguin, L. (2008). The intersection between differential response and family involvement approaches. *Protecting Children, 23*(1–2), 88–95.

Cingolani, J. (1984). Social conflict perspective on work with involuntary clients. *Social Work, 29*, 442–6.

Cleaver, H., & Freeman, P. (1995). *Parental perspectives in cases of suspected child abuse.* London, England: HMSO.

Collins-Camargo, C., & Millar, K. (2010). The potential for a more clinical approach to child welfare supervision to promote practice and case outcomes: A qualitative study in four states. *Clinical Supervisor, 29*(2), 164–87. http://dx.doi.org/10.1080/07325223.2010.517491

Comer, D., & Vassar, D. (2008). Six principles of partnership: Building and sustaining system-wide change. *Protecting Children, 23*(1–2), 96–104.

Conley, A. (2007). Differential response: A critical examination of a secondary prevention model. *Children and Youth Services Review, 29*(11), 1454–68. http://dx.doi.org/10.1016/j.childyouth.2007.06.003

Conrad, D., & Kellar-Guenther, Y. (2006). Compassion fatigue, burnout, and compassion satisfaction among Colorado child protection workers. *Child Abuse & Neglect, 30*(10), 1071–80. http://dx.doi.org/10.1016/j.chiabu.2006.03.009

Cook, K. S., & Rice, E. (2006). Social exchange theory. In J. Delamater (Ed.), *Handbook of social psychology* (pp. 53–76). New York, NY: Springer. http://dx.doi.org/10.1007/0-387-36921-X_3

Corcoran, J. (2005). *Building strengths and skills: A collaborative approach to working with clients*. New York, NY: Oxford University Press.

Corcoran, J., & Pillai, V. (2009). A review of the research on solution-focused therapy. *British Journal of Social Work, 39*(2), 234–42. http://dx.doi.org/10.1093/bjsw/bcm098

Corley, M. C., Minick, P., Elswick, R., & Jacobs, M. (2005). Nurse moral distress and ethical work environment. *Nursing Ethics, 12*(4), 381–90. http://dx.doi.org/10.1191/0969733005ne809oa

Crampton, D. (2007). Research review: Family group decision-making: A promising practice in need of more programme theory and research. *Child & Family Social Work, 12*(2), 202–9. http://dx.doi.org/10.1111/j.1365-2206.2006.00442.x

Croft, S., & Beresford, P. (1994). A participatory approach to social work. In C. Hanvey & T. Philpot (Eds.), *Practising social work* (pp. 49–66). London, England: Routledge.

Dale, P., Davies, M., Morrison, T., & Waters, J. (1986). *Dangerous families: Assessment and treatment of child abuse*. London, England: Tavistock.

Davies, P. (2011). The impact of a child protection investigation: A personal reflective account. *Child & Family Social Work, 16*(2), 201–9. http://dx.doi.org/10.1111/j.1365-2206.2010.00732.x

Davis, E. B. (1995). *The use of authority with involuntary clients in child protective investigations* (Doctoral dissertation). Retrieved from Proquest Dissertations and Theses Global. (Order No. 9530865)

de Boer, C., & Coady, N. (2007). Good helping relationships in child welfare: Learning from stories of success. *Child & Family Social Work, 12*(1), 32–42. http://dx.doi.org/10.1111/j.1365-2206.2006.00438.x

De Jong, P., & Berg, I. K. (2001). Co-constructing cooperation with mandated clients. *Social Work, 46*(4), 361–74.

De Jong, P., & Hopwood, L. (1996). Outcome research on treatment conducted at the Brief Family Therapy Center, 1992–1993. In S. D. Miller, M. A. Hubble, and B. L. Duncan (Eds.), *Handbook of solution-focused brief therapy: Foundations, applications, and research* (pp. 272–98). San Francisco, CA: Jossey-Bass.

De Jong, P., & Miller, S. D. (1995). How to interview for client strengths. *Social Work, 40*(6), 729–36.

De Leon, G. (1988). Legal pressure in therapeutic communities. In C. G. Leukefeld & F. M. Tims (Eds.), *Compulsory treatment of drug abuse: Research and clinical practice* (Vol. 86, pp. 160–76,). Rockville, MD: National Institute on Drug Abuse.

Department for Child Protection. (2010). *A report on the 2010 Signs of Safety survey.* Perth: Department for Child Protection, Government of Western Australia.

Department for Child Protection (2012). *2012 Signs of Safety evaluation report.* Perth: Department for Child Protection, Government of Western Australia.

de Shazer, S. (1982). *Patterns of brief family therapy: An ecosystemic approach.* New York, NY: The Guilford Press.

de Shazer, S., Berg, I. K., Lipchik, E., Nunnally, E., Molnar, A., Gingerich, W., & Weiner-Davis, M. (1986). Brief therapy: Focused solution development. *Family process, 25*(2), 207–21.

Dill, K., & Bogo, M. (2009). Moving beyond the administrative: Supervisors' perspectives on clinical supervision in child welfare. *Journal of Public Child Welfare, 3*(1), 87–105. http://dx.doi.org/10.1080/15548730802695105

Dillman, D. A. (2007). *Mail and internet surveys: The tailored design method.* John Wiley & Sons Inc.

Dingwall, R., Eekelaar, J., & Murray, T. (1995). *The protection of children: State intervention and family life.* Aldershot, England: Avebury.

Doek, J. E. (1991). Management of child abuse and neglect at the international level: Trends and perspectives. *Child Abuse & Neglect, 15*, 51–6. http://dx.doi.org/10.1016/0145-2134(91)90008-2

Douglas, E. M., McCarthy, S. C., & Serino, P. A. (2014). Does a social work degree predict practice orientation? Measuring strengths-based practice among child welfare workers with the strengths-based practices inventory – provider version. *Journal of Social Work Education, 50*(2), 219–33.

Drake, B. (1996). Consumer and worker perceptions of key child welfare competencies. *Children and Youth Services Review, 18*(3), 261–79. http://dx.doi.org/10.1016/0190-7409(96)00004-7

Drake, R. E., Bond, G. R., & Becker, D. R. (2012). *Individual placement and support: An evidence-based approach to supported employment.* http://dx.doi.org/10.1093/acprof:oso/9780199734016.001.0001

Dreyfus, H. L., & Dreyfus, S. E. (2005). Peripheral vision expertise in real world contexts. *Organization Studies, 26*(5), 779–92. http://dx.doi.org/10.1177/0170840605053102

Dumbrill, G. C. (2006). Parental experience of child protection intervention: A qualitative study. *Child Abuse & Neglect, 30*(1), 27–37. http://dx.doi.org/10.1016/j.chiabu.2005.08.012

Early, T. J., & GlenMaye, L. F. (2000). Valuing families: Social work practice with families from a strengths perspective. *Social Work, 45*(2), 118–30.

Eraut, M. (2000). Non formal learning and tacit knowledge in professional work. *British Journal of Educational Psychology, 70*(1), 113–36. http://dx.doi .org/10.1348/000709900158001

Eva, K., Armson, H., Holmboe, E., Lockyer, J., Loney, E., Mann, K., & Sargeant, J. (2012). Factors influencing responsiveness to feedback: On the interplay between fear, confidence, and reasoning processes. *Advances in Health Sciences Education: Theory and Practice, 17*(1), 15–26. http://dx.doi.org /10.1007/s10459-011-9290-7

Faller, K. C. (1985). Unanticipated problems in the United States child protection system. *Child Abuse & Neglect, 9*(1), 63–9. http://dx.doi.org/10.1016 /0145-2134(85)90093-6

Featherstone, B., White, S. & Morris, K. (2014). *Re-imagining child protection: Towards humane social work with families*. Bristol: Policy Press. http://dx.doi .org/10.1332/policypress/9781447308027.001.0001

Ferguson, H. (2005). Working with violence, the emotions and the psycho-social dynamics of child protection: Reflections on the Victoria Climbié case. *Social Work Education, 24*(7), 781–95. http://dx.doi.org/10.1080 /02615470500238702

Ferguson, H. (2009). Performing child protection: Home visiting, movement and the struggle to reach the abused child. *Child & Family Social Work, 14*(4), 471–80. http://dx.doi.org/10.1111/j.1365-2206.2009.00630.x

Ferguson, H. (2016). What social workers do in performing child protection work: Evidence from research into face-to-face practice. *Child & Family Social Work, 21*(3), 283–94. http://dx.doi.org/10.1111/cfs.12142

Festinger, L. (1962). *A theory of cognitive dissonance* (Vol. 2). Redwood City, CA: Stanford University Press.

Figley, C. R. (1995). *Compassion fatigue: Coping with secondary traumatic stress disorder in those who treat the traumatized*. New York, NY: Routledge.

Figley, C. R. (2002). Compassion fatigue: Psychotherapists' chronic lack of self care. *Journal of Clinical Psychology, 58*(11), 1433–41. http://dx.doi.org /10.1002/jclp.10090

Fisher-Borne, M., Cain, J. M., & Martin, S. L. (2015). From mastery to accountability: Cultural humility as an alternative to cultural competence. *Social Work Education, 34*(2), 165–81. http://dx.doi.org/10.1080/02615479 .2014.977244

Forrester, D., Kershaw, S., Moss, H., & Hughes, L. (2008). Communication skills in child protection: How do social workers talk to parents? *Child & Family Social Work, 13*(1), 41–51.

Franklin, C., Trepper, T., McCollum, E., & Gingerich, W. (2012). *Solution-focused brief therapy: A handbook of evidence-based practice*. New York, NY: Oxford University Press.

Frederico, M., Jackson, A., & Dwyer, J. (2014). Child protection and cross-sector practice: An analysis of child death reviews to inform practice when multiple parental risk factors are present. *Child Abuse Review, 23*(2), 104–15. http://dx.doi.org/10.1002/car.2321

Freedberg, S. (2009). *Relational theory for social work practice: A feminist perspective*. New York, NY: Routledge.

Frey, L., LeBeau, M., Kindler, D., Behan, C., Morales, I. M., & Freundlich, M. (2012). The pivotal role of child welfare supervisors in implementing an agency's practice model. *Children and Youth Services Review, 34*(7), 1273–82. http://dx.doi.org/10.1016/j.childyouth.2012.02.019

Fricker, R. D. (2008). Sampling methods for web and e-mail surveys. In N. Fielding, R. Lee, & G. Blank (Eds.), *The SAGE handbook of online research methods* (pp. 195–216). London, England: Sage Publications Inc. http://dx.doi.org/10.4135/9780857020055.n11

Gallagher, M., Smith, M., Wosu, H., Stewart, J., Hunter, S., & Cree, V. E. (2011). Engaging with families in child protection: Lessons from practitioner research in Scotland. *Child Welfare, 90*(4), 117–34.

Gambrill, E. (2006). *Critical thinking in clinical practice: Improving the quality of judgments and decisions*. Hoboke, NJ: John Wiley & Sons.

Ghaffar, W., Manby, M., & Race, T. (2012). Exploring the experiences of parents and carers whose children have been subject to child protection plans. *British Journal of Social Work, 42*(5), 887–905. http://dx.doi.org/10.1093/bjsw/bcr132

Gibbons, J., & Gray, M. (2002). An integrated and experience-based approach to social work education: The Newcastle model. *Social Work Education, 21*(5), 529–49. http://dx.doi.org/10.1080/0261547022000015221

Gibbs, J. A. (2001). Maintaining frontline workers in child protection: A case for refocusing supervision. *Child Abuse Review, 10*(5), 323–35. http://dx.doi.org/10.1002/car.707

Gibson, M. (2014). Narrative practice and the Signs of Safety approach: Engaging adolescents in building rigorous safety plans. *Child Care in Practice, 20*(1), 64–80. http://dx.doi.org/10.1080/13575279.2013.799455

Gillingham, P. (2014). Electronic information systems in human service organisations: The what, who, why and how of information. *British Journal of Social Work*. http://dx.doi.org/10.1093/bjsw/bcu030

Gingerich, W. J., & Eisengart, S. (2000). Solution-focused brief therapy: A review of the outcome research. *Family Process, 39*(4), 477–98. http://dx.doi.org/10.1111/j.1545-5300.2000.39408.x

Gingerich, W. J., & Peterson, L. T. (2013). Effectiveness of solution-focused brief therapy: A systematic qualitative review of controlled outcome studies. *Research on Social Work Practice, 23*(3), 266–83. http://dx.doi.org/10.1177/1049731512470859

Goddard, C., & Tucci, J. (1991). Child protection and the need for the reappraisal of the social worker-client relationship. *Australian Social Work, 44*(2), 3–10.

Gorin, S. (2004). *Understanding what children say: Children's experience of domestic violence, parental substance misuse and parental health problems.* London, England: National Children's Bureau.

Gottlieb, L. (2012). *Strengths-based nursing care: Health and healing for person and family.* New York, NY: Springer Publishing Company.

Gottlieb, L. N., Gottlieb, B., & Shamian, J. (2012). Principles of strengths-based nursing leadership for strengths-based nursing care: A new paradigm for nursing and healthcare for the 21st century. *Canadian Journal of Nursing Leadership, 25*(2), 38–50. http://dx.doi.org/10.12927/cjnl.2012.22960

Grant, J., & Cadell, S. (2009). Power, pathological worldviews and the strengths perspective in social work. *Families in Society, 90*(4), 425–30. http://dx.doi.org/10.1606/1044-3894.3921

Gray, M. (2010). Moral sources and emergent ethical theories in social work. *British Journal of Social Work, 40*(6), 1794–811. http://dx.doi.org/10.1093/bjsw/bcp104

Gray, M. (2011). Back to basics: A critique of the strengths perspective in social work. *Families in Society, 92*(1), 5–11. http://dx.doi.org/10.1606/1044-3894.4054

Graybeal, C. (2001). Strengths-based social work assessment: Transforming the dominant paradigm. *Families in Society, 82*(3), 233–42. http://dx.doi.org/10.1606/1044-3894.236

Green, G. P., & Haines, A. (2012). *Asset building & community development.* Thousand Oaks, CA: Sage.

Greenberg, S. A., & Shuman, D. W. (1997). Irreconcilable conflict between therapeutic and forensic roles. *Professional Psychology: Research and Practice, 28*(1), 50–7.

Greenberg, S. A., & Shuman, D. W. (2007). When worlds collide: Therapeutic and forensic roles. *Professional Psychology: Research and Practice, 38*(2), 129–32.

Gross, J. J. (2013). Emotion regulation: Taking stock and moving forward. *Emotion (Washington, D.C.), 13*(3), 359–65. http://dx.doi.org/10.1037/a0032135

Hair, H. J. (2013). The purpose and duration of supervision, and the training and discipline of supervisors: What social workers say they need to provide

effective services. *British Journal of Social Work, 43*(8), 1562–88. http://dx.doi
.org/10.1093/bjsw/bcs071

Haley, J. (1993). *Uncommon therapy: The psychiatric techniques of Milton H.
Erickson, MD.* New York, NY: W.W. Norton & Co.

Hall, C., Parton, N., Peckover, S., & White, S. (2010). Child-centric information
and communication technology (ICT) and the fragmentation of child welfare
practice in England. *Journal of Social Policy, 39*(03), 393–413. http://dx.doi
.org/10.1017/S0047279410000012

Harbert, A., & Tucker-Tatlow, J. (2012). *Review of child welfare risk assessments.*
Retrieved from https://theacademy.sdsu.edu/wp-content/uploads/2015
/02/SACHS_Risk_Assessment_Report_and_Appendices_11_2012.pdf

Harlow, E. (2003). New managerialism, social service departments and social
work practice today. *Practice. Social Work in Action, 15*(2), 29–44. http://dx.doi
.org/10.1080/09503150308416917

Harmon-Jones, E., Amodio, D. M., & Harmon-Jones, C. (2009). Action-based
model of dissonance: A review, integration, and expansion of conceptions of
cognitive conflict. *Advances in Experimental Social Psychology, 41,* 119–66.

Harris, B., & Leather, P. (2012). Levels and consequences of exposure to service
user violence: Evidence from a sample of UK social care staff. *British Journal
of Social Work, 42*(5), 851–69. http://dx.doi.org/10.1093/bjsw/bcr128

Harris, P. (2008). Engaging substance misusers through coercion. In M. Calder (Ed.),
*The carrot or the stick? Towards effective practice with involuntary clients in
safeguarding children work* (p. 277). Dorset, England: Russell House Publishing.

Healy, K. (1998). Participation and child protection: The importance of context.
British Journal of Social Work, 28(6), 897–914. http://dx.doi.org/10.1093
/oxfordjournals.bjsw.a011407

Healy, K., Meagher, G., & Cullin, J. (2009). Retaining novices to become expert
child protection practitioners: Creating career pathways in direct practice. *British
Journal of Social Work, 39*(2), 299–317. http://dx.doi.org/10.1093/bjsw/bcm125

Herbert, M. (2003). *Child welfare project: Creating conditions for good practice.*
Ottawa, ON: Canadian Association of Social Workers.

Hetherington, R. (1998). Issues in European child protection research.
European Journal of Social Work, 1(1), 71–82. http://dx.doi.org/10.1080
/13691459808414724

Hetherington, R. (2002). *Partnerships for children and families project. Learning
from difference: Comparing child welfare systems.* Waterloo, ON: Wilfrid Laurier
University.

Hetherington, T. (1999). Child protection: A new approach in South Australia.
Child Abuse Review, 8(2), 120–32. http://dx.doi.org/10.1002/(SICI)1099
-0852(199903/04)8:2<120::AID-CAR524>3.0.CO;2-F

Hodges, T., & Clifton, D. (2004). Strengths-based development in practice. In P. A. Linley & S. Joseph (Eds.), *Positive psychology in practice*, (pp. 256–68). Hoboken, NJ: John Wiley & Sons.

Hogg, M. A., & McGarty, C. (1990). Self-categorization and social identity. In D. Abrams & M. A. Hogg (Eds.), *Social identity theory: Constructive and critical advances* (Vol. 10, pp. 10–27). London, England: Harvester Wheatsheaf.

Hogg, V., & Wheeler, J. (2004). Miracles R them: Solution-focused practice in a social services duty team. *Practice: Social Work in Action, 16*(4), 299–314. http://dx.doi.org/10.1080/09503150500046202

Holmgård Sørensen, T. (2013). *When parents and network create safety for the child – an evaluation of "safety plans" as part of working with children at risk in department of social services city of Copenhagen*. Copenhagen, Denmark: Socialforvaltnin-gen, Københavns Kommune.

Hope, B. (2011). *All in a day's work. No child should ever be forgotten*. London, England: Hodder & Stoughton.

Hosman, C. M. H., van Doesum, K. T. M., & van Santvoort, F. (2009). Prevention of emotional problems and psychiatric risks in children of parents with a mental illness in the Netherlands: I. The scientific basis to a comprehensive approach. *Advances in Mental Health, 8*(3), 250–63.

Hotho, S. (2008). Professional identity – product of structure, product of choice: Linking changing professional identity and changing professions. *Journal of Organizational Change Management, 21*(6), 721–42. http://dx.doi .org/10.1108/09534810810915745

Houston, S., & Griffiths, H. (2000). Reflections on risk in child protection: Is it time for a shift in paradigms? *Child & Family Social Work, 5*(1), 1–10. http://dx.doi.org/10.1046/j.1365-2206.2000.00145.x

Howe, D. (1992). Child abuse and the bureaucratisation of social work. *Sociological Review, 40*(3), 491–508. http://dx.doi.org/10.1111/j.1467-954X.1992.tb00399.x

Howe, D. (1996). Surface and depth in social work practice. *Social theory, social change and social work*, 77–97.

Howe, D. (1998). Relationship-based thinking and practice in social work. *Journal of Social Work Practice, 12*(1), 45–56.

Howe, D. (2010). The safety of children and the parent-worker relationship in cases of child abuse and neglect. *Child Abuse Review, 19*(5), 330–41. http://dx.doi.org/10.1002/car.1136

Howe, D., Batchelor, S., & Bochynska, K. (2009). Estimating consumer parenthood within mental health services: A census approach. *Advances in Mental Health, 8*(3), 231–41. http://dx.doi.org/10.5172/jamh.8.3.231

Hunter, B. A., Lanza, A. S., Lawlor, M., Dyson, W., & Gordon, D. M. (2016). A strengths-based approach to prisoner reentry: The Fresh Start Prisoner

Reentry Program. *International journal of offender therapy and comparative criminology, 60*(11), 1298–314.

Huuskonen, S., & Vakkari, P. (2011). Client's temporal trajectory in child protection: Piecing information together in a client information system Human-Computer Interaction. In P. Campos, N. Graham, J. Jorge, N. Nunes, P. Palanque, & M. Winckler (Eds.), *Human-Computer Interaction – INTERACT 2011: 13th IFIP TC 13 International Conference, Lisbon, Portugal, September 5-9, 2011, Proceedings, Part IV* (pp. 152–69). Springer. http://dx.doi.org/10.1007/978-3-642-23768-3_13

Huxley, P., Evans, S., Beresford, P., Davidson, B., & King, S. (2009). The principles and provision of relationships: Findings from an evaluation of support, time and recovery workers in mental health services in England. *Journal of Social Work, 9*(1), 99–117. http://dx.doi.org/10.1177/1468017308098434

Ibrahim, N., Michail, M., & Callaghan, P. (2014). The strengths based approach as a service delivery model for severe mental illness: A meta-analysis of clinical trials. *BMC Psychiatry, 14*(1), 243. http://dx.doi.org/10.1186/s12888-014-0243-6

Idzelis Rothe, M., Nelson-Dusek, S., & Skrypek, M. (2013). *Innovations in child protection services in Minnesota: Research chronicle of Carver and Olmsted Counties.* St Paul, MN: Wilder Research.

Ivanoff, A. M., Blythe, B. J., & Tripodi, T. (1994). *Involuntary clients in social work practice: A research-based approach.* Hawthorne, NY: Aldine de Gruyter.

Jack, R. (2005). Strengths-based practice in statutory care and protection work. In M. Nash, R. Munford & K. O'Donoghue (Eds.), *Social work theories in action* (pp. 174–88). London, England: Jessica Kingsley Publishers.

Jimenez, J. (2006). The history of child protection in the African American community: Implications for current child welfare policies. *Children and Youth Services Review, 28*(8), 888–905. http://dx.doi.org/10.1016/j.childyouth.2005.10.004

Jobe, A., & Gorin, S. (2013). "If kids don't feel safe they don't do anything": Young people's views on seeking and receiving help from Children's Social Care Services in England. *Child & Family Social Work, 18*(4), 429–38. http://dx.doi.org/10.1111/j.1365-2206.2012.00862.x

Jones, N. J., Brown, S. L., Robinson, D., & Frey, D. (2015). Incorporating strengths into quantitative assessments of criminal risk for adult offenders: The Service Planning Instrument. *Criminal Justice and Behavior, 42*(3), 321–38. http://dx.doi.org/10.1177/0093854814547041

Juarez, J. A., Marvel, K., Brezinski, K. L., Glazner, C., Towbin, M. M., & Lawton, S. (2006). Bridging the gap: A curriculum to teach residents cultural humility. *Family Medicine-Kansas City, 38*(2), 97.

Kaplan, C., & Merkel-Holguin, L. (2008). Another look at the national study on differential response in child welfare. *Protecting Children, 23*(1/2), 5–22.

Keddell, E. (2012). Going home: Managing "risk" through relationship in returning children from foster care to their families of origin. *Qualitative Social Work: Research and Practice, 11*(6), 604–20. http://dx.doi.org/10.1177/1473325011411010

Kemp, S. P., Marcenko, M. O., Lyons, S. J., & Kruzich, J. M. (2014). Strength-based practice and parental engagement in child welfare services: An empirical examination. *Children and Youth Services Review, 47*, 27–35. http://dx.doi.org/10.1016/j.childyouth.2013.11.001

Kempe, C. H., Silverman, F. N., Steele, B. F., Droegemueller, W., & Silver, H. K. (1962). The battered-child syndrome. *Journal of the American Medical Association, 181*(1), 17–24. http://dx.doi.org/10.1001/jama.1962.03050270019004

Kennealy, P. J., Skeem, J. L., Manchak, S. M., & Eno Louden, J. (2012). Firm, fair, and caring officer-offender relationships protect against supervision failure. *Law and Human Behavior, 36*(6), 496–505. http://dx.doi.org/10.1037/h0093935

Kisthardt, W. E. (1997). *The impact of the strengths model of case management with adults with serious and persistent mental illness.* (Doctoral dissertation). Retrieved from ProQuest Dissertations & Theses Global. (Order No. 981134)

Kisthardt, W. (2012). Integrating the core competencies in strengths-based, person-centered practice: Clarifying purpose and reflecting principles. In D. Saleebey (Ed.), *The strengths perspective in social work practice.* Upper Saddle River, NJ: Pearson Education Inc.

Korthagen, F., & Vasalos, A. (2005). Levels in reflection: Core reflection as a means to enhance professional growth. *Teachers and Teaching, 11*(1), 47–71. http://dx.doi.org/10.1080/1354060042000337093

Kretzman, J. P., & McKnight, J. L. (1993). *Building communities from the inside out: A path toward finding and mobilizing a community's assets.* Evanston, IL: The Asset-Based Community Development Institute, Institute for Policy Research, Northwestern University.

Kyte, A., Trocme, N., & Chamberland, C. (2013). Evaluating where we're at with differential response. *Child Abuse & Neglect, 37*(2-3), 125–32. http://dx.doi.org/10.1016/j.chiabu.2012.10.003

Laming, H. B. (2009). *The protection of children in England: A progress report* (Vol. 330). London, England: The Stationery Office.

LeBlanc, V. R., Regehr, C., Shlonsky, A., & Bogo, M. (2012). Stress responses and decision making in child protection workers faced with high conflict situations. *Child Abuse & Neglect*, *36*(5), 404–12. http://dx.doi.org/10.1016/j.chiabu.2012.01.003

Lefevre, M. (2008). Assessment and decisionmaking in child protection: Relationship-based considerations. In M. Calder (Ed.), *The carrot or the stick: Towards effective practice with involuntary clietns in safeguarding children work* (pp. 78–92). Dorset, England: Russell House.

Lietz, C. A. (2009). Critical thinking in child welfare supervision. *Administration in Social Work*, *34*(1), 68–78. http://dx.doi.org/10.1080/03643100903432966

Lietz, C. A. (2011). Theoretical adherence to family centered practice: Are strengths-based principles illustrated in families' descriptions of child welfare services? *Children and Youth Services Review*, *33*(6), 888–93. http://dx.doi.org/10.1016/j.childyouth.2010.12.012

Lietz, C. A. (2013). Strengths-based supervision: Supporting implementation of family-centered practice through supervisory processes. *Journal of Family Strengths*, *13*(1), 6.

Lietz, C. A., & Rounds, T. (2009). Strengths-based supervision: A child welfare supervision training project. *Clinical Supervisor*, *28*(2), 124–40. http://dx.doi.org/10.1080/07325220903334065

Littlechild, B. (2008). Social work with involuntary clients in child protection work. In M. C. Calder (Ed.), *The carrot or the stick: Towards effective practice with involuntary clients in safeguarding children work* (pp. 141–51). Dorset, England: Russell House Publishing.

Lipsky, M. (2010). *Streel-level bureaucracy: Dilemmas of the individual in public services*. New York, NY: Russell Sage Foundation Publications.

Lohrbach, S., Sawyer, R., Saugen, J., Schmitt, K., Worden, P., & Xaaji, M. (2005). Ways of working in child welfare: A perspective on practice. *Protecting Children*, *20*(2/3), 93–100.

Lonne, B., Parton, N., Thomson, J., & Harries, M. (2008). *Reforming child protection*. New York, NY: Routledge.

Lwin, K., Versanov, A., Cheung, C., Goodman, D., & Andrews, N. (2014). The use of mapping in child welfare investigations: A strength-based hybrid intervention. *Child Care in Practice*, *20*(1), 81–97. http://dx.doi.org/10.1080/13575279.2013.847055

Macias, C., William Farley, O., Jackson, R., & Kinney, R. (1997). Case management in the context of capitation financing: An evaluation of the strengths model. *Administration and Policy in Mental Health*, *24*(6), 535–43. http://dx.doi.org/10.1007/BF02042831

Maidment, J. (2006). The quiet remedy: A dialogue on reshaping professional relationships. *Families in Society*, *87*(1), 115–21. http://dx.doi.org/10.1606/1044-3894.3491

Mandell, D. (2008). Power, care and vulnerability: Considering use of self in child welfare work. *Journal of Social Work Practice, 22*(2), 235–48. http://dx.doi.org/10.1080/02650530802099916

Marshall, S. K., Charles, G., Kendrick, K., & Pakalniskiene, V. (2010). Comparing differential responses within child protective services: A longitudinal examination. *Child Welfare, 89*(3), 57–77.

Maruna, S., & LeBel, T. P. (2015). 5 strengths-based restorative approaches to reentry. *Positive Criminology,* 65.

Maslach, C. (2003). Job burnout: New directions in research and intervention. *Current Directions in Psychological Science, 12*(5), 189–92. http://dx.doi.org/10.1111/1467-8721.01258

Maybery, D., & Reupert, A. (2006). Workforce capacity to respond to children whose parents have a mental illness. *Australian and New Zealand Journal of Psychiatry, 40*(8), 657–64. http://dx.doi.org/10.1080/j.1440-1614.2006.01865.x

Maybery, D., & Reupert, A. (2009). Parental mental illness: A review of barriers and issues for working with families and children. *Journal of Psychiatric and Mental Health Nursing, 16*(9), 784–91. http://dx.doi.org/10.1111/j.1365-2850.2009.01456.x

Mayer, J. E., & Timms, N. (1970). *The client speaks: Working class impressions of casework.* New York, NY: Atherton.

McAuliffe, D., & Sudbery, J. (2005). "Who do I tell?" Support and consultation in cases of ethical conflict. *Journal of Social Work, 5*(1), 21–43. http://dx.doi.org/10.1177/1468017305051362

McCoyd, J. L., & Kerson, T. S. (2013). Teaching reflective social work practice in health care: Promoting best practices. *Journal of Social Work Education, 49*(4), 674–88.

McFadden, P., Campbell, A., & Taylor, B. (2015). Resilience and burnout in child protection social work: Individual and organisational themes from a systematic literature review. *British Journal of Social Work, 45*(5), 1546–63. http://dx.doi.org/10.1093/bjsw/bct210

McGarrigle, T., & Walsh, C. A. (2011). Mindfulness, self-care, and wellness in social work: Effects of contemplative training. *Social Thought, 30*(3), 212–33.

Meagher, G., & Parton, N. (2004). Modernising social work and the ethics of care. *Social Work and Society, 2*(1), 10–27.

Medina, A., & Beyebach, M. (2014a). How do child protection workers and teams change during solution-focused supervision and training? A brief qualitative report. *International Journal of Solution-Focused Practices, 2*(1), 9–19. http://dx.doi.org/10.14335/ijsfp.v2i1.17

Medina, A., & Beyebach, M. (2014b). The impact of solution-focused training on professionals' beliefs, practices and burnout of child protection workers in Tenerife Island. *Child Care in Practice, 20*(1), 7–36. http://dx.doi.org/10 .1080/13575279.2013.847058

Merkel-Holguín, L. A., Kaplan, C., & Kwak, A. (2006). National study on differential response in child welfare: American Humane Association/ Child Welfare League of America. Washington, DC: American Humane Association and Child Welfare League of America.

Michalopoulos, L., Ahn, H., Shaw, T. V., & O'Connor, J. (2012). Child welfare worker perception of the implementation of Family-Centered Practice. *Research on Social Work Practice, 22*(6), 656–64. http://dx.doi.org/10.1177 /1049731512453344

Mildon, R., & Shlonsky, A. (2011). Bridge over troubled water: Using implementation science to facilitate effective services in child welfare. *Child Abuse & Neglect, 35*(9), 753–56. http://dx.doi.org/10.1016/j.chiabu .2011.07.001

Miller, G., & de Shazer, S. (1998). Have you heard the latest rumor about…? Solution-focused therapy as a rumor. *Family Process, 37*(3), 363–77. http://dx.doi.org/10.1111/j.1545-5300.1998.00363.x

Miller, S. D., Hubble, M. A., & Duncan, B. L. (1996). *Handbook of solution-focused brief therapy.* San Francisco, CA: Jossey-Bass Publishers.

Ministry for Children and Family Development. (2012). *Child and youth safety and family support policies.* Victoria, BC: British Columbia Ministry for Children and Family Development.

Mirick, R. G. (2013). An unsuccessful partnership: Behavioral compliance and strengths-based child welfare practice. *Families in Society, 94*(0), 1–8.

Modrcin, M., Rapp, C., & Poertner, J. (1988). The evaluation of case management services with the chronically mentally ill. *Evaluation and Program Planning, 11*(4), 307–14. http://dx.doi.org/10.1016/0149 -7189(88)90043-2

Morgan, S., & Hemming, M. (1999). Balancing care and control: Risk management and compulsory community treatment. *Mental Health and Learning Disabilities Care, 3*, 19–21.

Morrison, T. (1990). The emotional effects of child protection work on the worker. *Practice. Social Work in Action, 4*(4), 253–71. http://dx.doi.org /10.1080/09503159008416902

Morrison, T. (1997). Emotionally competent child protection organizations: Fallacy, fiction or necessity? In J. Bates, R. Pugh, & N. Thompson (Eds.), *Protecting children: Challenges and change* (pp. 193–211). Aldershot, England: Arena.

Moulton, C. E., Regehr, G., Mylopoulos, M., & MacRae, H. M. (2007). Slowing down when you should: A new model of expert judgment. *Academic Medicine, 82*(10 Supplement), S109–S116. http://dx.doi.org/10.1097 /ACM.0b013e3181405a76

Moyle, W., Parker, D., & Bramble, M. (2014). *Care of older adults: A strengths-based approach.* Port Melbourne, Australia: Cambridge University Press.

Mullins, J. L. (2011). A framework for cultivating and increasing child welfare workers' empathy toward parents. *Journal of Social Service Research, 37*(3), 242–53. http://dx.doi.org/10.1080/01488376.2011.564030

Munro, E. (1999). Common errors of reasoning in child protection work. *Child Abuse & Neglect, 23*(8), 745–58. http://dx.doi.org/10.1016/S0145-2134(99)00053-8

Munro, E. (2005). Improving practice: Child protection as a systems problem. *Children and Youth Services Review, 27*(4), 375–91. http://dx.doi.org /10.1016/j.childyouth.2004.11.006

Munro, E. (2008). *Effective child protection* (2nd ed.). Thousand Oaks, CA: Sage.

Munro, E. (2011). *The Munro review of child protection: Final report. A child-centred system.* London: Department for Education.

Murphy, D., Duggan, M., & Joseph, S. (2013). Relationship-based social work and its compatibility with the person-centred approach: Principled versus instrumental perspectives. *British Journal of Social Work, 43*(4), 703–19. http://dx.doi.org/10.1093/bjsw/bcs003

Myers, J. E. B. (2004). *A history of child protection in America.* Bloomington, IN: Xlibris Corporation.

Nadeem, E., Gleacher, A., & Beidas, R. S. (2013). Consultation as an implementation strategy for evidence-based practices across multiple contexts: Unpacking the black box. *Administration and Policy in Mental Health, 40*(6), 439–50. http://dx.doi.org/10.1007/s10488-013-0502-8

Newberger, E. H., & Bourne, R. (1978). The medicalization and legalization of child abuse. *American Journal of Orthopsychiatry, 48*(4), 593–607. http://dx.doi.org/10.1111/j.1939-0025.1978.tb02564.x

O'Leary, P., Tsui, M.-S., & Ruch, G. (2013). The boundaries of the social work relationship revisited: Towards a connected, inclusive and dynamic conceptualisation. *British Journal of Social Work, 43*(1), 135–53. http://dx.doi .org/10.1093/bjsw/bcr181

O'Rourke, L. (2010). *Recording in social work: Not just an administrative task.* Bristol, England: The Policy Press.

Orsi, M. M., Lafortune, D., & Brochu, S. (2010). Care and control: Working alliance among adolescents in authoritarian settings. *Residential Treatment for Children & Youth, 27*(4), 277–303. http://dx.doi.org/10.1080 /0886571x.2010.520637

Oliver, C. (2012). The relationship between Symbolic Interactionism and Interpretive Description. *Qualitative Health Research, 22*(3), 409–15. http://dx.doi.org/10.1177/1049732311421177

Oliver, C. (2013). Including moral distress in the new language of social work ethics. *Canadian Social Work Review, 30*(2), 203–16.

Oliver, C. (2014). *Making strengths-based practice work in child protection: Frontline perspectives.* (Unpublished doctoral dissertation). University of British Columbia, Vancouver, BC.

Oliver, C., & Charles, G. (2015). Which strengths-based practice: Reconciling strengths-based practice and mandated authority in child protection work. *Social Work, 60*(2), 135–43. http://dx.doi.org/10.1093/sw/swu058

Oliver, C., & Charles, G. (2016). Enacting firm, fair and friendly practice: A model for strengths-based child protection relationships? *British Journal of Social Work, 46*(4): 1009–26. http://dx.doi.org/10.1093/bjsw/bcv015

Ornstein, E., & Ganzer, C. (2005). Relational social work: A model for the future. *Families in Society, 86*(4), 565–72. http://dx.doi.org/10.1606/1044-3894.3462

Ortega, R. M., & Faller, K. C. (2010). Training child welfare workers from an intersectional cultural humility perspective: A paradigm shift. *Child Welfare, 90*(5), 27–49.

Osteen, P. J. (2011). Motivations, values, and conflict resolution: Students' integration of personal and professional identities. *Journal of Social Work Education, 47*(3), 423–44. http://dx.doi.org/10.5175/JSWE.2011.200900131

Palys, T., & Atchison, C. (2003). *Research decisions: Quantitative and qualitative perspectives.* Toronto, ON: Nelson.

Parton, N. (1979). The natural history of child abuse: A study in social problem definition. *British Journal of Social Work, 9*(4), 431–51.

Parton, N. (1994). "Problematics of government," (post)modernity and social work. *British Journal of Social Work, 24*(1), 9–32.

Parton, N. (1998). Risk, advanced liberalism and child welfare: The need to rediscover uncertainty and ambiguity. *British Journal of Social Work, 28*(1), 5–27. http://dx.doi.org/10.1093/oxfordjournals.bjsw.a011317

Parton, N. (2008). Changes in the form of knowledge in social work: From the social to the informational? *British Journal of Social Work, 38*(2), 253–69. http://dx.doi.org/10.1093/bjsw/bcl337

Parton, N. (2011). Child protection and safeguarding in England: Changing and competing conceptions of risk and their implications for social work. *British Journal of Social Work, 41*(5), 854–75. http://dx.doi.org/10.1093/bjsw/bcq119

Parton, N. (Ed.). (1997). *Child protection and family support: Tensions, contradictions, and possibilities.* London, England: Routledge.

Pauly, B., Varcoe, C., Storch, J., & Newton, L. (2009). Registered nurses' perceptions of moral distress and ethical climate. *Nursing Ethics, 16*(5), 561–73. http://dx.doi.org/10.1177/0969733009106649

Pearson, G. S. (2013). Strengths-based nursing care for psychiatric nurses. *Perspectives in Psychiatric Care, 49*(1), 1. http://dx.doi.org/10.1111/ppc.12007

Pease, B. (2011). Men in social work: Challenging or reproducing an unequal gender regime? *Affilia, 26*(4), 406–18. http://dx.doi.org/10.1177/0886109911428207

Pipkin, S., Sterrett, E. M., Antle, B., & Christensen, D. N. (2013). Washington State's adoption of a child welfare practice model: An illustration of the Getting to Outcomes implementation framework. *Children and Youth Services Review, 35*(12), 1923–32. http://dx.doi.org/10.1016/j.childyouth.2013.09.017

Pollack, S. (2010). Labelling clients "risky": Social work and the neo-liberal welfare state. *British Journal of Social Work, 40*(4), 1263–78. http://dx.doi.org/10.1093/bjsw/bcn079

Rapp, C. (Ed.). (1993). *Theory, principles, and methods of the strengths model of case management.* Amsterdam, the Netherlands: Harwood Academic Publishers.

Rapp, C., & Chamberlain, R. (1985). Case management services for the chronically mentally ill. *Social Work, 30*(5), 417–22.

Rapp, C., Saleebey, D., & Sullivan, W. (2005). The future of strengths-based social work. *Advances in Social Work: Special Issue on the Futures of Social Work, 6*(1), 79–90.

Rapp, C. A., & Sullivan, W. P. (2014). The strengths model: Birth to toddlerhood. *Advances in Social Work, 15*(1), 129–42.

Rapp, R., & Lane, D. (2012). "Knowing" the effectiveness of strengths-based case management with substance abusers. In D. Saleebey (Ed.), *The strengths perspective in social work practice* (pp. 149–160). Upper Saddle River, NJ: Pearson Education Inc.

Rath, T., & Conchie, B. (2009). *Strengths based leadership: Great leaders, teams, and why people follow.* New York, NY: Gallup Press.

Reder, P., & Duncan, S. (2003). Understanding communication in child protection networks. *Child Abuse Review, 12*(2), 82–100. http://dx.doi.org/10.1002/car.787

Regehr, C., & Antle, B. (1997). Coercive influences: Informed consent in court-mandated social work practice. *Social Work, 42*(3), 300–6. http://dx.doi.org/10.1093/sw/42.3.300

Regehr, C., Hemsworth, D., Leslie, B., Howe, P., & Chau, S. (2004). Predictors of post-traumatic distress in child welfare workers: A linear structural equation model. *Children and Youth Services Review, 26*(4), 331–46. http://dx.doi.org/10.1016/j.childyouth.2004.02.003

Rex, S., & Hosking, N. (2013). A collaborative approach to developing probation practice skills for effective engagement, development and supervision (SEEDS). *Probation Journal, 60*(3), 332–8. http://dx.doi.org/10.1177/0264550513499002

Rice, K., Girvin, H., & Primak, S. (2014). Engaging adolescent youth in foster care through photography. *Child Care in Practice, 20*(1), 37–47. http://dx.doi.org/10.1080/13575279.2013.847054

Richards, S., Ruch, G., & Trevithick, P. (2005). Communication skills training for practice: The ethical dilemma for social work education. *Social Work Education, 24*(4), 409–22. http://dx.doi.org/10.1080/02615470500096928

Richmond, M. E. (1917). *Social diagnosis*. New York, NY: Russell Sage Foundation.

Rodney, P., Doane, G. H., Storch, J., & Varcoe, C. (2006). Toward a safer moral climate. *Canadian Nurse, 102*(8), 24–7.

Rogowski, S. (2012). Social work with children and families: Challenges and possibilities in the neo-liberal world. *British Journal of Social Work, 42*(5), 921–40. http://dx.doi.org/10.1093/bjsw/bcr129

Rooney, R. H. (2009). *Strategies for work with involuntary clients* (2nd ed.). New York, NY: Columbia University Press.

Roose, R., Roets, G., & Schiettecat, T. (2014). Implementing a strengths perspective in child welfare and protection: A challenge not to be taken lightly. *European Journal of Social Work, 17*(1), 3–17. http://dx.doi.org/10.1080/13691457.2012.739555

Ross, E. C., Polaschek, D. L. L., & Ward, T. (2008). The therapeutic alliance: A theoretical revision for offender rehabilitation. *Aggression and Violent Behavior, 13*(6), 462–80. http://dx.doi.org/10.1016/j.avb.2008.07.003

Ruch, G. (2005). Relationship based practice and reflective practice: Holistic approaches to contemporary child care social work. *Child & Family Social Work, 10*(2), 111–23. http://dx.doi.org/10.1111/j.1365-2206.2005.00359.x

Ruch, G. (2007). Reflective practice in contemporary child-care social work: The role of containment. *British Journal of Social Work, 37*(4), 659–80. http://dx.doi.org/10.1093/bjsw/bch277

Ruch, G., & Murray, C. (2011). Anxiety, defences and the primary task in integrated children's services: Enhancing inter-professional practice. *Journal of Social Work Practice, 25*(4), 433–49. http://dx.doi.org/10.1080/02650533.2011.626648

Ryan, M. (2013). The pedagogical balancing act: Teaching reflection in higher education. *Teaching in Higher Education, 18*(2), 144–55. http://dx.doi.org/10.1080/13562517.2012.694104

Sabalauskas, K. L., Ortolani, C. L., & McCall, M. J. (2014). Moving from pathology to possibility: Integrating strengths-based interventions in child welfare provision. *Child Care in Practice, 20*(1), 120–34. http://dx.doi.org /10.1080/13575279.2013.847053

Saleebey, D. (1992). *The strengths perspective in social work practice* (1st ed.). White Plains, NY: Longman.

Saleebey, D. (1996). The strengths perspective in social work practice: Extensions and cautions. *Social Work, 41*(3), 296–305.

Saleebey, D. (1997). The strengths approach to practice. In D. Saleebey (Ed.), *The strengths perspective in social work practice* (2nd ed.) (pp. 49–57). White Plains, NY: Longman.

Saleebey, D. (2006). *The strengths perspective in social work practice* (4th ed.). Boston, MA: Allyn and Bacon.

Saleebey, D. (2012). *The strengths perspective in social work practice* (6th ed.). Upper Saddle River, NJ: Pearson Education Inc.

Sandelowski, M., Voils, C. I., & Knafl, G. (2009). On quantitizing. *Journal of mixed methods research, 3*(3), 208–22.

Scarth, S., & Sullivan, R. (2007). Child welfare in the 1980s: A time of turbulence and change. In L. T. Foster & B. Wharf (Eds.), *People, politics and child welfare in British Columbia* (pp. 83–96). Vancouver, BC: UBC Press.

Schreiber, J. C., Fuller, T., & Paceley, M. S. (2013). Engagement in child protective services: Parent perceptions of worker skills. *Children and Youth Services Review, 35*(4), 707–15. http://dx.doi.org/10.1016/j.childyouth.2013.01.018

Scourfield, J., & Welsh, I. (2003). Risk, reflexivity and social control in child protection: New times or same old story? *Critical Social Policy, 23*(3), 398–420. http://dx.doi.org/10.1177/02610183030233005

Scriven, A., & Smith-Ferrier, S. (2003). The application of online surveys for workplace health research. *Journal of the Royal Society for the Promotion of Health, 123*(2), 95–101. http://dx.doi.org/10.1177/146642400312300213

Shear, N. W. (2015). *Successful implementation of Solution-Based Casework: A child welfare casework practice model?* New York, NY: The City University of New York.

Shennan, G. (2006). "Doing it" in child protection. *Solution News, 2*(3), 15–19.

Sidebotham, P. (2013). Authoritative child protection. *Child Abuse Review, 22*(1), 1–4. http://dx.doi.org/10.1002/car.2261

Sims-Gould, J., Byrne, K., Hicks, E., Khan, K., & Stolee, P. (2012). Examining "success" in post-hip fracture care transitions: A strengths-based approach. *Journal of Interprofessional Care, 26*(3), 205–11. http://dx.doi.org/10.3109 /13561820.2011.645090

Skeem, J. L., Louden, J. E., Polaschek, D., & Camp, J. (2007). Assessing relationship quality in mandated community treatment: Blending care with control. *Psychological Assessment, 19*(4), 397–410. http://dx.doi.org/10.1037/1040-3590.19.4.397

Skrypek, M., Idzelis, M., & Pecora, P. (2012). *Signs of Safety in Minnesota: Parent perceptions of a Signs of Safety child protection experience.* St. Paul, Minnesota: Wilder Research.

Skrypek, M., Otteson, C., & Owen, G. (2010). *Signs of Safety in Minnesota. Early indicators of successful implementation in child protection agencies: Wilder Research.* St. Paul, Minnesota: Wilder Research, in collaboration with Casey Family Programs and Minnesota Department of Human Services.

Smalley, R. E. (1967). *Theory for social work practice.* New York, NY: Columbia University Press.

Smith, B. D., & Donovan, S. E. F. (2003). Child welfare practice in organizational and institutional context. *Social Service Review, 77*(4), 541–63. http://dx.doi.org/10.1086/378328

Sprang, G., Craig, C., & Clark, J. (2011). Secondary traumatic stress and burnout in child welfare workers: A comparative analysis of occupational distress across professional groups. *Child Welfare, 90*(6), 149–68.

Stanford, S. (2010). "Speaking back" to fear: Responding to the moral dilemmas of risk in social work practice. *British Journal of Social Work, 40*(4), 1065–80. http://dx.doi.org/10.1093/bjsw/bcp156

Stanley, J., Goddard, C., & Sanders, R. (2002). In the firing line: Violence and power in child protection work. *Child & Family Social Work, 7*(4), 323–4.

Stanley, T., & Mills, R. (2014). "Signs of Safety" practice at the health and children's social care interface. *Practice, 26*(1), 23–36. http://dx.doi.org/10.1080/09503153.2013.867942

Statistics Canada (2012). 2011 Census of Canada profile tables: Vancouver, British Columbia (Code 5915022) and British Columbia (Code 59). (Catalogue number 98–316-XWE). Retrieved April 17, 2015, from Statistics Canada: http://www12.statcan.gc.ca/census-recensement/2011/dp-pd/prof/index.cfm?Lang=E

Staudt, M., Howard, M. O., & Drake, B. (2001). The operationalization, implementation, and effectiveness of the strengths perspective: A review of empirical studies. *Journal of Social Service Research, 27*(3), 1–21.

Storch, J., Rodney, P., Pauly, B., Fulton, T., Stevenson, L., Newton, L., & Makaroff, K. (2009). Enhancing ethical climates in nursing work environments. *Canadian Nurse, 105*(3), 20–5.

Strasburger, L. H., Gutheil, T. G., & Brodsky, A. (1997). On wearing two hats: Role conflict in serving as both psychotherapist and expert witness. *American Journal of Psychiatry, 154*(4), 448–56. http://dx.doi.org/10.1176/ajp.154.4.448

Svensson, K. (2003). Social work in the criminal justice system: An ambiguous exercise of caring power. *Journal of Scandinavian Studies in Criminology and Crime Prevention*, 4(1), 84–100. http://dx.doi.org/10.1080/14043850310011126

Tajfel, H. (1978). *Differentiation between social groups: Studies in the social psychology of intergroup relations*. London, England: Academic Press.

Tajfel, H. (Ed.). (2010). *Social identity and intergroup relations* (2nd ed., Vol. 7). Cambridge, England: Cambridge University Press.

Tew, J. (2006). Understanding power and powerlessness: Towards a framework for emancipatory practice in social work. *Journal of Social Work*, 6(1), 33–51. http://dx.doi.org/10.1177/1468017306062222

Tham, P. (2007). Why are they leaving? Factors affecting intention to leave among social workers in child welfare. *British Journal of Social Work*, 37(7), 1225–46. http://dx.doi.org/10.1093/bjsw/bcl054

Thomas, C., & Davis, S. (2005). Bicultural strengths-based supervision. In M. Nash, R. Munford, & K. O'Donoghue (Eds.), *Social work theories in action* (pp. 189–204). London, England: Jessica Kingsley Publishers.

Thorne, S. (2008). *Interpretive description*. Walnut Creek, CA: Left Coast Press.

Thorne, S., Kirkham, S. R., & MacDonald Emes, J. (1997). Interpretive description: A noncategorical qualitative alternative for developing nursing knowledge. *Research in Nursing & Health*, 20(2), 169–77.

Travis, D. J., Lizano, E. L., & Mor Barak, M. E. (2016). "I'm So Stressed!": A longitudinal model of stress, burnout and engagement among social workers in child welfare settings. *British Journal of Social Work* 46(4), 1076–95. http://dx.doi.org/10.1093/bjsw/bct205

Trevithick, P. (2003). Effective relationship-based practice: A theoretical exploration. *Journal of Social Work Practice*, 17(2), 163–76. http://dx.doi.org/10.1080/026505302000145699

Trocmé, N., Knoke, D., & Blackstock, C. (2004). Pathways to the overrepresentation of Aboriginal children in Canada's child welfare system. *Social Service Review*, 78(4), 577–600. http://dx.doi.org/10.1086/424545

Trocmé, N., Knott, T., & Knoke, D. (2003). *An overview of differential response models*. Toronto, ON: Centre of Excellence for Child Welfare, Faculty of Social Work, University of Toronto.

Trotter, C. (1997). Working with mandated clients: A pro-social approach. *Australian Social Work*, 50(2), 19–28. http://dx.doi.org/10.1080/03124079708414082

Trotter, C. (2002). Worker skill and client outcome in child protection. *Child Abuse Review*, 11(1), 38–50. http://dx.doi.org/10.1002/car.719

Trotter, C. (2004). *Helping abused children and their families: Towards an evidence-based practice model*. Thousand Oaks, CA: Sage Publications.

Trotter, C. (2006). *Working with involuntary clients: A guide to practice.* Thousand Oaks, CA: Sage Publications.

Trotter, C. (2009). Pro-social modelling. *European Journal of Probation, 1*(2), 142–52. http://dx.doi.org/10.1177/206622030900100206

Trotter, C., & Ward, T. (2013). Involuntary clients, pro-social modelling and ethics. *Ethics & Social Welfare, 7*(1), 74–90. http://dx.doi.org/10.1080/17496535.2012.666753

Tuck, V. (2013). Resistant parents and child protection: Knowledge base, pointers for practice and implications for policy. *Child Abuse Review, 22*(1), 5–19. http://dx.doi.org/10.1002/car.1207

Turnell, A. (2004). Relationship-grounded, safety-organised child protection practice: Dreamtime or real-time option for child welfare. *Protecting Children, 19*(2), 14–25.

Turnell, A. (2012). *The Signs of Safety: A comprehensive briefing paper.* Perth, Australia: Resolutions Consultancy.

Turnell, A., & Edwards, S. (1999). *Signs of Safety: A safety and solution oriented approach to child protection casework.* New York, NY: W. W. Norton & Co.

Turnell, A., & Essex, S. (2006). *Working with "denied" child abuse: The resolutions approach.* Maidenhead, England: Open University Press.

Turnell, A., Lohrbach, S., & Curran, S. (2008). Working with involuntary clients in child protection: Lessons from successful practice. In M. Calder (Ed.), *The carrot or the stick? Towards effective practice with involuntary clients in safeguarding children work* (pp. 104–15). Dorset, England: Russell House.

Turpel-Lafond, M. E. (2013). *Who protected him? How B.C.'s child welfare system failed one of its most vulnerable children.* Victoria, BC: Representative for Children and Youth.

Turpel-Lafond, M. E. (2014). *Lost in the shadows: How a lack of help meant a loss of hope for one First Nations girl.* Victoria, BC: British Columbia Representative for Children and Youth.

van Nijnatten, C., Hoogsteder, M., & Suurmond, J. (2001). Communication in care and coercion: Institutional interactions between family supervisors and parents. *British Journal of Social Work, 31*(5), 705–20. http://dx.doi.org/10.1093/bjsw/31.5.705

van Zyl, M. A., Barbee, A. P., Cunningham, M. R., Antle, B. F., Christensen, D. N., & Boamah, D. (2014). Components of the solution-based casework child welfare practice model that predict positive child outcomes. *Journal of Public Child Welfare, 8*(4), 433–65. http://dx.doi.org/10.1080/15548732.2014.939252

Waldfogel, J. (1998). Rethinking the paradigm for child protection. *Future of Children, 8*(1), 104–19. http://dx.doi.org/10.2307/1602631

Weakland, J. H., Fisch, R., Watzlawick, P., & Bodin, A. M. (1974). Brief therapy: Focused problem resolution. *Family process, 13*(2), 141–68.

Weaver, D., Moses, T., Furman, W., & Lindsey, D. (2003). The effects of computerization on public child welfare practice. *Journal of Social Service Research, 29*(4), 67–80. http://dx.doi.org/10.1300/J079v29n04_04

Weick, A. (2000). Hidden voices. *Social Work, 45*(5), 395–402. http://dx.doi.org/10.1093/sw/45.5.395

Weick, A., Rapp, C., Sullivan, W. P., & Kisthardt, W. (1989). A strengths perspective for social work practice. *Social Work, 34*(4), 350–4.

Weld, N. (2008). The three houses tool: Building safety and positive change. In M. Calder (Ed.), *Contemporary risk assessment in safeguarding children* (pp. 224–31). Dorset, England: Russell House Publishing.

Wells, G., Shields, L., Hauck, Y., & Bennett, E. (2014). Do we make a difference?: Parents' and nurses' experiences of using a strengths-based, solution-focused approach to care. *Australian Journal of Child and Family Health Nursing, 11*(2), 5–10.

Wheeler, J., & Hogg, V. (2012). Signs of Safety and the child protection movement. In C. Franklin, T. Trepper, W. Gingerich, & E. McCollum (Eds.), *Solution-focused brief therapy: A handbook of evidence-based practice* (pp. 203–15). New York, NY: Oxford University Press.

White, S., Wastell, D., Broadhurst, K., & Hall, C. (2010). When policy o'erleaps itself: The "tragic tale" of the Integrated Children's System. *Critical Social Policy, 30*(3), 405–29. http://dx.doi.org/10.1177/0261018310367675

Williams, L. M., Kemp, A. H., Felmingham, K., Liddell, B. J., Palmer, D. M., & Bryant, R. A. (2007). Neural biases to covert and overt signals of fear: Dissociation by trait anxiety and depression. *Journal of Cognitive Neuroscience, 19*(10), 1595–608. http://dx.doi.org/10.1162/jocn.2007.19.10.1595

Wilson, T. G. (2013). *The impact of the frequency of technology use on client engagement behavior exhibited by child welfare workers.* Atlanta, GA: Clark Atlanta University.

Winefield, H. R., & Barlow, J. A. (1995). Client and worker satisfaction in a child protection agency. *Child Abuse & Neglect, 19*(8), 897–905. http://dx.doi.org/10.1016/0145-2134(95)00052-A

Woods, M. E., & Hollis, F. (1990). *Casework: A psychosocial therapy* (4th ed.). Boston, MA: McGraw-Hill.

Wright, D., & Odiah, C. (2000). Forensic practice in the helping professions: Advocate and adversary roles as a threat to therapeutic alliances and fiduciary relations. *Journal of Offender Rehabilitation, 31*(1/2), 57–68.

Yamatani, H., Engel, R., & Spjeldnes, S. (2009). Child welfare worker caseload: What's just right? *Social Work, 54*(4), 361–68. http://dx.doi.org/10.1093 /sw/54.4.361

Yatchmenoff, D. K. (2005). Measuring client engagement from the client's perspective in nonvoluntary child protective services. *Research on Social Work Practice, 15*(2), 84–96. http://dx.doi.org/10.1177/1049731504271605

Index

Figures and tables indicated by page numbers in italics.